T0113497

Mirror, Mirror on the Wall

✳ ✳ ✳ ✳ ✳ ✳

Mirror, Mirror on the Wall

* * * * * *

WOMEN WRITERS

EXPLORE THEIR FAVORITE

FAIRY TALES

* * * * * *

EDITED BY Kate Bernheimer

ANCHOR BOOKS

A DIVISION OF RANDOM HOUSE, INC.

NEW YORK

SECOND ANCHOR BOOKS EDITION, JULY 2002

Copyright © 1998, 2002 by Kate Bernheimer

All rights reserved under International and Pan-American Copyright Conventions. Published in the United States by Anchor Books, a division of Random House, Inc., New York, and simultaneously in Canada by Random House of Canada Limited, Toronto. Originally published in softcover in slightly different form in the United States by Anchor Books, a division of Random House, Inc., New York, in 1998.

All of the individual essays which appear in this work, with the exception of the titles noted below, are copyright © 1998 by its respective author. The following essays are copyright © 2002 by its respective author: "The Wilderness Within," "The Monkey Girl," and "Transformations."

Grateful acknowledgment is made to Georges Borchardt, Inc., for permission to reprint "Exquisite Hour" from *Aureole* by Carole Maso. Copyright © 1996 by Carole Maso. Reprinted by permission of Georges Borchardt, Inc., on behalf of the author.

Anchor Books and colophon are registered trademarks of Random House, Inc.

Library of Congress Cataloging-in-Publication Data

Mirror, mirror on the wall: women writers explore their favorite fairy tales / edited by Kate Bernheimer. — 2nd Anchor Books ed.
p. cm.
1. American literature—Women authors. 2. Fairy tales—History and criticism. 3. Women—Folklore. 4. Women—Psychology.
I. Bernheimer, Kate.
PS508.W7M57 1998
810.9'9287—dc21 97-42242
CIP

Anchor ISBN: 978-0-385-48681-1

Book design by Mia Risberg

www.anchorbooks.com

FOR MY SISTERS
AND FOR MY BROTHER

After being conditioned as a child to the lovely never-never land of magic, of fairy queens and virginal maidens, of little princes and their rosebushes, of poignant bears and Eeyore-ish donkeys, of life personalized, as the pagans loved it, of the magic wand, and the faultless illustrations—the beautiful dark-haired child (who was you) winging through the midnight sky on a star-path in her mother's box of reels—of Griselda in her feather-cloak, walking barefoot with the Cuckoo in the lantern-lit world of nodding mandarins, of Delight in her flower garden with the slim-limbed flower sprites . . . all this I knew, and felt, and believed. All this was my life when I was young. To go from this to the world of "grown-up" reality . . . To feel the sexorgans develop and call loud to the flesh; to become aware of school, exams (the very words as unlovely as the sound of chalk shrilling on the blackboard), bread and butter, marriage, sex, compatibility, war, economics, death, and self. What a pathetic blighting of the beauty and reality of childhood. Not to be sentimental, as I sound, but why the hell are we conditioned into the smooth strawberry-and-cream Mother-Goose-world, Alice-in-Wonderland fable, only to be broken on the wheel as we grow older and become aware of ourselves as individuals with a dull responsibility in life? To learn snide and smutty meanings of words you once loved, like "fairy."

—From *The Journals of Sylvia Plath*

ANNOTATED CONTENTS

✳ ✳ ✳ ✳ ✳ ✳

I was drawn to both "Little Red Riding Hood" and "Goldilocks and the Three Bears" as fantasies of escape, and, curiously, when recently I began to think of them again, I could not remember how either of them ended—until I asked my son, who set me straight.

Once upon a time, I lived in another country and in another language under a cruel dictatorship which my father was plotting to overthrow. This is not a made-up story, this is not a fairy tale. This is the autobiography of my childhood in the Dominican Republic under the dictatorship of El Jefe.

I was not a well-brought-up little girl of the fifties. I had been born in 1939, just after the outbreak of the Second World War, and there was no hope then of sweeping the darker emotions under the rug. There they were on the world stage, displayed for all to see: fear, hatred, cruelty, blood and slaughter. A few fairy tale hanged corpses and chopped-off heads were, by comparison, nothing to get squeamish about.

As a culture, we are fairly preoccupied with sleep. In spite of the media's insistence to the contrary, I maintain that we don't really wonder, very often, who's having lots of sex; we wonder, more often, who might be getting lots of sleep. . . . In our exhaustion, we emphatically do not wish for Prince Charming to come. If he isn't already in bed with us, to hell with him.

And then there was "The Little Mermaid," far more complex but equally brutal and—I was nothing if not consistent—a painful story "redeemed" (I see now) by another noble ending which I didn't remember because its fake good cheer never registered on me. "There is a view poetry should improve your life," the poet John Ashbery once said. "I think people confuse it with the Salvation Army."

A. S. BYATT

Ice, Snow, Glass 60

Science and reason are bad, kindness is good. It is a frequent but not a necessary opposition. And I found in it, and in the dangerous isolation of the girl on her slippery shiny height a figure of what was beginning to bother me, the conflict between a female destiny, the kiss, the marriage, the child-bearing, the death, and the frightening loneliness of cleverness, the cold distance of seeing the world through art, of putting a frame around things.

KATHRYN DAVIS

Why I Don't Like Reading Fairy Tales 80

A dancer inside a castle inside a book inside a bookcase inside a cupboard inside a castle-studded landscape: how deftly the Nordic Paper Industry managed to convey the terror I knew lurked at the heart of the Christian message. Your tenure on this earth, where you might actually prefer to stay (despite its perils, the perverse machinery of cause and effect embodied in snuffbox goblins and gumdrop poodles), would be finite, yet once you died you'd have no choice but to go on forever and ever.

The Princess lives in an underwater palace filled with snakes. We do not know who she is, or how she came there. Do not feel sorry for her. She is happy enough. The snakes are not horrid . . . and play with her and sing her to sleep. She has never left the palace, has never wanted to. . . . As you might guess, there is in the story a prince. And his friend, the minister's son.

Any child who considers herself a candidate for expulsion from the human race is certain to tremble reading about Kay. And though I was brought up in a largely secular, Jewish home, and, as I remember, was always in some way aware that according to any strict interpretation of "The Snow Queen" I was out of luck, I always longed to reach the moment in the story of Gerda's tears, when Kay would be returned to himself.

I recognized how many instances these fairy tales addressed situations like mine. In order for girl children to survive their sexual maturation, they would have to escape from their malevolent matriarchs. My sister Karen had disappeared. From what poison apple had she sampled? What spell had been cast upon her?

His eyes move over me with the same entranced gaze as if we're magnets, attracted by an inexplicable force. The intimacy is eerie, almost unbearable. I know he has something important to show me, something that will change me, making me indifferent to trees and sky and heat. But to my surprise, he whips out a mirror. *See a monkey see a monkey see a monkey*, he whispers, thrusting the mirror up close to my face.

The elusive right man became our obsessive preoccupation. Not finding him was the defining experience. It is the same with the princess on the pea. She's not after the prince, she's after the pea.

I hated fairy tales as a child because they had nothing to do with reality. Not because they spoke of goblins and elves and giants, not because of such obvious unreality. It had more to do with their neatly packaged morals. Mostly, I hated the notion that you got what you deserved. As I understood life, you rarely got what you deserved, and if you did, you'd better start looking over your shoulder.

Fairy tales . . . sanctioned all that was taboo in the family. Fantasy was often seen by Christian folks as dangerous, as potentially Satanic. My love of fairy tales was accepted as long as it was not much talked about. I liked to lie in a dark room and daydream my favorite stories, making self the center of the drama.

When I was a child in Killiney, south of Dublin, I saw a fairy on a stone wall—a tiny fellow in green and brown—but my mother, close by, didn't see him or believe me. We were on our way to visit the Druid chair that faces the rising sun under some sacred oak trees (now encircled by suburban housing, but left alone) to make parting wishes before our return to America.

Seven years ago, I married for the second time. Joe had custody of his two daughters—Megan, thirteen, and Katie, ten—and had lived alone with them for most of their lives. Right before I married Joe, my mother had sent me an article stating that ten and thirteen were the worst ages for children to adjust in a second marriage. Thanks, Ma, I said. I also began to rethink the role when the wicked stepmother herself *c'est moi*.

If acknowledging the influence of great writers makes some authors feel threatened, what about *fairy tales*? That should bring on a regular panic attack. . . . That the accepted notion of literary influence is appallingly simplistic is shown, I think, by the fact that it overlooks—ignores—disdains—the effect of "pre-literature"—oral stories, folk tales, fairy tales, picture books—on the tender mind of the pre-writer.

And she slips into the white of herself—into the white—her life snowing. A muffled, peaceful sound and she feels could it be? slightly aroused by the white, by the taking away finally of everything as she falls into some infinite. Voice 3 said something about pearls once. And the little girls danced all night—remember? Until their shoes were thin.

When I first read the poet Federico García Lorca's legends, I understood that there is no story, there are only moments. And I broke from narrative finally, and felt that precipitous falling that is dangerous only as long as one believes in gravity.

Blue Beard wanted his new wife to find the corpses of his former wives. He *wanted* the new bride to discover their mutilated corpses; he *wanted* her disobedience. Otherwise he wouldn't have given her the key to the forbidden closet; he wouldn't have left on his so-called business trip; and he wouldn't have stashed the dead Mrs. Blue Beards in the closet in the first place. Transparently, it was a setup. In the postmodern world Mrs. Blue Beard doesn't take the bait.

What is troubling about the fairy tale world and its long association with women is precisely its condition as mythical and stereotypical, a rigidly schematized counterworld to the "real"; an enchanted, or accursed, world whose relationship to reality is analogous to that of our dreams to our waking lives. As if the province of women must be unreal, trivial.

Despite what Einstein says about the impossibility of time travel, the barrier of the speed of light, I've traveled through time.

Maybe that is why I don't expect questions about baldheaded girls. It would seem that black girls would be beyond that now, especially these girls, wealthy and privileged and beautiful. It would seem they would not be part of the cult of Rapunzel, paying homage to some girl in a fairy tale.

Back to Sleeping Beauty, then. By now it's probably clear that what I'm talking about is a sort of modified necrophilia: not exactly sex with a corpse—literal graveyard amour—but sex with a woman who only *appears* to have left the world of the living. . . . The surest route to a man's (or to some men's) heart is to pretend to be unconscious: I'm asleep, dear . . . and actually, to tell the truth, I may not even be . . . real.

In our home, language itself was of prime importance: my mother labored long and hard over each syllable she wrote; my father gloried in crossword puzzles; when my sister or I asked the meaning of a word, we were told to go and look it up in the big dictionary that lay conveniently open on the counter in my mother's writing room. Yet in "The Juniper Tree," the townspeople do not hear the words the bird is singing; they do not want, or are not psychologically equipped—like the townspeople of Oswiecim in World War II, who watched the cattle cars stuffed full of Jews clatter down the steel rails, who lived next to Auschwitz's ovens and pretended not to notice the black stench that filled the sky.

The beastly bride, while she may shed her skin or commit herself as a sensual partner, never surrenders her power and therefore always remains a little dangerous, a little unpredictable. There are beastly brides who hide their scales, their fur, and don the bodies of women in order to marry men for their own reasons and have children. Perhaps these brides should come with warning labels—disrespect us at your own peril!

The effect of these tales, so far as I could see, was to fill the heads of little girls with mystery, and provide them with those archetypes which make for unease—why am I not as slim as the Fairy Princess? why are the Fairy Godmotherly gifts I proffer not magic? why do I stay the beggar-girl and the Prince just looks the other way? why if I'm Cinderella is there no ball to go to? why are my good deeds not rewarded by fate? why does my goose not lay golden eggs? and so forth.

Even for a particularly shy and thoughtful only child growing up in a parsonage in Maine, vaguely aware of those other horsemen, the four from Revelation—the fourth one, the pale one being You Know Who—this was probably odd, this equanimicable attitude toward Baba Yaga, this happy fascination.

You must not speak. That's what my stepfather said: don't speak, don't cry, don't tell. That's what my mother said as well, as we sat in hospital waiting rooms—and I obeyed, as did my brothers. We sat still and silent as stone while my mother spun false tales to explain each break and bruise and burn.

INTRODUCTION

✻ ✻ ✻ ✻ ✻ ✻

Why break the spell?
——H.D.

This volume offers a specific moment of self-reflection for women—a gaze into the mirror through the lens of the fairy tale. It is my hope that this collection of essays will gain as much value to readers of fairy tales—those who read them to their children or to themselves, those who read them as scholars or students—as those favorite fairy tale volumes on their shelves, those books with faded ink and illustrations. Perhaps you, as I do, have on your shelves a cherished fairy tale book, one with a blue fabric cover and broken, beaten-up spine. Perhaps this book will gain a place beside it.

I am pleased therefore to have the chance to introduce a second edition of *Mirror, Mirror on the Wall: Women Writers Explore Their Favorite Fairy Tales* with some general words about its contents. As you may have gathered, this volume collects essays from authors about their memories and ideas of fairy tales. I imagine you have your own. Let me begin with a little personal history.

When I was young, each and every Sunday in Brookline, Massachusetts, my sisters and brother and I would march down to the basement at my grandparents' house to watch fairy tale movies on a big screen. My grandfather, a publicist for a movie company, had put up big letters at the entrance to the steep, creaky stairs. MOGER MOVIES, they read. Glazed with pizza and raspberry soda, we'd line up on the couch in the basement and wait for the show to begin. From the projection room, my grandfather would call out a few words I can't quite recall, perhaps simply "Let the show begin." The lights would dim, and on would come the most frightening and beautiful movies. These were fairy tales, direct to us from Walt Disney Studios. We'd sit there for hours, our eyes shining bright. The palest blues and pinks you could imagine, the warbling girls' voices, and oh, talking mice! Often I wish I could climb back into those days, when fairy tales were just for escaping.

The only word I can think of to describe how I felt is *transfixed*. And while that was thirty years ago, these stories still have their hold. But to choose a favorite? It was Andy Warhol who said, when once asked which artists he liked, "I like them all." Though the contributors to this volume express a range of reactions to hearing fairy tales as a child—and revisiting them as adults—everyone represented in this volume suggests a certain, similar enchantment with tales.

The fairy tale is a particular form of literature—a lovely, strange kind of story. For the reader, fairy tales offer both wildly familiar and familiarly wild terrain. In fairy tales, houses on chicken legs spin in the woods. The bones of a child bloom into a tree. A young girl indolently pulls wings off of flies. Queens seek to eat stepdaughters' livers and hearts. Those details, and the predictably unpredictable structure of the stories in which they are contained, are a great influence on my fictional writings.

Years ago, I began to notice how often other writers seemed impacted, too. The idea for *Mirror, Mirror on the Wall* was to begin a conversation among writers about how fairy tales affected their thinking. I asked specifically for contributors to muse upon emotion, gender, culture and self. As I too began to explore the very same questions and turned to the fairy tales themselves for some answer, I started to see how very intricately *literary*—how completely innovative—fairy tales are simply as stories. Each version of a tale stands alone, but also gels with tradition. This quality—separate, but entwined—reminds me of the essays in this volume. I encouraged each author to write in a mode that was natural for her, the fairy tales themselves being our glue.

Hearing people, big and small, discuss the pleasure and horror in fairy tale fiction never ceases to give me a thrill. Just recently, I gave a reading at a small bookstore near my home. A friend brought her two-year-old daughter. When I finished reading—from my first novel, which is based on fairy tales—some people lined up for a book signing. Lily, my friend's daughter, stood patiently in line for ten minutes, clutching a thin, hardcover volume. When she came up to the table, she stood looking shyly up at me, pressing the book to my hands. It was a picture book from Walt Disney's "Snow White" movie. "Lily!" I exclaimed. "Look, Snow White has a hair ribbon just like yours!" And it's true: Snow White had the same exact bow tied around her black hair. Lily blushed as furiously as a two-year-old can, and I can confidently say that the look crossing her face was *ecstatic*.

Like Lily, and others in this volume, I was infatuated with

fairy tales as a very young girl, even after we left my grandparents' house. I had many dolls and insisted on calling all of my rag dolls Elizabeth—Ella for short, from Cinderella. And for many years, I insisted on being Cinderella for Halloween, *before* she was saved. I'd go in the yard and toss dirt in my hair and rip a party dress (I thought it would be more authentic if my clothes were ruined, just as hers were). My older sister had her fairy tale obsession too, but in a different way. She was a bride for no fewer than *six* Halloweens, I remember. I could be exaggerating here, but that's how it felt.

In these twenty-eight essays, you will find the suggestive detail and intricate ideology of fairy tales as the contributors reflect on their own favorites. I was surprised when, in researching my idea for this book, I did not come upon a complete collection that gathered personal responses. (*The Reception of Grimms' Fairy Tales: Responses, Reactions, Revisions*, a very nice volume edited by Donald Haase, gathers four pieces about German tales, and that book gave me confidence that an entire collection devoted to personal responses would be quite powerful.) Surely, given fairy tales' glittering presence in so many cultural forums—from film to advertising to popular fiction to games—a collection of personal responses might find a place. This particular moment in time also seems ripe for the book. Fairy tales themselves are obsessed with ends and beginnings—*once upon a time . . . they lived happily ever after*—and the contrived drama of the turn of the century lends itself well to the artifice and excess of enchantment literature. (In fact, history has seen at least one other movement of this sort of fin de siècle interest in the fairy tale: England's nineteenth-century Pre-Raphaelites, an association that helped produce Christina Rossetti's great fairy tale–inspired work, *Goblin Market*.)

Perhaps no explanation is necessary as to why I asked women specifically to respond to the tales. However, the more I know about fairy tales in their traditional forms, the more mystified I am when people cast fairy tales as antiwoman. Admittedly, fairy tale plots, as we receive them in popular culture, are often lacking or flat. There is a girl, victimized but pleasant, who likes to clean. Some things happen to her—often involving jealousies of women—and eventually she is saved from suffering by a handsome man. Although Disney's versions tend to follow that mold, I feel they sometimes get short shrift. As animated stories, their artistry is astounding. I find them delightfully—almost wickedly—bright. (Though admittedly, a five-year-old girl won't see the perverse hilarity in a warbling, singing, downtrodden girl. I simply thought Cinderella was *great*.) The original fairy tales include many of these elements, in fact.

If we look closely at the history of fairy tales, they are clearly not antiwoman. Many folklorists believe that a vast number of them were authored by women over the course of centuries. From this enormous body of work, however, only those stories dramatically revised by men have dominated popular culture until *very* recent days. For example, most of us know the Brothers Grimm, Hans Christian Andersen, and Charles Perrault. But actually, the oldest known versions of European fairy tales (those published by Straparola and Basile in sixteenth-century Italy) were based on oral tales by woman storytellers and were far more sensual and violently realistic than the stories we see on the screen and in popular books. How to explain that, in the early versions of "Sleeping Beauty," the Prince does not save her—he rapes her? In "The Story of Grandmother," an Italian story widely considered the first "Little Red Riding Hood," our young heroine performs a striptease for the wolf.

But she escapes his advances, all on her own. (Male authors such as Perrault added the hunter who saves her.)

For this reason, I decided to ask women how they felt about fairy tales. This is, in a sense, going right to the source. The exaggerated characters and plots in fairy tales provide interesting mirrors to complex cultural ideas about women. Fairy tales were often turned into writing from an oral tradition intended to secretly educate girls about the ways of the world. Perhaps this secrecy lends to their otherworldly sensation. Perhaps this is what we mean by *enchantment*.

Needless to say, asking women how fairy tales have impacted their thinking about the feminine self is not to herald nostalgically the myth that little girls like dolls and fairies (nor to reject categorically that possibility) but to wonder about wonder, about *being*. It is to look at the act of looking at ourselves inside stories, to regard the tradition and stereotype of female reflection on self. In this, there is power for all sorts of readers.

I think the idea that fairy tales are ambiguously exciting has long been "in the air." Sometime in the late 1960s, I had a doll that was on one side Little Red Riding Hood, and on the other side the Wolf and the Grandmother. You flipped Little Red Riding Hood's skirt right over her head to reveal the Grandmother, whose bonnet you could shift to reveal a wolf face. This was the one doll I feared, and I would hide it wherever I could. Something about flipping the girl's *skirt* just seemed wrong. But soon after I would hide the doll my curiosity would overtake me. I'd find it again and flip that skirt over. This never ceased to titillate me. (I did not know about "The Story of Grandmother" then.)

Of course, just as the responses in *Mirror, Mirror on the Wall* vary wildly, so do the original fairy tales themselves. Readers are familiar only with the homogenized, popularized tales compiled for print—and cleaned up—by Victorian editors such as Andrew Lang (who did the *Blue Fairy Book, Green Fairy Book*, etc., series) and the vaguely modest Grimm brothers. In fact, the oldest versions of fairy tales were much darker than those we commonly find in bookshops, and not always meant for children's consumption at all. Many female artists have dealt with these darker versions over and over in their work: in literature by Christina Rossetti, Angela Carter, Anne Sexton, Marina Warner and Rita Dove, as well as by the writers in this volume and countless others; in film by Caroline Thompson, Jane Campion and Penny Marshall; in music from Liz Phair, Courtney Love and Madonna (and Anne Sexton, who briefly toured with a rock group, Our Kind). *Mirror, Mirror on the Wall* emerges from a curiosity about how women, and artists in particular, have been intimately shaped by the tales. It is meant to exclude no reaction to them, nor prescribe one. Fairy tales themselves often place reader and heroine alike in a great hall of mirrors, reflecting forever and ever without closure. And this is good.

I feel I ought to repeat that the hall of mirrors is not meant to exclude anyone. Indeed, men could also be included here. Someday I would like to do a volume of essays that includes men's responses. I have a wish list, too: creative artists Tim Burton, American McGee, Neil Gaiman, Robert Coover, Stephen King, William Wegman, Charles Vess—I could go on and on. But the idea of *Mirror, Mirror* is to go as close to the source as we can—to go into the mirror, in a sense. When it comes to fairy tales, we ought start with *women*, as traditionally they were the major tellers and authors of the folk stories on which today's literary fairy tales are based.

Mirror, Mirror on the Wall seeks to return us to that tradition, as a beginning of protecting our knowledge of it. During time periods when written literature was almost exclusively the province of men, disenfranchised populations such as women, peasants and gypsies used oral stories as metaphoric ways of addressing their own concerns and speaking of their lives. But while the written versions we know are largely authored by men, this does not mean that women disappeared from the literary tradition of the fairy tale. Not at all. Women writers in the seventeenth-century salons of Paris created an enormously popular vogue for such tales among educated adults. This is, in fact, when the name *fairy tale* was coined! The vast majority of stories published at that time in *forty-one* volumes (*The Fairies' Cabinet*) were authored by women. Sadly, the women working in the salon tradition were overlooked by fairy tale editors in the following centuries. Let us not continue the error.

For there is a resurgence in our time of fairy tale prose. The authors in this volume are representative of that: A. S. Byatt's novel *Possession* contains a retelling of "The Glass Coffin"; Kathryn Davis's intricate novel *The Girl Who Trod on a Loaf* is based on the Andersen tale of the very same name; Midori Snyder's *The Innamorati* draws from traditional Italian lore; and Lydia Millet's *My Happy Life* contains a classic fairy tale heroine—downtrodden but full of hope. (My own novel is based on German, Russian and Yiddish tales.)

It is important to note that many authors of contemporary fairy tales have published in the "fantasy" genre—some of whom are not included in this book (Delia Sherman, Tanith Lee, Patricia McKillip, Kelly Link and others) and some who are (Terri Windling, Midori Snyder and others). Still others have published sophisticated works of children's and young adult fiction (Robin McKinley, Francesca Lia Block and Jane Yolen, for instance). Highbrow readers quick to dismiss these tales because of the genre labels might consider that these writers are also following in the footsteps of the salon writers of Paris, working subversively in fields often dismissed by the literary establishment, and staking out territory in books that have wide appeal. These authors often acknowledge their debt to a range of influences from Madame D'Aulnoy to Angela Carter. Of course, for the purposes of this collection I was limited in the *number* of authors who could participate. This expanded edition attempts to broaden its scope. Readers are encouraged not only to seek out the original tales discussed, but the multitude of contemporary writings influenced by the tales.

Readers of all educational backgrounds may also find a great wealth of information in critical works by Marina Warner, Cristina Bacchilega, Nancy Canepa, Maria Tatar, Elizabeth Wanning Harries and Jack Zipes. These writers have worked to uncover the proper history and significance of fairy tales, confronting two centuries of gender bias in fairy tale canon formation. Their writings prove that contemporary authors—many of them represented in this volume—who use fairy tales in subversive ways to create stories for adults are in fact working in a long historical tradition that will only gain in importance.

Angela Carter, perhaps the most significant twentieth-century fairy tale writer, whose presence is sorely missed on this planet, offers this passage in a collection of her own tales, *Fireworks*. It synoptically describes the connection between women and fairy tales—the first premise for this collection.

Then the city vanished; it ceased, almost immediately, to be a magic and appalling place. I woke up one morning and found it had become home. Though I still turn up my coat collar in a lonely way and am always looking at myself in mirrors, they're only habits and give no clue at all to my character, whatever that is.

These scant lines—however mysterious—might act as a metaphor for what it is like to hear fairy tales as a child, and then revisit them as an adult. When we look at them as adults, fairy tales are magic and appalling. They can give us a chill, the kind that comes from strange recognition. Like mirrors, fairy tales are suggestive openings into the self—never final answers, but only reflections.

I hope this volume makes a contribution to your appreciation of fairy tales in all their odd brilliance, as well as provides an opportunity to revisit the stories that you cherish from some moment in your life. I also hope it contributes to a historical literary tradition of women and fairy tales, which began long ago and far away, but which we can bring to the foreground again.

KATE BERNHEIMER
Portland, Oregon
December 2001

AUTHOR'S NOTE: I would like to thank Megan Hustad, Brent Hendricks and Terri Windling for their editorial generosity in connection with this second edition of *Mirror, Mirror on the Wall*.

Mirror, Mirror
on the Wall

* * * * * *

ALICE ADAMS

✳ ✳ ✳ ✳ ✳ ✳

The Three Bears and Little Red Riding Hood in the Coffin House

It is odd, I think: one's tendency to locate the imaginative literature that one reads in one's own known, familiar sites. (Or am I the only one who does this? Come to think of it, I've never mentioned this habit to another person.) In any case, for me, both "The Three Bears" and "Little Red Riding Hood" take place in a neighborhood shack that we all, as children, called "the coffin house." As much of D. H. Lawrence happened in a boathouse in Maine, but that was much later on, and not really a part of this story.

The coffin house, then, was a garage-like structure some distance off in the woods (I should note that I am speaking of the thirties, in the very rural countryside that surrounded the very small, at that time, town of Chapel Hill, North Carolina). Our neighborhood of pleasant faculty houses was out in this countryside. This fact of its being out in the woods of course lent validity to my situating such stories there; both Goldilocks and

3

Little Red Riding Hood would indeed have to walk through woods to get to the coffin house.

Actually in this storage shed there were the wooden plank cases in which coffins were transported; I cannot now imagine how we children had come by this fact, and, as I think of it, I wonder if it was even true. But we called it the coffin house, and we convinced ourselves that all those tall, upright boxes were coffins, and we also believed that the various bits of trash we found around that house were the leavings of the dead: an occasional magazine, a candy wrapper ("He must have been eating this candy bar when he died!") or a half-smoked cigarette. Going to the coffin house was always a good adventure; anything at all might be there. I suppose the ultimate hope was of finding a "dead person," somehow left behind from the funeral rites.

When I thought of Goldilocks arriving at this house, I imagined that the cases had been pushed aside and indeed thinned out to make room for the table at which the Three Bears had been eating—at which Goldilocks found the porridge of the Little Bear so delicious. I believe that I added an upstairs room for the sake of the beds. However, when I came to Little Red Riding Hood, I placed the Grandmother's bed squarely out among the coffin boxes, their looming, shadowy presences as frightening as the grotesque face of the Grandmother-wolf.

Both of these stories can be viewed as cautionary: Do not go off into the woods, and especially not by yourself—and, certainly, do not go to a house where coffins are stored, where you might just possibly find a dead body.

None of us ever mentioned the coffin house to our parents, I believe for two reasons: one, that we would be forbidden to go there; and two, that we would be exposed as credulous, and told, "Of course those aren't real coffins, they're just big empty boxes." It was infinitely preferable to cling to our myth, our titillating terror.

The worst possible crime available to a child, back then, was to run away from home. This was always a thrilling possibility—no wonder we were so frequently warned against any version thereof, like walking off into the woods by yourself. I, of course, a rebellious and in many ways discontented child who longed for a change of scene—I was enthralled by the notion of running away. But I was also a fearful child, and I never got much farther than the woods with which I was deeply familiar.

I was drawn to both "Little Red Riding Hood" and "Goldilocks and the Three Bears" as fantasies of escape, and, curiously, when recently I began to think of them again, I could not remember how either of them ended—until I asked my son, who set me straight.

There are, as I now understand it, at least two accepted versions of how things turned out for Little Red Riding Hood. In one, the Grandmother reveals her true character as the predatory, carnivorous wolf who gobbles up the child. In the other, a kindly woodsman, fortuitously in the neighborhood, comes along to save the little girl. In some versions he comes before, in others after she is eaten alive; in the latter story she is removed with an ax from the stomach of the wolf—dead wolf, happily rescued little girl. In psychoanalytic terms, I take this to mean that your mother will get you in the end, probably; your father might or might not save you. In any case, it seemed too dangerous a chance for me to take.

In most versions of "The Three Bears," at the end the intruding little girl, Goldilocks, is somehow ejected from the home of the bears, sometimes thrown from an upstairs window;

other stories have her peaceably leaving through the front door, with polite and friendly parting waves.

But I seem to have found or invented still a third version of my own, in which having at last come upon such a warm and congenial family, Goldilocks is adopted by that family, with the Littlest Bear for her brother (something I very much wished I had).

The coffin house, then, contained infinite possibility, either bloody death at the hands (or teeth!) of the ultimate witch— or, conversely, a brand-new warm and affectionate family.

I do not think I really believed that stuff about coffins and dead people for a minute, but I did believe in the possibility of change—and in fantasy.

JULIA ALVAREZ

✳ ✳ ✳ ✳ ✳ ✳

An Autobiography
of Scheherazade

Once upon a time, I lived in another country and in another
language under a cruel dictatorship which my father was
plotting to overthrow. This is not a fairy tale. This is the story of
my childhood in the Dominican Republic under the dictatorship of El Jefe. But what I remember is not the cruel dictator,
not the disappearances, not my parents' nervous voices behind
closed doors, but the storybook that helped me get through the
long, dull schooldays that were my understanding of what dic-
tatorships made children do.

I lay on my stomach under my bed, a six-, seven-, eight-,
nine-, ten-year-old girl—this went on for a long time as long
times do during childhood. With the bedskirt providing a perfect cover, I felt as if I had actually been transported to a silken
tent in a faraway country with nothing but my wits to keep me
alive. The storybook I was reading was one that my maiden
aunt Titi, the only reader I knew, had given me. *The Thousand
and One Nights*, it was called, and on its cover sat a young girl

with a veil over her long dark hair and beside her, reclining on one elbow and listening to what she was saying, was a young man with a turban wound around his head. What I liked about this young girl was that unlike the fair princesses and pale blond and brunette heroines in the other storybooks, Scheherazade could have been a Dominican girl: dark-skinned, dark-haired, almond-eyed. She was the only heroine who looked like another smart girl from the Third World.

This book was the only voluntary reading I did, for I was a poor student and poorly behaved. In fact, if you want to know the truth, the reason I was hiding under the bed this early in the morning instead of reading my book openly on top of my bed was to avoid having to go to school that day.

Every morning after breakfast my mother and aunts rounded up my sisters and cousins for the drive to the Carol Morgan School. There was a crowd of us—three cars were needed—and by the time one car was filled up and on its way, the aunts weren't quite sure who had already gone and who was left to transport. So, if I slipped away from my sisters and cousins, and hightailed it to my bedroom, and threw myself under the bed, and stayed there, quietly reading my book of stories, it would not be until midday, when the school crowd returned for *la comida del mediodía*, that my mother realized that I had played hooky again right under her very nose.

Why did I do this? School was deadly. I thought I would surely die of boredom sitting on that hard chair listening to Mrs. Brown talk about the pilgrims or *i* before *e* or George Washington cutting down a cherry tree. We were attending the Carol Morgan School because my parents had decided that we should learn English and get "an American education" rather than a Dominican one. To this day, they say this choice eventually made our transition to the United States so much easier. But how could they have known back then that we would be going into exile in a few years?

So what I was learning in school had nothing to do with the brilliantly colored, tropical, and dangerous world around me. We were living in a dictatorship, complete with spies, late-night disappearances, torture, and death. What, indeed, did this world have to do with the capital of Alabama and Dick and Jane and a big red bouncing ball? And what on earth was apple pie? Was it anything at all like a *pastel de tamarindo?* No wonder I shut the doors to my attention and refused to do my homework. My education was a colonialist one: not imposed from the outside but from within my own family. I was to learn the culture, tongue, manners of the powerful country to our north who had put our dictator in place and kept him there for thirty-one years. Maybe my parents did know what they were doing.

And maybe I, sensing the unspoken world of intrigue and danger around me, where El Jefe ruled supreme, found kinship with the girl on the cover of my storybook.

Certainly she had more to say to me than Dick and Jane.

I am Scheherazade, she would always begin. *I am a girl stuck in a kingdom that doesn't think females are very important.*

Why, that's just like me, I'd pipe up. It's always the boy cousins who are asked what they want to do with their lives. We girls are told we are going to be wives and mothers. If we're asked anything at all, it's how many children we want and whom we might want to marry.

But even though I am a girl, Scheherazade went on, *I am ambitious and clever and I've found ways of getting around the restraints put upon me.*

Why, that's just like me, I put in. Here I am, hiding under this bed in the middle of a school day, doing what I please. And I've found other ways of getting around things as well. I can learn any poem by heart if I hear it read out loud a few times. When company comes, Mami dresses me up in my first-communion dress and takes me out to recite in front of everyone. They reward me with *pesetas* and sometimes a whole *peso*. I've already told Mami that when I grow up, I'll go ahead and have those half-dozen babies I'm supposed to have, but I'm also going to become a famous actress who gets to travel around the world and do whatever she wants—

Very recently, I had a shock, Scheherazade interrupted. (*Pobrecita*, she could hardly get a word in edgewise!) *I found out that I am living in a country where our cruel sultan is killing all my girlfriends. First he marries them, then the next day he kills them. I've been racking my brains, trying to figure out a way to stop all this killing, and I think I've finally got a plan.*

Far off in the direction of the *palacio nacional*, a siren sounded. I wasn't sure what it meant. Sometimes the siren meant a "resignation," with the retiree appearing in the papers a few days later in a black-outlined box with a crucifix and *Que descanse en paz* above a blurry photo of his face. Sometimes the siren meant our *jefe*, Rafael Leonidas Trujillo, was going out, and so the streets had to be cleared. I am sure that siren also meant other things my parents were afraid to tell me.

What I am going to do, Scheherazade confided, *is marry the sultan and then before he can kill me the next morning, I'm going to tell him a story.*

That's worked for me, I said, nodding at her bright-eyed face on the cover. Many, many times I had escaped punishment with a story. Just last week Mami came rushing to find out who had broken my grandmother's blue crystal ball that sat on a pedestal under the tamarind tree. Of course, it seemed pretty obvious to her when she found my cousin Ique and me holding rakes, but I set her straight. I told Mami that the reason we were holding rakes was that we had just chased off the man who had broken the ball.

"And what man would that be?" my mother asked, eyes narrowed.

Hmm, I thought. What man would that be? I knew my parents were afraid of the *guardia* who periodically came on the property searching for an acquaintance or just asking for *un regalito* to buy their *cigarillos*. So, I explained that the man we had chased off was a *guardia* whom we had caught snooping around the property.

That sent a volley of scared looks among the adults who had followed my mother outside at the sound of breaking glass. How was I supposed to know that my father and uncles had joined the underground and were plotting the overthrow of the dictator? That my parents' seeming compliance was all show. That *guardia* on the grounds meant my family's participation had been uncovered. The adults went off in a cold sweat to a private conference behind locked doors while Ique and I were left to enjoy the tamarinds we had knocked down with our rakes.

I finally talk my father into going along with my plan, Scheherazade continued, *and so after my first night with the sultan, just as the sun is coming up, I say to the sultan, Oh, sultan, would you like to hear one of my wonderful stories? And the sultan shrugs, sure, go ahead—*

Just then, the bedskirt was lifted up. My mother's face peered angrily at me. "So, this is where you are. Come out this instant!" I crept out slowly, hunching my shoulders as if to take up less space on this earth. My mother shook me by the arm. "You better have a good explanation as to what you're doing under that bed instead of at school with your sisters."

Her yanking shook the book out of my hands. It fell, face up, on the floor. Scheherazade gazed up at me with an eager look in her eye as if to say, "Go ahead, girl. Think up something!"

Early on I learned that stories could save you. That stories could weave a spell even over powerful adults and get them off your case and on to other things like talking politics behind closed doors or making a tamarind *pastel* in the kitchen.

The power of stories was all around me, for the tradition of storytelling was deeply rooted in my Dominican culture. With more than eighty percent illiteracy when I was growing up, the culture was still an oral culture. Rarely did I see anyone reading a book, except for my aunt Titi—and that was the reason, everyone knew, why at twenty-five she wasn't yet married. (She also wore pajamas and knew Latin and read the dictionary, which didn't help matters any.) Mostly people listened to radio programs and to each other. Streets were known, not by street signs, but by the stories or characters or events associated with them. The street where Chucho lives. You know, Chucho, the man born with a sixth finger on each hand because when his mother was pregnant, she stole a piece of *pudín de pan* from a neighbor, and so God punished her by putting an extra, shoplifting finger on her son's hands.

Ah yes, *that* Chucho, *that* street!

So it is no surprise, given my island oral tradition, that I became a storyteller. But it is still a surprise to me—given my nonliterary childhood, my aversion to writing and to anything that smacked of a classroom—that I grew up to write books that students read and discuss, sitting at their desks in school, instead of lying on their stomachs under a bed with a stolen flashlight.

Of course, what made this second surprise happen was an even bigger surprise, the surprise of my life, you could call it: escaping to the United States in August 1960, with the SIM, the secret police, on my father's tail. Suddenly overnight, we lost everything: a homeland, an extended family, a culture, and yes, even a language, for Spanish was my mother tongue, the language I used inside my head. The classroom English I had learned at Carol Morgan had very little to do with the English being spoken on the streets and in the playgrounds of New York City. I could not understand most things the Americans were saying to me with their marbles-in-their-mouths, fast-talking, elided American English which Walt Whitman rightly termed "that barbaric yawp."

One thing I did understand. Boys at school chased me across the playground, pelting me with little stones, yelling, "Spic! Spic! Go back to where you came from!"

"I don't ehspeak een-gleesh," I lied, taking the easy way out instead of being brave and speaking up like Scheherazade.

But my silence was also strategy. Inside my head a rich conversation had started, inspired by the world of books. Not just *The Thousand and One Nights*, but Nancy Drew mysteries, *Little Women, Winnie-the-Pooh*. I was encouraged by teachers who asked me to write down what I remembered about that world I was so homesick for. I found that if I wrote down *the bright pink flowers in Mamita's garden*, I could summon up my grand-mother's back patio with the hot-pink bougainvillea dropping down through the slats of the overhead trellis. By rubbing the lamp of language I could make the genie appear: the sights, sounds, smells, the people and places of the homeland I had lost.

I realized something I had always known lying on my stomach under the bed: language was power. Written-down language was money in the bank.

Still, I remember their faces. The corners of their mouths were stained with egg yolk. Their eyes were pale blue or gray—some drained, bleached color without warmth or kindness. In their jeering voices I could hear some other voice—maybe a parent's—hurling the same kind of insults at them. I dreaded this playground gang because I could not speak *their* language clearly enough to make them understand that I was not the enemy. The little island with bombs aimed in the direction of New York City was our next-door neighbor Cuba, not the Dominican Republic. If anything, our dictator knew on which side his cassava was oiled and salted. But how could I make these boys understand these fine distinctions when the moment I opened my mouth, they made fun of me.

"I don't ehspeak een-gleesh," they taunted my accent. "I'm Chiquita Banana and I'm here to say . . ." They glared at me as if I were some repulsive creature with six fingers on *both* hands.

Sometimes the teacher caught them and gave them a talking-to or kept them after school. Finally, the pain of punishment must not have been worth the pleasure of watching me burst into tears, and so they gave up picking on me and started in on someone else.

Looking back now, I can see that my path as a writer began in that playground. Somewhere inside, where we make promises to ourselves, I told myself I would learn English so well that Americans would sit up and notice. I told myself that one day I would express myself in a way that would make those boys feel bad they had tormented me. Yes, it was revenge that set me on the path of becoming a writer, but that only got me down a short way on that hard, lifetime road. At some point, revenge turned into redemption. Instead of pummeling those boys with my success, I began to want to save them. (I have not spoken of my Catholic background and my other great childhood heroine, Joan of Arc.) I wanted to change those looks of hate and mistrust, to transform the sultan's face into the beautiful face of the reclining prince on the cover of my childhood storybook.

Where did I get the idea that stories could do that? That *I* could do that?

I grew up hearing a different story about who I was and where I was going. Neither Scheherazade nor Joan of Arc, for that matter, were the approved heroines of my childhood. Instead, the ready-made autobiography I was given by my parents, my aunts, and teachers was the age-old fairy tale–princess story: Cinderella, mixed in with lots of Sleeping Beauty and the Virgin Mary.

Once upon a time there was a sweet, pretty, passive, powerless, and probably blond (stay out of the sun!) princess who never played hooky from school or told lies about who broke the crystal ball in her grand-mother's garden. The handsome (Catholic) prince of the land fell in love with her, married her, and she lived happily ever after as his lucky wife and the mother of his children.

This is the true shape of every happy woman's life, I was told. Give and take a few adjectives—maybe not so pretty, maybe not so passive—this is what you should aspire to be. Especially once I hit adolescence, I was told this story over and over.

But the problem was that there was another story in my head. In the back rooms of my mind, Scheherazade was recounting another version of my life: if I wanted to tell stories, I'd better get off my butt and write them down.

My mother and aunts shook their heads knowingly. "Be smart: get married while you're still young and pretty and can attract a good man. Have your children while you're still young and energetic and have the energy for children. You can always write." That is what they said. You can *always* write, as if writing were some automatic skill you could pick up when you wanted. As if it did not have to be cultivated, worked at, husbanded. As if you did not have to give your whole life over to it—isn't that what Scheherazade had done? And one life might not be enough. Even Chaucer, one of the masters of English literature, complained about how little time there was to master the craft of writing. "The lyf so short, the craft so long to lerne."

And so, I married, not once, but twice before I was thirty, searching for that right man, for that elusive happiness. With each marriage, I put aside my writing. It was nobody's fault, really. Back in those pre-women's-movement years, wives did not lock themselves up to write books. I'd sooner have had an affair than go off to my room to write and leave my husband to fend for himself.

Instead, I closed the door to that world of books. I wrote very little those years I was married. But she was back there in my head, Scheherazade, causing trouble, waking me up in the middle of the night with her stories of the life I could be living if I trusted myself, if I became my own woman, if I followed my heart's desire and brought forth what was inside me to bring forth.

Both marriages were brief. I was not yet thirty and I was *twice* divorced. No one we knew got divorced at all, and only movie stars got divorced more than once. I was a true failure at the fairy tale–princess story. There was no way to tidy up my messy life and come out with a happy ending. No one expected much from me anymore. Mami stopped making suggestions. The aunts sighed a lot, but said nothing.

And so ironically, my two failures freed me to be whoever I was. On my customs card coming back from the D.R., where I had gone after my second divorce, I wrote down *teacher* after *occupation*. Then I rethought my answer and made a slash mark and added *writer*.

"Oh?" the customs officer asked me when he had skimmed through the card. "What have you written? Anything I've heard of?"

"Not yet," I murmured.

That summer I enrolled in a fiction workshop and began writing stories. I set up a writing schedule and I kept to it. I began to make decisions based not on how to make my life safe and cushioned so that I could accommodate my princess fears and fantasies, but on what choices would allow me to pursue the dream in my heart. Many times I made what looked like seemingly foolish choices, giving up "perfectly good" jobs or turning down job offers because during the interview with prospective employers it would become clear that I would have no time for writing during the school year. "You can always write summers," they suggested.

But I wanted to write right *now*. And so I made a space for it in my head, my heart, and in my working day. I wrote every morning, even if it was only for a brief half hour or hour before I turned to my stack of papers to correct or lesson plans to prepare. The days I absolutely could not write because there was no time, I felt off balance, defeated, as if I were one of the damsels who had not gotten away from the sultan. It was turning out to be true, what William Carlos Williams had said, that "one cannot get the news from poems, but men [and women] die daily for lack of what is found there."

Years went by, and I kept on writing, and teaching at whatever institution would allow me that little extra time every day to write. These jobs were mostly adjunct instructor jobs at local colleges, teaching however many sections of freshman composition would pay the rent and put food on the table and still give me time to write. As I published more, I managed to get jobs as a visiting writer. These positions were never secure, funded according to the vagaries of class enrollments or arts funding. And so I moved across America from colleges to old-age homes to poets-in-the-schools programs to private schools to universities, replacing someone on his Guggenheim or staffing an extra fiction-writing course that had been added at registration. I should have gotten vanity plates for my ancient yellow VW that read HAVE TYPEWRITER/WILL TRAVEL. And I continued to publish, to send out my poems and stories.

Among my circle of friends, everyone had married, once, or

if twice, they stayed married. Many had children and seemed to be settled down for the rest of their lives. And here I was, still on the road, in a rusted old car, supporting myself with hand-to-mouth jobs. Many nights I woke up at three in the morning in Illinois or Washington, D.C., or Delaware or Vermont and wondered if I was fooling myself. Maybe I was a deluded Scheherazade? The few single men I was now meeting looked over my shoulder at the pretty, young arrivals in the field of time. It was just as well, I told myself (not fully convinced). I had never been successful at picking a lover with whom I could be both a wife *and* a writer.

Ten years after the fairy tale fiasco of my second marriage, happiness surprised me. A feisty Scheherazade-type agent found a good publisher for my first novel. I also found a true *compañero* for the woman I had become. The first night we went out we stayed up late telling each other the story of our lives. Since we were already middle-aged, we needed a second night to continue the narrative, and a third, and a fourth. We found that our individual narratives could be woven into whole cloth with nothing important left out.

What if she hadn't been in that back room of my mind, under the bedskirt of my consciousness? What if early on I hadn't found Scheherazade's example to kindle in me the possibility of another choice? If I hadn't seen her reflection in the mirror: a woman who used words to weave a web of enchantment, a woman who was not going to be a victim, a woman who took matters into her own hands?

Maybe I would have found her anyway because, as I mentioned earlier, I was raised in a storytelling culture. Certainly, in coming to this country and this new language, I discovered new resources and the need for self-invention. What was already a natural love of words and their music, of narrative and its enchantments, might have come to the fore, and I would have become a writer anyhow.

But I am glad that she came so early into my life and into my imagination so that her voice was not completely drowned out by the other voices that were telling me something else. Early on I became Scheherazade—one of her thousand and one incarnations. I began to tell stories to anyone who would listen and even to those who would not. It was just a matter of time before I, too, listened to the story I was telling myself about who I really was.

MARGARET ATWOOD

✳ ✳ ✳ ✳ ✳ ✳

Of Souls as Birds

When she was little Frieda had loved the goblins, the princesses,
the old men of the sea, the water maidens, the raven brothers,
the haunted woods. Yet the stories were often absurd, often
inconsequential. Frieda's literal, logical battleaxe of a mind had
been bemused and entangled by these tales. She had tried to
chop her way through the briars. She did not like nonsense.
There was a mystery there, forever beyond her grasp.
——MARGARET DRABBLE, The Witch of Exmoor

The French writer Colette believed that you should have either too many truffles, or none at all. Just one would not suffice; and so it is with fairy tales. One or two won't do it. But what is "it"? Think of a Bible that contained only the story of Cain and Abel, or an *Odyssey* that began and ended with the cave of the Cyclops. The body of folktale is indeed a body, an organic structure made of its many component parts. One story alone is only a finger or a toe.

Once upon a time, long, long ago—to be precise, in the 1950s—the body of European folktale as it was known in North America was severely constricted; most of it was kept veiled from view, and only a few tales were popularly circulated. These were pinkly illustrated versions of "Cinderella" or "The Sleeping Beauty," stories whose plots were dependent on female servility, immobility or even stupor, and on princely rescue; and it's entirely understandable that women for whom "fairy tale" meant this sort of thing would have objected to it as encouraging girlie inertia. Even these few stories had been censored—all vengefulness, all pecked-out eyes and nail-studded barrels removed: The wicked sisters danced at the wedding, but not in red-hot shoes. It was thought wrong at that time to encourage or even to acknowledge the darker emotions. For well-brought-up little girls of the fifties, the main point of these stories was the outfits. Ruffles were all.

I was not a well-brought-up little girl of the fifties. I had been born in 1939, just after the outbreak of the Second World War, and there was no hope then of sweeping the darker emotions under the rug. There they were on the world stage, displayed for all to see: fear, hatred, cruelty, blood and slaughter. A few fairy tale hanged corpses and chopped-off heads were, by comparison, nothing to get squeamish about.

Also, I was exposed to a large chunk of these tales at an early age, before the manicured versions had hit the stands. When I was five or six, my parents sent away by mail-order for *The Complete Grimms' Fairy Tales.* This was the 1944 Pantheon edition, with an excellent translation by Padraic Colum and a commentary by Joseph Campbell, and it was flagrantly unexpurgated.

The illustrations were by Josef Scharl, and they were not at all pretty, not even in the Arthur Rackham gnarly-goblin way, but they were very forceful, emerging as they did straight from the same traditions of peasant folk art that had shaped the tales themselves.

This was a tradition that called a spade a spade, a wart a wart, and an ugly sister an ugly sister, and most likely a witch into the bargain. Your starving parents might leave you in the woods, to save the last bit of food for themselves. Your stepmother might plot to get rid of you so her own kid would inherit the loot. For the most part, life was hard, and lived close to the rock, and driven by the *sauve-qui-peut* variety of common sense; temptations to evil abounded, and were frequently heeded. There was many a skeleton in a dress, many a heart on a plate, many a hairy pot-bellied devil; blood gushed from loaves of bread, coal-eyed cats breathed fire. It was a long way from outfits: there was not a ruffle to be seen.

This wasn't a book designed to please every small child. To some it would have given screaming nightmares. Possibly it had in mind a more adult audience. My parents were taken aback when the book arrived, and contemplated withholding it, at least until my brother and I were older; but it was no use. We could both read by that time, and we ate this book up. Not one truffle at a time: the whole basketful.

What was the appeal? It's hard to be definite about that. The stories didn't have any direct application to our real lives. They weren't much good from a practical point of view. At this time we were living for half the year in the Canadian north woods, and we knew that if we went for a walk there we were unlikely to come upon any castles, if we met any bears or wolves they wouldn't be the talking kind, if we kissed a frog it would most likely pee on us, and if we got lost we wouldn't find any short-sighted, evil old women with patisserie cottages and child-sized ovens. Rescue, if any, would not be supplied by princes.

So it wasn't our outer lives that the Grimms' tales addressed: it was our inner ones. These stories have survived as stories, over so many centuries and in so many variations, because they do make such an appeal to the inner life—you could say "the dreaming self" and not be too far wrong, because they are the stuff both of nightmare and of magical thinking. As Margaret Drabble says, there's a mystery in such stories which is beyond the grasp of the rational mind. There's also a large element of the haphazard. The rules—about elderly people in forest settings, about speaking to shabby-looking although prestidigitous strangers, about animals gifted with large vocabularies—are arbitrary, and they vary from tale to tale. In one story, a talking wolf is your friend; in another, he's out to eat your granny. In one, old folks in the shrubbery must be given your lunchtime sandwich or bad luck will befall you; in another, they're just waiting to turn you into stone, or into dinner. Things happen in fairy tales because they happen, as in dreams; and as in dreams, there are large anxieties, and sudden victories, and serendipitous gifts; and as in dreams, there are recurring patterns.

Fairy tales were a taste that stayed with me; but although I went on to read all of the Andrew Lang *Blue, Green, Red* and *Yellow Fairy Books* that I could get my hands on, as well as the Arabian Nights and Lamb's *Tales of the Gods and Heroes*, and Dickens's *Christmas Carol* and Ruskin's *King of the Golden River*, and the complete tales of Edgar Allan Poe, and *The Wizard of Oz*, and anything else of that kind I might stumble across, I kept returning to the Grimms' stories. By the age of nine or ten I'd memorized a good many of them.

Asking which story was my favorite might seem like asking Colette which was her favorite truffle; yet I did have favorites. Thinking back some fifty years later, trying to pinpoint which these were, I'd have to say they were the ones with birds in them.

Now, in real life birds were birds. They cawed, hooted, quacked and chirped, and, if they were loons, made eerie sounds at night that caused the hair to stand up on your arms. But in fairy tales, birds were either messengers that led you deeper into the forest on some quest, or brought you news or help, or warned you, like the bird at the robbers' house in "The Robber Bridegroom," or meted out vengeance, like the eye-pecking doves at the end of "Cinderella"; or else they were something you could be transformed into. These last were my kind of birds.

For instance? There are a lot of for instances. In "The Singing, Soaring Lark," the bridegroom is a Cupid figure who is transformed into a white dove because his bride has disobeyed his orders to let no ray of light fall on him; she must follow his trail of blood and feathers until she can change him back through her devotion. In "Jorinda and Joringel," the beloved is transformed into a caged nightingale by a malicious witch, and can be freed only if her lover can recognize her in her bird form. In "The Six Swans," "The Seven Ravens" and "The Twelve Brothers," various assortments of brothers are changed into swans or ravens—usually through some indiscretion or ill will on their father's part—and are rescued by their only sister, who must undergo some radical ordeal on their behalf. She must keep silent, she must not laugh, she must make little shirts for them, she must risk being burnt at the stake as a witch, until the time comes when they may be released. "The Twelve Brothers" is the most complex of these three, and is noteworthy because the brothers are to be killed by their parents—who are having twelve creepy little coffins made in secret, each with a little death pillow in it—if the expected thirteenth baby is a girl, because the king wants her alone to inherit. So much for the supposed universal sexism of fairy tales.

Two of the most compelling bird-transformation tales are "The Juniper Tree" and "Fitcher's Bird." In ordering their collection, the Grimm brothers placed them back to back, as if they knew the two had something to do with each other. "The Juniper Tree" features one of the most memorable of evil stepmothers—memorable not only because she's so well rendered, but because at the end you actually feel sorry for her.

In this story, it's not Snow White who is as red as blood and as white as snow. Instead it's a little boy, who is wished into being when his mother cuts her finger and sees the red blood on the white snow, and who is born after an especially lyrical passage detailing each month of his mother's pregnancy, which parallels the springtime, the summer, and the ripening fruit of the juniper tree that stands outside her house. This, then, is to be a year-boy, called into being by blood on the snow, nourished by the growing seasons, and doomed to sacrifice. I didn't think this as a child, of course. I was just sad when the mother died.

The father marries again, and the stepmother favors her own daughter. They tend to, in the world of the Grimms. She thinks of ways to get rid of the little boy so her daughter can inherit everything, and finally entices him to a large chest where she keeps apples and suggests he pick out an apple for himself. (It's apple time, autumn time, end of the road for little year-boys.) Then she lets the sharp lid fall on his neck, and off comes his head. Terrified by what she has done, she sets the boy's head back on the body, winds a handkerchief around the neck, puts an apple in his hand, and fools her daughter into giving him a box on the ear when he won't speak to her.

(In the early sixties I published a poem based on this story, which began, "I keep my brother's head among the apples." My friend Beverly, who worked at the same market-research company as I did, has recently confessed to me that she came across this poem and was badly frightened by it. She didn't know about the original story; she thought I might just be too weird for words. Such are the hazards of mythopoetry.)

The story continues. What is to be done with the dead boy, so as to conceal the awful deed from his father? The poor little girl is in an agony of sorrow and guilt, as she thinks she's done it, and the mother lets her think so. (*Sauve qui peut.*) Nothing for it but to make the boy into black-puddings, bones and all. At dinner, the father gobbles up everything, declaring that this is the most delicious food he's ever tasted. But Marlinchen, the sister, gathers up all the bones and ties them into her best silk handkerchief, and carries them outside, "weeping tears of blood." (Those tears of blood haunted me as a child; I could picture them all too well, and certainly hoped I would never weep any.) She buries them under the juniper tree, where the dead mother is already buried; and the tree which is really the mother gives birth to her son again, this time in the form of a bird:

*The juniper tree began to stir itself, and the branches parted asun-
der, and moved together again, just as if someone were rejoicing. . . . At the same time a mist seemed to arise from the tree,
and at the centre of this mist it burned like fire, and a beautiful
bird flew out of the fire singing magnificently . . . and when he
was gone, the juniper tree was just as it had been before, and the
handkerchief with the bones was no longer there. Marlinchen,
however, was as gay and happy as if her brother were still alive.*

Which he is, but in a soul-form. He signs a song, which recounts his own murder, the way he was cannibalized, and how
his bones were gathered together and buried under the juniper
tree; his song is so splendid that it compels all who hear it to
listen, and to reward him for singing it a second time. In this
way he collects a golden chain from a goldsmith, a pair of red
shoes from a shoemaker, and a millstone from a miller. Then he
returns home and sings to entice his family members outside.
The father is rewarded with the gold chain and the sister with
the red shoes. The stepmother, who by this time is in a state of
extreme terror, with her hair standing up "like flames of fire"—
only she, it appears, knows who the bird really is and what the
words of his song signify—is compelled to rush outside as well,
and is crushed by the millstone. Pyrotechnics occur, one dead
person is exchanged for another, and when the smoke clears
there is the little brother again; he takes the hands of his father
and sister, and in a spirit of joy and renewal, and not at all dis-
concerted by the fiery end of the wife of one and the mother of
another, they all go into the house and eat. The year-boy has
been resurrected, and the story fittingly concludes with a feast.
(The first mother however is not restored. She remains a tree.
As a child, I experienced that as an omission.)

What I liked about this story—and about all the stories in which people were changed into birds and then changed back—is that there was in fact a formula for changing them back. They could be *brought* back, out of that other form within which their real selves were concealed. At some level it did not escape me that those changed into birds in fairy tales were in fact not just changed but dead. The swan brothers had evaded their little coffins only to be put into coffins of another sort— they were imprisoned in the bodies of an alien species. At that time I knew nothing about the many legends and the many cultures in which the souls of the dead become birds of various kinds; but I knew that the people transformed to birds in these stories were dead people, and that the act involved in changing them back to human beings was an act not only of metamorphosis but of resurrection. The white feathery swan bodies are shed like shrouds as the brothers step back into the ordinary light of daily life.

Nor was it lost on me that in most of the tales I've mentioned, the rescuer was a sister. I was a sister myself, and was pleased to be assigned such an active role. For others—for brothers—the transformation into swans; for me, the task of knitting little shirts in order to magic these swan-brothers back from the dead. All my skill and tenacity would be needed, but if I stuck at it long enough I would get results.

Why was I interested in bringing the dead back to life? Most children are, especially if they've known someone who has died, or who has threatened to. Their understanding of death doesn't usually go so far as nonbeing; especially at a time when children were told that dead people had gone to Heaven, or had gone away, or had become angels, children were not likely to believe that a dead person was not; instead, they believed that the dead were somewhere else, or possibly something else. Dying was a major—the major—form of transformation. It meant that the dead went away, right out of their bodies, and who knows what shape they might assume then? In any case, wherever or whatever they were, they could no longer speak to you, they could no longer communicate. (Hence, no doubt, the fairy tale prohibition against speaking, for so many of those who assume the task of rescue: The rescuer has to identify partially with the one to be rescued—has to have, as it were, one foot in the grave.)

I wasn't much worried about dying myself; I didn't consider it likely. But I was worried about others. My father gave me no concern; he was dependable, and appeared to be quite solidly planted to this earth; but not so my mother and my brother. For the most part it was mothers and brothers who died in the stories, not fathers and daughters, and my mother and my brother seemed more likely candidates. When I was nine, my mother had been carted off to the hospital under mysterious circumstances involving blood. My brother had almost drowned—when I was too young to remember, but I'd been told about it—and had narrowly avoided death by lightning, an event I'd witnessed; so he didn't seem to me to have an unchallenged grip on life. Should he slip away somehow, or should my mother vanish a second time in an ambulance, it would be useful to know what to do. Or to know that there was something to be known, if only I could find it out; some cave to descend into, something to weave, a set of instructions to follow; a way of calling back. Resurrection is an idea which is very attractive to children. It means that nothing and nobody will ever be permanently lost. So this was the appeal of "The Juniper Tree."

"Fitcher's Bird" was quite different. It concerns a wizard who takes the form of a poor man and goes begging, carrying a large basket on his back. Those who give him bread, and whom he touches, are forced to jump into his basket. His victims are pretty girls, and when he hits a family with three of them in it, he starts off with the eldest.

Once in his basket, she is carried away to his magnificent house in the middle of a dark forest. Here she is showered with "whatsoever she could possibly desire," until the day when he says he has to go away on a visit, and hands her the keys to the house—along with an egg, which is to be carefully preserved, and a command that she shall not enter one forbidden room. Of course she does enter it; and when she sees that it contains an ax, and a large basin full of blood, and the cut-up bodies of previous curious girls, she drops the egg in terror. It falls into the basin, and the bloodstains will not come off it. Back comes the wizard, demanding keys and egg; when he sees the evidence of the girl's disobedience, it's off with her head and other appendages, and into the basin she goes.

It's the same with the second pretty sister; but the third one is "clever and wily." After the wizard leaves the house, this girl puts the egg away carefully on a shelf, and not until then does she examine the forbidden room. She's horrified to discover her two sisters cut into pieces; but when she puts them together in the right order, the pieces join themselves together and the girls come alive again (thus recapitulating the behavior of slaughtered and eaten prey animals when their bones are set in order, in the ancient shamanistic rituals of northern Europe; but I didn't know that as a child). The third sister hides her two revived siblings, and awaits the wizard's return.

When he sees the spotless egg, he declares that the third girl has passed the test: first prize, marriage to him. But somehow he has lost his former powers over her, and is "forced to do whatever she wished." (Once the question is popped, it's wedding-rehearsal time, and the former Svengali turns instantly into a Ken doll.) The girl orders him to carry a basketful of gold to her parents; but in the basket she hides her two sisters. She warns the wizard that she'll have her eye on him, and will know if he's slacking. Every time the poor man sits down to rest, one of the sisters orders him to go on, and the unfortunate man thinks it's his bride-to-be nagging.

Meanwhile the girl is keeping busy. She takes a skull—there must have been plenty lying around—and dresses it up in bridal ornaments and flowers, and sets it in a window, looking out. Then she gets into a barrel of honey, and after that she rolls in the contents of a featherbed, until she looks like a "wondrous bird." Thus disguised, she makes her escape from the forest. On her way she encounters the wizard's friends, going to the wedding; when questioned by them, she replies with a bird-like song, which instructs them to look up at the house and see the bride peeping out of the window. Even the wizard is fooled. When all the wizardly crew is in the house, the "brothers and kinsmen" of the girl arrive, summoned by the two sisters, and burn down the house, with the whole evil crew inside it.

This is of course a version of the Bluebeard story. When I came across the Perrault rendition a couple of years later, I was somewhat disappointed. Although there's the added feature of a blue beard—the "Fitcher's Bird" wizard lacks this growth—I found the story somewhat preachy, with various tut-tuts about female curiosity. Also there's a Sister Anne present in the house—who invited *her*, I wondered—and the heroine is powerless to help herself, but after many tears and considerable whining, must be rescued by her brothers. Brothers feature in

"Fitcher's Bird" too—in stories as in real life, they're useful for setting fires—but not until the very end, when the clever third sister has outsmarted the wizard and has made her escape through the forest, alone, with the aid of nothing but wits and guts and a talent for improvised costumes. Nobody raps *her* knuckles for being curious.

Not everyone prefers the Grimms' variant to the Perrault: Marina Warner, in her fairy tale magnum opus, *From the Beast to the Blonde*, calls the Grimms' story "a rummage bag," "eerie, volatile and curiously unfocussed socially and politically"; and there are indeed some puzzling things in it. Who, for instance, is Fitcher? Why does the heroine disguise herself as a bird? Why the egg? None of these things troubled my sleep as a child— "Fitcher" was obviously the name of the wizard, an egg was a good choice as a telltale object, since stains are notoriously difficult to get off an egg—I knew this from Easter egg painting— and a bird seemed as good a disguise as any, although I did wonder whether the girl dipped herself in the honey with or without her own clothes on; without, I suspected.

However, as an adult I had second thoughts. Marina Warner calls the bloody egg "a queasy female symbol," which it well may be; but it's also a queasy male one, as I learned from my German publisher. The story had stayed with me, and over the years I'd written several variations on it, including a story called "Bluebeard's Egg," which also became the title of a story collection; but this title could not be directly translated into German, as "eggs" in German is a slang word for "testicles," and the title would have meant "Bluebeard's Testicle," or something more like "Bluebeard's Single Ball," which would not—I was assured—have been dignified. In this light the egg in the story can be seen as the repository of the man's sexual honor, and the entry into the forbidden room and the dirtying of the egg is not only disobedience—a Pandora curiosity-thy-name-is-woman motif—but sexual treachery. The man, wizard or not, is still a man, and like most men is seeking a bride who will be true to him and not besmirch his eggs. Thus his motive for chopping up the egg-dirtying girls: they've sullied his honor. Eggs can be many other things as well, but it seems to me that a reading of this particular story should include the testicle connection.

As for the name: the wizard's name in German is not "Fitcher," but "Fichter." A search through my German dictionary gave me no "Fichter" as a noun, but it did give me *ficht* as a past tense of the irregular verb *fechten*, to fight, and *fechten gehen*, to go begging. (The English "fight" and "fetch" are probably relatives of this verb.) Since the wizard disguises himself as a beggar, I'd guess that the meaning of "Fichter," in the context of the story, lies somewhere in this area.

But what about the girl's own disguise? Hers is actually twofold: as a "wondrous bird"—like the dead boy's other form in "The Juniper Tree"—and as her alter ego, the decked-out death's-head posing as her bridal self which is an integral part of the deception, and thus of the girl's successful flight. Take the wizard's house "in a dark forest" as the realm of death, with the wizard as a sort of Pluto who carries Persephone-maidens off to it. Then what you have is a girl who is forced to enter the place of death, and acquires a bodily death-form which she leaves behind her (the beflowered skull appropriate, as it is indeed Death who is the wizard's ultimate bride), and a soul-form (the wondrous bird). Then she makes good her own escape, and—presumably after a good hot shower—her return to human form. In fact, she accomplishes her own resurrection. It's a powerful feat, and if this is how it's done, we should all start collecting honey and featherbeds immediately.

Why do souls so often become birds rather than something else? They can of course take the form of other creatures as well—frogs, bears, foxes, trees, butterflies, and so forth; though such things as slugs and hookworms are not favored. Birds and souls, however, seem to have a natural affinity—it must be the airiness, the seeming weightlessness, the wings, the singing. But according to Carlo Ginzburg, all animal and bird forms in myth and folk tradition exist in a borderland—the borderland between the world of the living and the world of the dead. One of the great tasks of the ancient shamans was to send the soul out of the body, after which it could assume animal form and visit the world of the dead. What for? To gather information useful to the world of the living (which is what Odysseus, Aeneas and Dante are also up to); or to commune once more with those who have become incommunicado—with the loved and the lost. Consider Orpheus.

These bird-transformation stories of the Grimms are thus part of a much larger structure. The sisters who take a vow of silence and who knit and conjure their brothers back from the twilight life-death borderland of animal forms, the questers who enter the dark death-houses of witches and wizards in order to rescue their beloveds, or else to rescue themselves, inherit a long tradition; as we do when, as children, we hear and claim these stories. According to Carlo Ginzburg in *Ecstasies: Deciphering the Witches' Sabbath*, "going to the beyond, returning from the beyond" is not just one motif among many: it is the ur-motif, the "elementary narrative nucleus" which "has accompanied humanity for thousands of years." The "participation in the world of the living and of the dead, in the sphere of the visible and the invisible," is "a distinctive trait of the human species."

No wonder then that these bird-stories, these stories of the journey into death and back from it, intrigued me as a child. They are part of the story that has intrigued us all, as human beings, for much longer than anyone can remember.

BOOKS CITED

Ginzburg, Carlo. *Ecstasies: Deciphering the Witches' Sabbath*. New York: Penguin Books, 1992.

Warner, Marina. *From the Beast to the Blonde: On Fairy Tales and Their Tellers*. New York: Farrar, Straus & Giroux, 1994.

ANN BEATTIE

✳ ✳ ✳ ✳ ✳ ✳

John, Whose Disappearance Was Too Bad

I have a small green book written by Horace E. Scudder and published in Cambridge, Massachusetts, in 1864, called *Dream Children*. A fragile, wrinkly-as-the-bottom-of-the-sea piece of paper protects the etching on the title page, and it was this title page that led me to buy the book. It depicts two lovely young girls slumbering peacefully, their faces all blank repose, their long hair artfully arranged on the pillows. There is a bedside table, on which sits another book and what might be an hourglass, and behind them grows a tree whose leaves tickle the columns of some structure that is only partially visible. Leaves and flowers coil upward on their bedcovers, leading us to question whether they are truly asleep outdoors, or whether the idealized external world might not be part of their dream. Either way, it is a wonderfully, and elegantly persuasive, cameo: these girls are at peace; no visions of wicked witches flicker underneath those eyelids. It is the sleep of perfect repose—a state no adult finds credible, except that anyone who has ever seen a child who has fallen into exhausted, deep sleep will have to admit that yes—there is a period in one's life when fortunate children, who do not yet understand the extent of their good fortune, really do sleep this way.

As a culture, we are fairly preoccupied with sleep. In spite of the media's insistence to the contrary, I maintain that we don't really wonder, very often, who's having lots of sex; we wonder, more often, who might be getting lots of sleep. In the city, as the early morning trash compactors crush and clatter, we imagine our country cousins still blissfully slumbering. No matter that we may not have any country cousins, or that if we do, they may be inhaling carcinogenic fumes wafting downwind from the nearby nuclear facility, thoughtfully built near their obscure small town. In our imagination, people are always living where the air is purer, the days are less hectic, the nights star-spattered and silent. Somebody, somewhere, must be getting some rest, we think, as we swab on the under-eye cover stick and scorch our tongues on the daily Styrofoam caffeine drip. In our exhaustion, we emphatically do not wish for Prince Charming to come. If he isn't already in bed with us, the hell with him (okay, we'll continue to read articles about adjusting our expectations when we wake up). When we turn in for the night, we say a silent prayer that our hair-trigger security system will stay silent, hope that the batteries in the smoke detectors have been changed recently enough that we won't have a midnight chirping fest. Then—like the famous song in which the jukebox will be turned "way down low"—we slide the volume control button to silent on the answering machine and turn the ringer off . . . all in preparation for dreamy dreamland: you know; what eventually happens after you've relived the day's setbacks and thought of the clever ripostes you might have made if only you hadn't been so damned tired. After we've worked on perfect nutrition, exercised our way to the perfect body, assimilated Martha Stewart's quest for perfection in all things from driveway repaving to pound-cake making . . . after all that tiring (a.k.a. *challenging*) striving for excellence, hasn't it sort of been implied that we're supposed to get a good night's sleep?

In short, no; that's the stuff of fairy tales. And even there, sleep often is a simple plot device that takes place primarily so it can be interrupted. So the story I've decided to write about, called "John's Nap," is in some ways rather unusual, because while John does indeed sleep, and then sleep some more, and, finally, for all intents and purposes, sleep forever, the sleeping John has the ability to both experience and to assess his situation, though he is powerless to do anything about it; while he is asleep, he reflects that he is asleep, and in spite of everything, he repeatedly vows to continue sleeping. While this paradox of conscious unconsciousness contradicts our notion of what "sleep" is, it nevertheless resonates with frustrating, convincing persuasiveness. (Remember the drugs Sylvia Plath's narrator in *The Bell Jar* fears, because while under their influence you feel the pain, but afterward you forget that you've felt it?)

Here is what happens in "John's Nap": There is a little girl who has a sort of doll's house in the form of a grocery store. Everything is in its place—spices in drawers, etc., and, in fact, the entire grocery store could be said to be in its place, too, because it is in her father's library, which places it in a safe context. Still, while there may be organization—while things may be in their drawers, or set out correctly on the counter, and while a man named John guards this store, which is in turn guarded by being located in the context of Father's real-life library, there is no such thing, really, as safety, so this is what the little girl worries about. She has done what she can: she has put everything in its place, but still: constant vigilance is required, and like everyone else who can afford to, she passes the buck. John becomes her stand-in; he not only has to work all day, but he has to guard the store all night ("he stood behind the window to keep thieves away"). And if staying up all night isn't enough of a problem, John has yet another: his arm that used to hold the candlestick has fallen off, so he is a one-armed would-be protector—a bit vulnerable (to say nothing of what a good Freudian would make of the phallic imagery of loss of candle + limb). Also, the little girl, Mary, is his only customer, and the truth is, she's only a browser; nothing sells from this store—it remains where she put it, in place, to be checked on and worried about. Though Mary neglects to send John to the hospital when he has a broken arm, eventually she realizes that at the very least, he must be tired and needs some sleep. But she also thinks that if a customer should want something ("one of their rich customers"), John should be nearby. (Money talks, regardless of the fact that money does not speak, per se, in this particular story.) Just as Mary has attempted to order everything in her grocery store, so Mary's father has ordered his possessions: his books (the metaphor used is "like old soldiers, who had retired from active service on half-pay"—can't say there isn't a concern with economics here) sit on the bookshelves, and it is after Mary lifts the dustcloth that she lays John out—doing a bad job of it, as it turns out, because he falls off his "bed" onto the shelf behind the books. By this point, though, we already know that John is a very literal-minded fellow ("he did precisely what he was told to do, without asking any questions. Accordingly, he went to sleep immediately. . . ."). Is this a young girl's dream come true? Will she ever find a John in real life? At this point, we begin to experience John's conscious knowledge in his unconscious state ("It was rather trying not to wake up, but . . . he had been told to sleep. . . ."). The books, at first analogous to soldiers, and eventually personified, question the fallen John about what he thinks he's doing, first lying on them, then rolling off. The soldier-books are not nice. They are old and forgotten and not rich. They are what most of us are, or might become. They are slightly more outspoken than most, however. They say: "Did you break your arm? We hope so!" But John—a precursor of Gerald Ford, or at least Ford as described by LBJ—cannot do two things at one time; he cannot figure out whether his remaining arm is broken at the same time he is obeying orders to sleep. This results in the further disdain of the soldier-books and also attracts quite a crowd: beetles and bookworms come out of hiding and regard John and his—we knew it all along—broken arm. Eventually something called a shiner appears and talks to the sleeping John, who answers him (" 'What's the matter with you?' he said, wriggling up. . . . 'I'm sleeping,' said John"). Quite aware of everything that is happening, though unable to communicate, John hears the discussion of what will become of his arm (There are plans to bury it, and when he hears this, "he began to have bad dreams in his sleep"). As the arm is taken away by twelve beetles, things go from bad to worse: two mice enter the grocery store—not rich people, but pilfering mice who simply help themselves to what they want, and who are caustic as well, telling John, who announces his presence at the same time he informs them that he is asleep, that "if you're asleep, we won't wake you." In fear of becoming a literal-minded, John-like figure himself or herself, the reader begins to suspect that the oddity of all this conscious desire to communicate while in an unconscious state is not just due to John's being asleep. He is actually under some sort of curse, able to experience but not to effectively react—but as the story progresses we begin to turn against the victim: what is all this determined resolve to sleep on just because he has been instructed to sleep? The mice are effective in their one-upsmanship because—we begin to suspect—John is in a state of self-willed paralysis; by being compliant, he has become the ultimate passive victim; he even listens to a debate about whether he should be buried, himself, and is saved from this only when the crowd loses interest, "for there seemed to be nothing further to see, and John was left entirely alone." Eventually, Mary comes for him, sees the wreckage of the store, but only observes matter-of-factly (the exclamation point doesn't take us very far): "The mice came while John slept! . . . That was too bad." All John's resolve, all he has endured, all his anxiety, all his verbal, yet mute, suffering, and she only thinks it's *too bad?* Though the books might tell Mary where John lies, "they despised him" (too regimented, like themselves?), so they do not. Time passes, and John is forgotten—though we, of course, do not forget him. We know this genre: it is inevitable that he must reappear. His disappearance is lamented by the voice of the narrator, who suddenly intrudes as easily as the mice once wandered in, with what seems to be a perfunctory "Alas, poor John!" and then goes on to tell us what might have been (more of the same). Through the years John continues to sleep, as cognizant as anyone awake, yet unwilling, or unable, to do anything about the predicament he is in, and when Mary does find him, much later, once she has grown, she recognizes him, but—at this point, it seems almost a reprieve—he does not recognize her. The final lines of the story are: "John had slept so long that he did not know her. 'Don't disturb me,' he said; 'I was told to sleep.' "

Hmmm. Is it better that he was deluded? Is that what it takes to enact a lifetime of dutifulness? (See also Kazuo Ishiguro's *The Remains of the Day*.) Or have we been presented with a tragedy tinged by an antiquated sort of nobility—the tale of an unimaginative person who knows his limitations and who decides— through no delusion at all—to do his best to get by by capitulating? Little girls get to tell their toys what to do, of course. They can dress them as they want to (early on, John is handsome) and move them around to occupy various positions in the stories they invent. It is natural that children, who are bossed around, in turn boss around inanimate objects (or smaller kids on the playground, but that's another story). To take the long view: under more auspicious circumstances, what reunion might the armless toy—the inadequate, ineffectual guard of a silly kingdom—and the young girl, let alone the grown-up woman, have had? We know little about her at story's end, except that years before she lost something and didn't search everywhere for it. We know that she is still to be seen in the context of her father's house (Mother was noticeably absent in this story), and that she eventually marries. I also remember that as a young person she quickly accepted the inevitable ("the mice came . . ."); wooden John followed orders, yet it is difficult not to be struck by the realization that he experienced extremes of emotion ("Tell her!" he cried to the old soldier-books. "Why don't you tell her?" he cries at one point), though Mary herself never lost any sleep over not being able to find the missing John.

As with a dream, the reader, like the dreamer, plays all parts:

the reader is Mary; the reader is John. We all have our roles and assignments in life, and we may very well do our best with them, but time will inevitably take away our capacities. It is, of course, also to be expected that the sacred store will eventually be broken into. (Gratifyingly, however, we are the mice too; as such, we occasionally get to utter a few ironic lines, and even to make off with the goods.) As for Mary and John, I will observe the obvious, and say that they seem to have been temperamentally unsuited—though we are all unsuited to the daunting task of both arranging some reality and also effectively standing guard to preserve it. (The soldier-books in the story already learned this, and that is why they have become bitter.) Jaded and weary, even the bugs eventually scatter: this is an old story, a rerun, something initially exciting that eventually dwindles into something not worth remarking on. Of course bad things happen while we sleep; our stores are metaphorically, when not literally, broken into—and we're helpless to do anything about it. (We're also pretty helpless in the daytime, but we usually choose not to think about that.) In sleep we're vulnerable; our elders, the book-soldiers, won't protect us, and onlookers reveal themselves to be callous as they gossip: worms, of a sort—like the ones who slow to a crawl to gawk at highway accidents. The etching of *Dream Children* is itself a dream—an idealization meant to reassure, composed by someone who knows better, and who must therefore pretend harder, depicting perfect, relaxed harmony, the natural world a beautiful backdrop that enfolds its sleeping children.

I suppose I could read "John's Nap" as a cautionary tale about the dangers of doing something unquestioningly. I could also— and the temptation is really there—read it, and even envy it, as the tale of a man who, in spite of adversity, manages to sleep for a very long time. But the sleep is disturbed, and disturbing; in a story that predates Freud's discussion of the way in which the subconscious permeates the conscious mind, John gives voice to the difficulty and the frustration of trying to reconcile two seemingly disparate states (sleeping and waking; unconscious and conscious) as he tries to accommodate the two extremes that make up his life. I can't let my observations go at that, though. I have to say one more thing that will leave me open to accusations of harmful sexual stereotyping. Who imagines that if *Mary* had been the grocer and *John* had been the little boy, he wouldn't have dismantled the room, if that's what it took, to find Mary again? Wouldn't things have gone differently if the roles had been reversed? I remark on this not because I believe men are heroic, or in any way nobler than women. I just believe that they often proceed differently, and that that difference has sometimes resulted in our observing their insistence on logical continuity and romanticizing it into the white-knight syndrome (which does them the same disservice, obviously, that it does women, whom it relegates to being needy damsels in distress). My feeling—probably much influenced by reading *Gatsby* at an early age, and no doubt reinforced by the trial of O. J. Simpson—is that men are tenacious about getting back what they think they shouldn't have lost. Because to have lost it reflects badly on *them*, whereas women *assume* they will lose things. (In our lifetime, it was once an unspoken assumption that a big part of women's so-called maturation was to lose their last names.) Was it her (presumably mature) sense of the inevitability of loss, or something else that allowed Mary not to think of John for so long? He is rediscovered after twenty years, when Mary's father reaches for a book in order to research something, so he can impart further knowledge to his daughter. It is at that same moment that she rediscovers John—whom we see more as a wounded, ineffectual guardian angel than a fun-providing plaything (clearly, slumbering through the years, John has been unlucky in love as well as unlucky in business). Her father does not remember him at all, which offers a nice irony, because John was always the stand-in for daddy: the protector of the fortress that revealed itself to be vulnerable; the guardian who, even if awake, would have had trouble repelling invaders, to say nothing of the impossibility of John's ever touching daddy's daughter—the missing arms took care of that. Earlier, we learned that Mary's father protected his books with a green dustcloth that, once lowered, became first John's room darkener to facilitate his nap, and eventually his final curtain. Though he was once larger than life, at story's end he is clearly smaller: a wooden miniature of what might have been; someone personified, though he was never a real person; a symbol of a broken man; a repository, perhaps, of good intentions, who, at the very least—and dull, dutiful John got *only* the very least—came to have a very long night's sleep, while the woman who was once so attentive to him went on to have another life: a life so usual, it bore no resemblance to a fairy tale.

ROSELLEN BROWN

* * * * * *

It Is You the Fable Is About

It's time to be honest about memory and memoir writing.

As published memoirs proliferate, it's not surprising that many readers are intimidated by their authors' seemingly perfect recall of conversations between their parents overheard at the age of four, or the conditions of the weather, the props on the stage of significant rooms on which the dramas of their childhood were played, and finally, the subtly tuned emotions of their long-gone youth. Who could blame anyone for thinking that the gene that carries the ability to write must carry this prodigious capacity for recollection as well?

I recently heard the author of a currently (and justly) popular book of family autobiography say, "The way it works is, one memory sort of leads to another," as if that would explain the exactitude of her representation of conversations I had assumed—and still stubbornly assume—were a product of a rather loosely invoked poetic license. With all due respect, a little humility is in order. Writers remember, I suspect, as vaguely as everybody else, only we reconstruct convincingly out of the rubble of all we've forgotten. Each *Remembrance of Things Past* is always, in any hands, a novel.

I hadn't intended to begin so defensively but the fact is, when I'm asked to reminisce about what something meant to me or how it looked or felt in childhood, I am at (or near) a loss. Of course I have memories of all sorts. I swear I can picture the day of my second birthday, chiefly a clear image of limes ripening on the wooden bulkhead of our basement in Allentown, Pennsylvania—limes?! Could a two-year-old tell a lime from a golfball, a mossy stone, a paperweight, not to mention a lemon?—but who's to tell me if I'm right or wrong, or if I've imagined the scene entirely? Such trivia are unlikely to show up on anyone else's memory screen; it isn't as if I'm remembering a dramatic incident or a momentous public occasion.

No, my memories are discontinuous, like snapshots. Even ongoing emotions—feelings I know I had over a period of time—are more absent than present, composed of a few specifics and much more contextual filling-in, most of it guesswork. I don't think I could honestly, literally, put quotation marks around a single conversation I had or heard as a child. (I'm not too good at last week either, but that's another, newer story!)

Which brings me, with apologies for still sounding a little bit truculent, to my memory of the fairy tales of my girlhood.

Most of what I can conjure up of those stories is as fractured as everything else my memory lays claim to—little green islands surface, surrounded by the deep blue watery haze of Everything Else. Mostly what I have is a strong recollection of a welling excitement when I was in the vicinity of certain stories. Like many who become writers, my adrenaline coursed hard in me when I was in their presence.

One memory: I had a book, a thick little square book of fairy tales that I think for some reason (true? not true?) was saved from the trash, though I don't know whose, or why it would have been on its way there—only that it had about it the air of something humbled, unwanted and rescued—which of course gave the book itself a near-fate in common with so many of the unappreciated heroes and heronies of the tales themselves. There were black-and-white line drawings in this book, simple and straightforward. The single illustration I can call up is from "The Twelve Dancing Princesses," their slippers lined up beside their beds, infirmary-style, in a long row. Just the beds, not the royal princesses, who like the proverbial cow who's not on the page because she's wandered away, were most certainly on the other side of the magic wall, dancing.

What else? Random recollections of reading in school: "The Tinder Box" and *The 500 Hats of Bartholomew Cubbins*, which for all I knew then or know now is not a fairy tale at all, but just a tale. The book they were in—this is the second grade, I'm fairly sure but not certain—was blue and brand-new, its covers waiting to be cracked for the first time. This was unprecedented: no one had written yet in the box of names inside the front cover. One day I delivered a message to the teacher of a class we called "the cardiac kids"—presumably a group of children with heart problems, something I've never heard of since—and somehow she discovered that I was a good reader. She invited me back to read for these kids from the new blue book, though given how little exertion it takes to read a story, I'm not sure why they needed me for that. In any event, although I remember the honor of the invitation I have no memory of ever having performed the heroic task. Which means nothing at all: I may have gone, I may not have. I surely got to initiate the blue book by writing my name in the Board of Education's little box but I don't recall that either.

Given the shakiness of these memories, which fairy tales can I remember with special feeling? Searching through the clutter of my brain for something other than that generally inflamed and ecstatic excitement, I've come upon two stories by Hans Christian Andersen that hugely moved me. Why I loved them tells me something about myself; so does the even more rudimentary fact that they've survived amidst the rubble of all I've forgotten.

Though most people tend to confound Anderson and the Brothers Grimm, lumping them together as the preservers of old passed-down tales, they are actually very different. Andersen was also not the delightful figure that Danny Kaye made him, singing "Thumbelina, Thumbelina, pretty little thing" and his other light-hearted Hollywood songs, any more than "The Little Mermaid" progresses quite as Disney would have us believe. Andersen was a maker of tales, some of which seem straight out of Kafka, some out of Márquez and the other magic realists, and then again out of Dickens and the class-tormented social documentarians. He is the author of stylized short stories, only a portion of which contain supernatural elements. Many of Andersen's characters are human and complex, full of sophisticated and often bitter humor, like the poet in "The Shadow" whose shadow trades places with him, usurping his humanity until the man is (yes, literally) less than a shadow of himself. This is not the place for a disquisition on Andersen's peculiar genius; suffice it to say, his tales have about them a darkness and a "reality" that is often unrelieved by any kind of happy resolution, just as fewer of the Grimms' *Household Tales* end with all's-well-that-ends-well symmetry than we tend to think. There are as many tragic rough-cutting edges in these stories as there are satisfying outcomes like marriages and reunions.

I was a very serious child, a child of gravity and—Rilke, I believe, called it "earthweight." Earnestness came easy to me, frivolity came hard. And "The Little Match Girl," whose sentimental young victim would be comfortable in *Bleak House*, was thrillingly heartbreaking to me. That Andersen would let his heroine die was shocking and—to some of us stories are exciting because they roil up our emotions, disturb our equilibrium even if they make us miserable—I would say *satisfying*. It happens that my own writing, as it's developed, has tended toward unhappy, or at best unresolved, endings. None of my four novels closes with a conventional "happily ever after" conclusion; I find myself astonished to discover that even as a child I was more than tolerant of painful outcomes. ("The Steadfast Tin Soldier" is another Andersen tale I loved and shivered at that ends with the death of the hero, whose stubbornly loyal heart does not melt when he is sacrificed in a fire.) The way I tend to remember these stories, the spiritual uplift with which I now see that Andersen concludes some of them, made absolutely no impression on me.

We are supposed to believe that the little match girl, who freezes to death when she is barred from the warmth and safety of others' houses, died happy: "No one knew the sweet visions she had seen, or in what glory she and her grandmother had passed into a truly new year." All I remember of this paragraph, these years later, were the dire words that preceded this sweet reunion: " 'She had been trying to warm herself,' people said." According to Andersen, the shivering child, head and feet bare on snowy New Year's Eve, lit her last matches (and thus froze to death) because with each strike of the match she was granted a lovely vision, apparently lovelier than mere survival; and finally, appealing to her beloved dead grandmother, she cried "Take me with you!" And here's the interesting, ambiguous sentence: "I know you will disappear when the match goes out, just like the warm stove, the goose and the beautiful Christmas tree." Is this joy or resignation, or maybe the madness of delirium?

Social realism battles here with the kind of fatalism (or is it transcendence?) that makes saints and martyrs, who trust their salvation lies elsewhere than on earth. Unlike Clarissa Pinkola Estés, who (in *Women Who Run with the Wolves*) writes about the dying girl as the brave possessor of a triumphant vision, I was a subscriber—still am—to the former attitude, unromantic, unassuagable, a damned liberal reformer: It's good to have a fire on a bone-cracking cold evening.

Perhaps I was a simple child to believe the worst; perhaps, as we know from, say, *Paradise Lost*, Satan (in the form of the uncharitable family behind the window) casts a stronger shadow than the best good angel. Perhaps it was the power of my politically left-leaning parents: one way or the other I remembered this only as the story of a child allowed to die of frostbite while the world ate its goose and Christmas pie behind closed doors. It was so fearfully poignant, it could bring tears to my eyes to imagine her cowering in an alley, invisible and abandoned. Her epiphany did not impress me: this was Little Nell without a bed to die in.

And then there was "The Little Mermaid," far more complex but equally brutal and—I was nothing if not consistent—a painful story "redeemed" (I see now) by another noble ending which I didn't remember because its fake good cheer never registered on me. "There is a view that poetry should improve your life," the poet John Ashbery once said. "I think people confuse it with the Salvation Army." Stories, too, of course; even among didactic tales, their true potency lies in their proximity to dream, and more particularly, to nightmare. Like deathbed conversions, last paragraph soul-saving does not convince.

I ask myself why "The Little Mermaid" so fascinated me that I shuddered and read it again and again. I don't remember when I met up with it; it may have been one of the stories in my square little book, but it may have come later when my own experience recommended it to me.

You remember the story: the little mermaid who lives with her sisters under the sea falls in love with a human prince whose life she has saved, an alien from such a different world that they literally breathe unlike elements. The wager she makes with the ubiquitous heartless challenger, her bad fairy, is twofold. First, she must endure the cruelest of punishments in exchange for a chance to be (or seem)—to borrow, really—the appearance of a human woman. Having exchanged her mermaid's tail for legs, every step she takes will torture her as if she were walking on razor blades. Worse, she must lose her tongue and, having yielded it up, of course, will not be able to present herself to the prince as she really is. And finally, stark and simple punishment, if she cannot convince the prince to love her more than any other creature, she will die. She is given the choice; not surprisingly, feisty and faithful to her dream, she chooses love and danger.

What a challenging story this is in its original non-Disney version. She is deprived of her voice, of her personality, her *self*, left only with her looks, which are captivating but (to the prince's eternal credit) insufficient compared to the pleasure of a complete speaking woman. The mermaid is a beautiful and loving husk and her longing is forever unrequited. Oh, the hideous irony, that in her desperation to attain love she has sacrificed the possibility of possessing it! Andersen has another story called "It Is You the Fable Is About."

The "happy ending" allows the mermaid to die, "but she did not feel death." Having failed to gain the love of a human being, she has not gained an immortal soul, though she is promised by the daughters of the air that if she does good deeds for three hundred years, she will (by default) be given her soul, a sort of alternatively certified booby prize. Worse, "if we find a good child who makes his parents happy and deserves their love, we smile and God takes a year away from the time of our trial. But if there is a naughty and mean child in the house we come to, we cry; and for every tear we shed, God adds a day to the three hundred years we already must serve."

I was not an irreverent or cynical child but I am proud to acknowledge that I so totally disregarded this ending that I am astonished now to discover it. Could the same vicious imagination that dreamed up the mermaid's tortures have cooked up such a mess of treacle? I wonder what kind of influence, inner or more likely outer, drove him to this cross between reduced jail time for good behavior and an out-of-season "Santa Claus is coming to town." (Yes, I've heard of Purgatory, but do people really get work-release if they show what good citizens they can be when their feet are being held to the fire? It's enough to make me hope she'll turn into a delinquent at her first opportunity.)

I think back to my attraction to this story and I truly can't reconstruct the way it made me feel. But this I can say: it was the mermaid's voicelessness that fascinated and panicked me. Or not so much her silence as her incapacity to *explain* herself. I have memories of writing poems as a teenager, and later—I even had one called, baldly, "Not to Know"—about the most painful scenarios I could imagine: Romeo and Juliet dying of misinformation; ditto Othello; the Wild Duck sacrificed in error; moments of my own life in which either I or someone else did not know something crucial. Such accidental ignorance has always been the worst catastrophe I could think of. Children recognize that they can't explain so much they would like to. I don't know that I felt particularly misunderstood but the threat is always there for children that they will be inadequate, possibly even speechless, when it's urgent that they be heard. So the idea that the mermaid, for love, would volunteer to lose her voice and thus yield up any chance to make her case—ah, this was so terrible to me I could hardly look it in the eye. And so, of course, I looked and looked. (As for consistency: I've recently been sent an essay that discusses "the price of speaking out" in my novels and traces many instances of self-imposed silence among my characters. Apparently the little mermaid has, unbeknownst to me, been my touchstone all along.)

My childhood was blessedly untraumatic. It was marred, if that's the word, by our moving a number of times, which left me standing at times on shifting sands. The hardest uprooting for me came after a record four years in one town during the crucial years between five and nine. I left the place where I had started school—the school library, by the way, is one of the few rooms I remember there. The town I lived in was where I'd learned to play the piano, where I made my first good friends. I don't remember directly much of what it felt like to be frightened and depressed, but I remember how I behaved: I can see myself from outside (and I recognize how exasperating I must have been). We were driving from New York to Los Angeles, my parents, my two older brothers, and I, and for most of the journey I simply couldn't eat. I remember lunches in the car—sandwiches and something in a thermos—but when we'd stop at night at the kind of mildewy bungalow motels that have since been replaced by neat and identical chains, without being able to explain what I was feeling I could not choke down a bite of dinner. Finally, after unyieldingly starving myself halfway across the continent, in Omaha at a place called Ye Olde English Inn— I do have occasional memories that are to the point—I was so distracted by some interesting game on a paper place mat that I forgot not to eat, and was saved from incipient starvation.

But once in Los Angeles, settled into a little white stucco house surrounded by alien vegetation like pomegranate bushes and palm trees, my wordless depression continued. My parents went out often at night in the first weeks, not to go dancing or partying but because my father was diligently searching for a business to invest in. L.A. in 1948 was full of what my father called "odd lots and broken sizes"—hustlers eager to make a deal, inventors of implausible gadgets looking for a backer, owners of losing enterprises desperate to unload them—and when my father found what looked like a plausible opportunity, he would bring my mother with him to check it out. It all sounded vaguely sinister to me. Left at home with my brothers, I was overwhelmed, night after night, by a profound depression—I have written about this, somewhat transformed, in my first novel, where it surfaces as a mournfulness, a deep red color like blood, perhaps, behind the eyes—and the best I could do to understand where it came from was to notice that it rolled over me, smothering, when I smelled night-blooming jasmine. I've since thought the heavy perfume might have been orange blossom. Whatever it was, I didn't think to associate it with my parents' nightly absence in this unfamiliar place, and I certainly didn't—couldn't—talk about it. My terror had no voice; even if I'd wanted to speak I don't think it occurred to me that there was anything to say in words about the desolation I was feeling. It was like drowning in ill omen.

This is a shaggy dog story: nothing desperate happened to me. Once my father settled on a business—as it turned out, for all that careful investigation he bought a shag carpeting factory of what turned out to be stunning unprofitability—my parents stayed home again. My depression lifted only to be borne back upon me at a few widely spaced moments in the future when I chanced to smell that perfume again, no longer as depression so much as the memory of where a wound had gaped and closed over. A scar, I suppose, though hardly lethal. I was its victim; I never agreed to it in return for something I wanted. But I emerged from this clouded time knowing I had been someone unfamiliar for a while, someone who'd walked through a different element, blind, deaf—all nose, led by the most primitive of the senses—and dropped down safe on the other side of it.

And what of "The Little Mermaid"? Possibly I read the story and loved it after these two experiences of wordless pain; perhaps I'd already read it. Wouldn't it be nice to be able to say and not be faking? I know that in the mermaid's voicelessness Andersen captured one of our—I mean humans'—primal terrors, that much I can vouch for. He gave us an implicit judgment of the limitations of mere beauty, beauty unendowed with self. He held forth an ideal of love and loyalty to the point of death and made us, while we're admiring it, wonder if the game is worth the candle. He suggested that too much wanting can change the one who desires (whatever her object) to the point of deformity. He reminded us how difficult, perhaps even how impossible, it is to try to leap certain barriers and successfully become something we are not.

Which of these, at age eight or nine, did I grasp? Which of them helped to form my storytelling soul and which did I respond to because I was already partway to who I was to become? I could write a convenient fiction here that would connect all these dots, Andersen's and mine, but I want to end where I began, invoking the modest truth and admitting how little of it I possess where my own childhood is concerned. How mysterious these stories were, that's all I know I felt, and how wonderfully dangerous and disorienting, coming at me out of nowhere. How amazing to break the silence, like the Ancient Mariner to lay a firm hand on a listener's arm and begin anywhere, anywhere at all: *"It was dreadfully cold, snowing, and turning dark." "Once there were five and twenty tin soldiers. They were all brothers because they had been made from the same old tin spoon." "Far,*

*far from land, where the waters are as blue as the petals of the corn-
flower and as clear as glass, there, where no anchor can reach the bottom, live the mer-people.*"

The author would like to acknowledge her use of *Hans Christian
Andersen: The Complete Fairy Tales and Stories* translated by Erik Christian
Haugaard (Anchor Books, 1974) for the quoted text in this essay.

A. S. BYATT

* * * * * *

Ice, Snow, Glass

One of the surprising things about glass, to northerners, must have been its resemblance to ice, and its difference from ice. Glass is made from sand, heated and melted; ice is a form of water, which shifts from solid to liquid with the seasons. The fairy stories which I now see provided much of my secret imagery as a child are northern tales about ice, glass and mirrors. It is surprising how often they go together. Hans Andersen's "The Snow Queen" opens with the splintering of a great mirror. "Snow White" has a heroine named for the whiteness of snow, a wicked stepmother entranced by a speaking mirror, and a glass coffin melted, so to speak, by a kiss. Then there is the Norwegian story, a version of the Atalanta myth, in which the unattainable princess sits at the top of a glass mountain, throwing down golden apples to the suitors who try to mount it. As a child I used to think of that great transparent spike indifferently as glass and ice, cold, hard, glittering. When I was grown-up I found the story "The Glass Coffin" in the

Brothers Grimm, and rewrote it into *Possession*. I shall start by looking at these tales, and then look at the sometimes paradoxical and private uses I made of them.

The Grimms' "Snow White" opens with falling snow. "It was once midwinter, and the snowflakes fell like feathers from the sky, and there sat a queen by a window, that had a frame of ebony, and she sewed. And whilst she sewed, and looked out at the snow, she pricked herself in the finger with the needle, and three drops of blood fell in the snow. And because the red looked so beautiful in the white snow, she thought to herself, 'if I were to have a child, white as snow, red as blood, and black as the ebony frame . . .' " Snow White is born and the Queen dies in the same moment. The king marries again, and the first thing we are told about the stepmother is that she is proud and beautiful and has a mirror that speaks the truth, and tells her that she is the fairest in the land. The story takes its way; Snow White grows to be the fairest; the stepmother orders her death; she lives with the dwarves, and is visited by the wicked queen, who tries to kill her with a colored lace, with a poisoned comb, and finally with a poisoned apple, "white with rosy cheeks," which causes her to fall down "dead." When the dwarves find her lying there, they cannot bury her "in the black earth" because she "still looks as fresh as a living person, and has still her beautiful red cheeks." So they make a transparent glass coffin, in which she lies "a long long time" still "as white as snow, as red as blood, and black-haired as ebony-wood." The Prince comes, says he cannot live out of her sight, carries away the coffin, and dislodges the poisoned apple, so that Snow White is restored to life, and becomes his wife. And the wicked queen's mirror tells her the young queen is a thousand times more beautiful, and she is made to dance herself to death in "red-glowing" heated iron shoes.

Even as a child I was entranced by the patterning of this, the weaving of the three colors, the framing in glass of faces and stages of lives. Andersen's tale is a literary work, and has, as Keats said of didactic poetry, designs on the reader. It comes out of the complex of stories about Snow White and Rose Red, and changes the imagery, adding a kind of personal terror to the elemental one. It opens, as readers do not always remember, with a wicked, mocking magician, who has invented a mirror which shrinks the good and beautiful, and magnifies the ugly and useless, making the loveliest landscapes look like boiled spinach. This mirror is carried into the sky by his magical pupils, dropped to earth and smashed into millions of fragments, which get into people's eyes, or are made into windows and spectacles, distorting everything to the "perverted and corrupted." "Some people were so unfortunate as to receive a little splinter into their hearts—that was terrible! the heart became cold and hard like a lump of ice."

The two children in the story, Kay and Gerda, tend beautiful rose trees on their roofs, and are happy until the arrival of the Snow Queen, who is queen of the "white bees," the snowflakes, and who "breathes with her frosty breath on the windows, and then they are covered with strange and beautiful forms, like trees and flowers." Kay sees the Snow Queen, who does not harm him—"there was a clear frost next day, and soon afterwards came spring—the trees and flowers budded, the swallows built their nest, the windows were opened . . . the roses blossomed beautifully that summer." But then Kay gets a splinter of the mirror in his eye and in his heart. He destroys the roses, tears up books of fairy tales, mocks Gerda, and becomes entranced by the mathematical beauty of the snowflakes seen through a "burning glass." The Snow Queen reappears, Kay attaches his sled to hers and is carried away. "A more intelligent, more lovely countenance he could not imagine; she no longer appeared to him ice, cold ice. . . ." They fly off into the raging storm, and Kay becomes obsessed with the beauty of maths, and statistics and puzzles.

Gerda, meanwhile, sets out to find him, and is entrapped by a kindly witch who has a lovely garden, and a cottage with high windows with panes of different colored glass, red, blue and yellow, so that when the bright daylight streamed through them, "various and beautiful were the hues reflected upon the room." She lives in a rosy enchantment, with cherries to eat and crimson silk cushions, but the witch waves her crutch and causes the roses to sink underground, in case they remind Gerda of her quest for Kay. Gerda's tears, however, when she sees the rose painted on the old lady's hat, cause the roses to spring up and talk to her—they tell her Kay is not dead underground, for they have been there, so she sets off again, on a series of comic adventures. Finally, aided by a Raven, a robber-maiden, a Lapland Woman and a Finland Woman, and a reindeer, she finds Kay in the Snow Queen's palace, after a very Victorian combat between an army of living snowflakes "like snakes rolled into knots, like great ugly porcupines, like little fat bears with bristling hair" and an "army of little bright angels" formed from the vapor of Gerda's breath as she prays. Kay is piecing together a jigsaw made of the fragments of a shattered frozen lake, which Andersen calls "the ice-puzzle of reason." He cannot form the word "Eternity," but when Gerda sings a hymn about the Infant Jesus, the word forms itself, and the children are able to escape back to the world of roses and summer. It seems significant that it is not the crucified God, but the Christ-child who initiates Kay and Gerda into the human perpetuity of birth after death—the earthly version of eternity, spring and rebirth, not the cold mathematical one.

The story of the princess on the glass mountain needs less elaboration—it is one of those about the third son, the Ash-Lad, who acquires three magic horses and suits of armor, rides up to the contest, each day, more glorious than the one before, and confounds the assembled suitors, including his lazy brothers. The princess sits on "a high hill, all of glass, as smooth and slippery as ice," with three gold apples in her lap, and watches her suitors. When she sees the Ash-Lad, she wants him to win, and throws the apples after him, one at each attempt. He reveals himself, much like the Ash-Girl, Cinderella, who reveals that she has the glass slipper in her possession, and when the king sees his golden mail under his sooty rags he says he well deserves the princess and half the kingdom.

The Grimms' "The Glass Coffin" is about an indomitable little tailor who discovers in an underground fastness not one but two glass cases, one containing a miniature palace with stables and outhouses "carefully and elegantly worked" and the other a beautiful maiden with long golden hair, wrapped in a rich cloak. He releases the maiden, who gives him "a friendly kiss on his mouth," calls him her heaven-sent husband, and tells him how she was imprisoned by a magician, a "*Schwarzkunstler*," or "Black-artist" who had turned her brother into a stag, and her servants into blue smoke imprisoned in glass flasks. After the rescue, the stag is turned back into a man, and the tailor and the lady are married.

There are obvious symbolic oppositions in all these stories, which I'll discuss first. Red and white, ice and fire, snow and blood life and death-in-life of the ice princess is a kind of isolation, a separate virginal state, from which she is released by the kiss, the opener, the knight on horseback. The combination of needle, blood and snow at the beginning of "Snow White" resembles the prick of the fairy spindle which begins the long sleep of Sleeping Beauty, amongst her hedge of roses and thorns, through which the prince breaks his way to wake her with a kiss. Snow White's mother bleeds, bears her desired daughter, and dies, and her daughter is red, white and black. The princess on the glass hill is isolated in her pride and her beauty, put at a distance by coldness and glitter, with golden apples in her lap. She throws down the apples to the handsome young man, and descends from the mountain. In Andersen's story, it is Gerda, the female child, who is in touch with warmth, flowering roses, cherries, and the human heart. The cold woman takes the young man away into her ice palace where she keeps him from the ordinary cycle of life and affection. Gerda rescues him for redness and warmth and the seasons. The ice palace is a false eternity, a duration outside time, to be escaped from. The lady in the glass coffin was bewitched because she hoped to have eternal happiness without marriage, communing with her beloved brother in their happy castle. The Black-artist's spell put her into a sleep resembling the sleep of Snow White and Sleeping Beauty, which Bettelheim has said may be a figure of the drowsiness and lethargy of girls at puberty; she is rescued by a husband, not a brother, to whom she offers the kiss of life.

But that wasn't how it felt to me as a girl, or not entirely, although I would probably have been able to explain the conventional "meaning" of the kiss, the awakening out of ice, the marriage and living happy ever after. I think I knew, even then, that there was something secretly good, illicitly desirable, about the ice hills and glass barriers. Snow White's mother died, and no one appears to have minded. It was natural. She was a woman, living a normal woman's fate. There was something wonderful about being beautiful and shining and high up with a lap full of golden fruit, something which was lost with human love, with the descent to be kissed and given away. Hans Andersen's Snow Queen was not only beautiful but intelligent and powerful; she gave Kay a vision of beauty and order, from which Gerda, with Andersen's blessing, redeemed him for the ordinary and the everyday. Andersen makes a standard opposition between cold reason and warm-heartedness and comes down whole-heartedly on the side of warm-heartedness, adding to it his own insistent Christian message. The eternity of the beautiful snow-crystals is a false infinity; only Gerda's invocation of the Infant Jesus allows a glimpse of true eternity. Andersen even cheats by making the beautiful, mathematically perfect snowflakes into nasty gnomes and demons, snakes, hedgehogs, bears, the things that torment the lazy daughter in the story of Mother Holle, who makes snow by shaking out her featherbed. Science and reason are bad, kindness is good. It is a frequent but not a necessary opposition. And I found in it, and in the dangerous isolation of the girl on her slippery shiny height a figure of what was beginning to bother me, the conflict between a female destiny, the kiss, the marriage, the childbearing, the death and the frightening loneliness of cleverness, the cold distance of seeing the world through art, of putting a frame around things.

All these stories have images of art, as well as of defloration and life and death. The queen in "Snow White" is entranced by a black frame around a window, making a beautiful image with red and white, warm blood and cold snow. Snow White herself is the creation of an aesthetic perception and she becomes an object of aesthetic perception, framed in her glass coffin, so beautiful that the Prince wants to carry the case everywhere. The wicked stepmother is also obsessed with beauty, of course—her own beauty, contemplated in the self-referring gaze of the mirror. There appears to be no glass between the first queen's ebony frame and the snow onto which she bleeds—she lives without glass between her and the world. It is the wicked wizard's mirror that has entered Kay's heart, making him cold, but the Snow Queen has a truth, an interest that Andersen is afraid of, which is not self-reflecting. Even as a little girl I could not see why the beauty of the snowflakes should be bad, or what was wrong with reason. Graham

Greene wrote that every artist has a splinter of ice in his heart, and I think artists recognize the distancing of glass and ice as an ambivalent matter, both chilling and life-giving, saving as well as threatening. When as a grown woman I first read "The Glass Coffin" I was entranced by the images of artistry the storyteller used to describe the miniature castle in the glass case, the craftsmanship the tailor sees in what is in fact a product of the Black Arts, a reduction of Life to Life-in-Death. A fabricated world in a glass case gives a delight an ordinary castle doesn't. When I rewrote the story in *Possession*, I made the tailor kill the Black-artist with an icesplinter that is not in the Grimms' tale, and I made him regret his own art when married to his rich lady. The story in *Possession* is told by Christabel LaMotte, woman and artist, who is deeply afraid that any ordinary human happiness may be purchased at the expense of her art, that maybe she needs to be alone in her golden hair on her glass eminence, an ice maiden.

A tale I always associated with the ice and glass was Tennyson's "The Lady of Shalott." I must have known it by heart as a small girl, since we had a coloring book with the poem and pages of Pre-Raphaelite images to color in. The Lady has things in common with the frozen death-in-life states of Snow White and of the lady and her castle in the glass coffins. She is enclosed in her tower, and sees the world not even through the window, but in a mirror, which reflects the outside life, which she, the artist, then weaves into "a magic web with colours gay." She is not the Wicked Queen; she does not reflect herself. She is "half-sick of shadows," which as a girl I always took to be a reflection of the sense that the life of books was more real and brighter than the everyday, but ought not to be. (There are other possible interpretations which I shan't go into on this occasion.) When the color of the outside life is specified (apart from the blue of the sky) it is red—the "red cloaks of market girls," or "long-haired page in crimson clad." Sir Lancelot is shining and flaming; he is a red-cross knight, whose "helmet and the helmet-feather / Burn'd like one burning flame together," and he has coal-black curls. This mixture of sun and flame causes the lady to leave her enclosed space, to look out of the window frame, which causes the mirror to crack from side to side, and the magic web to float wide. Once the Lady embarks on her last voyage she takes on the images of ice and glass.

And down the river's dim expanse
Like some bold seer in a trance
Seeing all his own mischance
With a glassy countenance
Did she look to Camelot.

She lies "robed in snowy white," and sings

Till her blood was frozen slowly
And her eyes were darken'd wholly . . .
A gleaming shape she floated by
Dead-pale between the houses high . . .

The Lady was solitary and alive, even if the magic colors bright were only shadows and reflections. Once she steps out toward flesh and blood she suffers part of the fate of Snow

White's mother who looked out, and desired a child. Her floating catafalque has a feeling of a glass coffin, and the illustrations of my childhood book corresponded to that feeling.

Preserving solitude and distance, staying cold and frozen, may, for women as well as artists, be a way of preserving life. A correlated figure who fascinated me and found her way into my work was Elizabeth I, the Virgin Queen, whose ambivalent image runs through "The Virgin in the Garden." Elizabeth preserved her power in the world by not bleeding in any sense— she preserved her virginity, and was not beheaded, like her mother and her great rival, Mary Queen of Scots, both of whom came down the ice mountain and tried to be passionate and powerful simultaneously. A poem written about her:

Under a tree I saw a Virgin sit
The red and white rose quartered in her face . . .

was ostensibly about her combination of York and Lancaster in the Tudor Rose, but I read it as a combination of Snow White and Rose Red in one self-sufficient person. She wrote a love lyric, I read, when turning away her suitors:

I am and am not, I freeze and yet am burned,
Since from my selfe another selfe I turned.

She was unchanging, *semper eadem*, as her motto said, a kind of Snow Queen. She made the opposite choice from Snow White's mother and the Lady of Shalott. And she wrote wonderful prose, and good poems; she was clever, and self-determined.

John Beer, in his interesting essay "Ice and Spring" on Coleridge's imaginative education, points out that ice in Coleridge's early thought was associated conventionally with "the icy dart of death" but that later he came to be more riddling and ambivalent about it, to be interested in the possibilities of preserving living things by freezing them, in ice as one extreme of the forms of the universe, so that frost at midnight is a "secret ministry" making beautiful forms of the "silent icicles / Quietly shining to the quiet Moon." The Ancient Mariner is becalmed on a hot slimy sea under a bloody sun, but the Albatross, the benevolent creature from the land of ice and snow, was sent by a good spirit, who "loved the bird that loved the man, who shot him with his bow." Kubla Khan builds a "miracle of rare device / A sunny pleasure-dome with caves of ice" and Coleridge is happier with the balance between the inanimate beauty of ice, crystalline forms, and warm organic ones than, as we have seen, Hans Andersen. Ice and snow are part of the cycle of the seasons, and life-forms frozen and dormant are also preserved in the cold. Neither Kay nor Snow White are dead; they are part of a vegetation myth, waiting for the spring. In this sense they are associated with another ambiguous figure, the Queen Hermione of *The Winter's Tale*, who does and does not die when her daughter is born. She is said to be dead, but at the miraculous ending she is restored in the form of a stone statue that has been kept hidden in a vault. I always see this statue as white marble, although it cannot be, and is described as painted. It is a dead woman preserved as a work of art, who then turns out to be a living woman. The connections of living blood and cold stone as Leontes looks at the "statue" are disturbing.

> LEONTES: Would you not deem it breath'd?
>   and that those veins
>   Did verily bear blood?
> POLIXENES: Masterly done
>   The very life seems warm upon her lip.
> LEONTES: The fixture of her eye has motion in't,
>   As we are mock'd with art.

And later, when Leontes tries to kiss the statue, to bring it to life with the kiss, in terms of the myth, he is warned off because the redness is only artfulness, paint.

> PAULINA: Good my lord, forbear:
>   The ruddiness upon her lips is wet;
>   You'll mar it if you kiss it, stain your own
>   With oily painting.

It is Hermione's son, Mamillius, who says "A sad tale's best for winter," and it is Mamillius who dies of grief when Hermione "dies" in giving birth to her daughter, the Perdita who makes the spring flower speech about the pale primroses that die unmarried (amongst others), invoking the flowers that Proserpina let fall when "gloomy Dis" was about to bear her away to his dark kingdom. Perdita is part of a consoling myth of renaissance and rebirth; Mamillius dies a real, final death of grief; Hermione is a riddle, a woman who has preserved herself by keeping herself apart from her life and its threats, though this has entailed the loss of one, possibly two, children. In my private iconography, which is of course very public, for myths have their life from general belief, Hermione's ruddy lips and stony figure are associated with the dead whiteness and red lips of the portraits of Elizabeth I, and with that most powerful of white faces, Keat's Moneta in "The Fall of Hyperion." Moneta is a figure for Mnemosyne, or memory.

> Then saw I a wan face,
> Not pined by human sorrows, but bright-blanched
> by an immortal sickness which kills not;
> It works a constant change, which happy death
> Can put no end to; deathwards progressing
> To no death was that visage; it had passed
> The lily and the snow; and beyond these
> I must not think now, though I saw that face
> But for her eyes I should have fled away.

Moneta is "visionless entire" "of all external things," and speaks to the artist in the poet——she has something in common with the Lady of Shalott, though she is more extreme. She is preserved again in a duration outside everyday time, like the Snow Queen; her sickness is also a strength and a wisdom.

Another pair of women I associate with the wisdom of the stories of Snow White and the Snow Queen are Dorothea and Rosamond in *Middlemarch*. There is a sense in which this pair of marriageable virgins, at the beginning of the story, are Snow White and Rose Red. Dorothea is white, has a nun-like quality, and is compared (ironically) to the Blessed Virgin in the second sentence of Chapter 1. She is also clever, interested in ideas and ideals, and will be interested in art. Rosamond's name itself is rose red, Rosa Mundi, the rose of the world, another way of referring to the Virgin, of course. In one of the scenes in which readers best, ironically remember Dorothea, she is seen on her return from her Roman wedding journey, imprisoned in her husband's house, Lowick Manor, in January. She looks out of the window. It is white and snowy. I give a long quotation because of the delicate way in which George Eliot has woven together the contrasts of red and white, fire and ice, blood and snow.

> *A light snow was falling as they descended at the door, and in the morning, when Dorothea passed from her dressing room into the blue-green boudoir that we know of, she saw the long avenue of limes lifting their trunks from a white earth, and spreading white branches against the dun and motionless sky. The distant flat shrank in uniform whiteness and low-hanging uniformity of cloud. The very furniture in the room seemed to have shrunk since she saw it before: the stag in the tapestry looked more like a ghost in his ghostly blue-green world; the volumes of polite literature in the bookcase looked more like immovable imitations of books. The bright fire of dry oak-boughs burning on the logs seemed an incongruous renewal of life and glow—like the figure of Dorothea herself as she entered carrying the red leather cases containing the cameos for Celia.*
>
> *She was glowing from her morning toilette as only healthful youth can glow; there was gem-like brightness on her coiled hair and in her hazel eyes; there was warm red life in her lips; her*

throat had a breathing whiteness above the differing white of the
fur which itself seemed to wind about her neck and cling down
her blue-grey pelisse with a tenderness gathered from her own, a
sentient commingled innocence which kept its loveliness against
the crystalline purity of the out-door-snow. (Chapter 28)

Rosamond is called Rosy by her husband and family; in Chapter 46, as one example, she appears in "her cherry-coloured dress with swansdown trimming about the throat." But her rosiness is not warmth; she is a parody of the domestic comfort of Gerda's homemaking. The fairy tale image most often applied to Rosamond, I imagine, is that of the water nixie, or melusine, or Lorelei, a cold-blooded fairy who entangles men to drown them, and has no soul. But in terms of the Snow White tales, she is not Rose Red but the wicked queen, and the opening of Chapter 27, which precedes the chapter in which Dorothea stares out of the window at the snow, Rosamond is associated with one of the most striking mirror-images in literature, which again I'll quote in full.

An eminent philosopher among my friends, who can dignify even
your ugly furniture by lifting it into the serene light of science,
has shown me this pregnant little fact. Your pier-glass or exten-
sive surface of polished steel made to be rubbed by a housemaid,
will be minutely and multitudinously scratched in all directions;
but place now against it a lighted candle as a centre of illumi-
nation, and lo! the scratches will seem to arrange themselves in a
fine series of concentric circles round that little sun. It is demon-
strable that the scratches are going everywhere impartially, and it
is only your candle which produces the flattering illusion of a

concentric arrangement, its light falling with an exclusive opti-
cal selection. These things are a parable. The scratches are events,
and the candle is the egoism of any person now absent—of Miss
Vince, for example. Rosamond had a Providence of her own who
had kindly made her more charming than other girls . . .

Rosamond is outwardly rosy and inwardly glassy; Dorothea is
outwardly pale, but inwardly "ardent" or burning. My friend,
the psychoanalyst Ignês Sodré, has written about a later moment when Dorothea, still trapped and now widowed, looks
out of a window after a sleepless night of decision, and sees "a
man with a bundle on his back and a woman carrying her baby"
and feels the desire to join "that involuntary palpitating life" and
no longer to be a spectator. As a result of this, she is able to approach Will Ladislaw, break the grip of her husband's dead
hand, and have everyday human happiness after all, the kiss of
the Prince, the husband, the child. George Eliot's last words
about her heroine are ambivalent. "Certainly those determining
acts of her life were not ideally beautiful . . ." "Her finely-
touched spirit still had its fine issues, though they were not
widely visible." She was, we are to believe, happy and good, and
alive, and that is much. But her creator chose differently,
though she also was ardent and passionate, and did not keep
herself to herself. There is a wonderful contrast of red and
white, when Dorothea, on her unhappy honeymoon journey in
Rome, is overwhelmed by the power of the layers of ancient
life and thought. She is a provincial innocent, "fed on meagre
Protestant histories and on art chiefly of the hand-screen sort."
(You can hear the curl of George Eliot's lip.) What she sees is
white and bloodless.

Ruins and basilicas, palaces and colossi, set in the midst of a sordid present, where all that was living and warm-blooded seemed sunk in the deep degeneracy of a superstition divorced from reverence; the dimmer but yet eager Titanic life gazing and struggling on walls and ceilings; the long vistas of white forms whose marble eyes seemed to hold the monotonous light of an alien world . . . Forms both pale and glowing took possession of her young sense, and fixed themselves in her memory even when she was not thinking of them, preparing strange associations which remained throughout her after-years.

And Dorothea sees this alien, monotonous whiteness through a threatening veil of red, the "red drapery" which in St. Peter's "was being hung for Christmas spreading itself everywhere like a disease of the retina." George Eliot, in her need to employ the red color, got the season wrong—the red drapery is for the Passion and resurrection at Easter. And the power of the writing is evidence that George Eliot, unlike her heroine, was shocked into excitement, into a desire to know, even into emulation, by the contrast between art of the handscreen sort and the power of European culture and history.

I always, for myself, associate Eliot's "white forms whose marble eyes hold the monotonous light of an alien world" with Keats's Moneta, who distinguishes between artists and dreamers. I also associate them with the more beautiful frozen white forms on Keats's ambiguous Grecian urn, those marble men and maidens who will love forever and never kiss, under dark eternal forest boughs, on a work of art which remains perpetually virginal, a "still unravished bride of quietness," a "silent form" which

dost tease us out of thought
As doth eternity: Cold Pastoral!
When old age shall this generation waste,
Though shalt remain, in midst of other woe
Than ours . . .

The child I was found an illicit encouragement (which was also a warning of coldness) under the ostensible message of the ice-tales. When I was an undergraduate I used to puzzle over W. B. Yeats's dictum

A man must choose
Perfection of the life, or of the work,
And if he choose the latter, must reject
A heavenly mansion, raging in the dark . . .

The frozen, stony women became my images of choosing the perfection of the work, rejecting (so it seemed to me then, though I have done my best to keep my apple and swallow it) the imposed biological cycle, blood, kiss, roses, birth, death and the hungry generations. These stories are riddles, and all readers change them a little, and they accept and resist change simultaneously.

BOOK LIST

1. The references to Snow White are from the three-volume Insel Taschenbuch edition of *Die Kinder und Hausmärchen gesammelt durch die Brüder Grimm* (1974). "*Sneewitchen*" is in the first volume, No. 112, p. 300. The translation is my own.

2. The edition I have used of Hans Andersen is the Bodley Head one of 1935 (reprinted London, 1967). Regrettably no translator is credited.

3. I have taken the story of the princess on the glass mountain from Joanna Cole, *Best-loved Folktales of the World*, New York: Doubleday Anchor, p. 78. I have played around with the language of this translation a bit—as a child I always thought of it as a glass mountain, not a hill, so I have used both. And I have substituted the Norwegian *Askelad* for the English "Boots" which gives a different feel from Ash-Lad. This is not the edition I originally met the story in, but the only one at hand.

4. "The Glass Coffin" (*"Der glaserne Sarg"*) is from the same edition of the Grimms, Vol. 3, No. 114, p. 97. Again the translation is my own, and I have twisted the Black-artist to suit my own purposes—one might well translate "magician" in most contexts.

5. When I checked this poem, which I had quoted from memory "I am fire and ice/I freeze and yet am burned," I found I had got it wrong, in the direction of the essay. It can be found (with modernized spelling) in the Carcanet anthology *Poetry by English Women: Elizabethan to Victorian*, edited by R. E. Pritchard, Manchester, 1990.

6. John Beer, "Ice and Spring: Coleridge's Imaginative Education" in *Coleridge's Variety* ed. John Beer, London: Macmillan, 1974, pp. 54 et seq.

7. I have used the Arden edition of "The Winter's Tale" (first published 1963), the Penguin *Complete Poems of Keats*, and the Penguin edition of *Middlemarch*.

KATHRYN DAVIS

✳ ✳ ✳ ✳ ✳ ✳

Why I Don't Like
Reading Fairy Tales

O f course this wasn't always the case. Once upon a time I
loved them more than anything; even before I could read
they were what I wanted to have read to me, especially the fairy
tales of Hans Christian Andersen. And though by now I've forgotten which were my first loves and which came later, I
think at least I've finally managed to expose (on irritated, even
painful rereading) the ardent heart of an otherwise stony aversion.

"There was once a little boy who had taken cold by going out
and getting his feet wet," begins "The Elder-Tree Mother." "No
one could think how he had managed to do so, for the weather
was quite dry . . ." You didn't have to be a genius to see that
this was the way I'd come down with pleurisy at Peggy Lentz's
seventh birthday party, or to realize that somehow the black-
gum-drop-and-toothpick poodle I'd been making when I suddenly started screaming was to blame. So it happened that I got
to spend the whole next month in bed, my mother beside me,

reading me one fairy tale after another. Every now and then she'd steal a glance in my direction to make sure I hadn't stopped breathing.

Downstairs the sun may have been shining, my sister playing her Mouseguitar, my father whistling, the dachshund racing mindlessly from one end of the house to the other. Downstairs it may have been noisy and bright but upstairs in my bedroom it was hushed and dark. My mother had drawn the venetian blinds and plugged in the raveling black-and-white-striped cord of the vaporizer, a queerly-shaped enamel-coated relic of her own sickly childhood. Puffs of yellowish steam came out of a hole in its top, musty and stale-smelling, as if the steam itself were a thing of the past, the bad breath of bygone fevers. "The little boy looked at the teapot and saw the lid raise itself gradually. Branches sprouted out, even from the spout, in all directions, till they became larger and larger, and there appeared, a large elder tree, covered with flowers white and fresh. . . ." Of course it was impossible not to confuse the teapot with the vaporizer.

Andersen goes on to describe an old man and woman on the occasion of their golden wedding anniversary, sitting under an elder tree, reminiscing. Long ago when they were children, long before the man sailed away and the woman pined for the letters he sent "from the land where the coffee berries grew," long long before he came back to her and they had children and grandchildren and great-grandchildren, they planted the twig that became that tree. " 'That is not a story,' " complains the little sick boy, reasonably enough, to which the Elder-Tree Mother replies, " 'Not exactly, but the story is coming now, and it is a true one. For out of truth grow the most wonderful stories, just as my beautiful elder bush has sprung out of the teapot.' " Then she takes the boy on a journey through his own life, through season after season, year after year, in the course of which he grows older and older and older—until he realizes that *he* is the old man celebrating his golden anniversary. "And the two old people sat in the red glow of the evening sunlight, and closed their eyes, and—and—the story was ended." Meanwhile the Elder-Tree Mother (whose real name is Memory) has remained a beautiful young girl. Where is she now? the boy wants to know. "She is in the teapot," his mother tells him. "And there she may stay."

How clearly Andersen expressed my own dawning sense of what it meant to be mortal. One day, before I even suspected what was happening, I'd be very old, at death's door (as those stuttering "and's" suggested), and I'd remember myself as a seven-year-old girl lying in a dark room in a maple bed, her mother (who'd have died years earlier) jumping up to begin dinner, leaving her alone with a puffing vaporizer. Unless you were a goddess and immortal, youth was no proof against death: to have been born was to have been set ticking like a watch or a time bomb. Though on reflection I'd have to say that it was probably less Andersen's view of mortality than his uncanny genius for conjuring a sense of *time*—of what constitutes the span of a human life—that I couldn't get enough of. Or, more precisely, that I couldn't remove my eyes from even for a second, like a spider perched on the ceiling right above your head, or approaching headlights on an icy road. . . .

In those days I had two editions of Andersen, the forest-green 1945 Grosset & Dunlap with the disturbing Arthur Szyk illustrations (including one showing a devil with an obscene sausage-like growth I've only just realized is a second devil's leg emerging from between the hairy cheeks of his bottom), and the baby-blue 1946 Rainbow Classic, with Jean O'Neill's insanely sweet-faced rendering of the Snow Queen. Or at least I thought that was the extent of my childhood collection until my friend Alexandra gave me an unusual boxed edition for my fiftieth birthday, causing Memory (still infuriatingly young) to leap all at once from her hiding place in the teapot.

Manufactured in 1950 by the Nordic Paper Industry of Viby, Jutland, Denmark, the set of twelve tiny volumes is housed in a slightly larger box with a picture on the cover of three incongruously American-looking children—dead ringers for Dick and Jane and Sally—listening as a thin fellow in a frock coat and jabot reads to them in front of a lopsided castle. Like cupboard doors the cover opens to reveal a king in a red ermine-trimmed robe, preparing to open a second pair of doors in a majestic mahogany cupboard. And behind that second pair of doors? A recessed shelf containing "Little Ida's Flowers," "The Happy Family," "The Wild Swans," "The Steadfast Tin Soldier" . . .

"He looked a little different as he had been cast last of all. The tin was short, so he had only one leg . . . On the table were many other playthings, and one that no eye could miss was a marvelous castle of cardboards . . . but prettiest of all was the little paper dancer who stood in the doorway with a dainty blue ribbon over her shoulders, set off by a brilliant spangle." The Nordic Paper Industry's translator wisely chooses to remain anonymous, unlike Mrs. E. V. Lucas & Mrs. H. B. Paull (translators of the Grosset & Dunlap edition) who offer instead: "There was not quite enough tin left," and "a delightful paper castle." And while the solecisms themselves don't ring any bells, there's no doubt in my mind that the memory summoned by the picture on the tiny book's cover—a row of soldiers standing at attention, oblivious to the "black bogey" who

has popped from his home in the snuffbox to engineer the soldier's tragic fate—is not only real but pristine, previously un-
recovered.

I can smell Vicks and Lipton noodle soup, hear my father tip-
toeing closer—is she awake? yes!—and then shyly handing me
a package containing a similar set of books. Maybe even this
precise set, banished to the cellar with the Mouseguitar when
my sister and I got too old, and dispatched after my father's
stroke (along with the venetian blinds and the vaporizer and the
dog dish) to the St. Martin's Christmas bazaar where it was
bought by a maiden aunt for her Vermont niece who one day
likewise grew too old and traded it for a copy of *The Spoils of
Poynton* at the used-book shop where eventually my friend
Alexandra would find it hidden under a pile of bellringers'
manuals.

Found it and bought it *for me*—ownership ultimately being
the explanation of both my obsession with Andersen's fairy
tales when I was a sickly pious girl in Philadelphia, and of my
inability to read them now.

"The Steadfast Tin Soldier" ends when a young man ("without rhyme or reason . . . no doubt the goblin in the snuffbox
was to blame") throws the tin soldier into the stove, and a
breeze blows the paper dancer in after it. "When the maid took
away the ashes the next morning, she found the soldier in the
shape of a little tin heart. But of the pretty dancer nothing was
left except her spangle, and that was burned as black as a coal."

A dancer inside a castle inside a book inside a bookcase inside a cupboard inside a castle-studded landscape: how deftly
the Nordic Paper Industry managed to convey the terror I
knew lurked at the heart of the Christian message. Your tenure
on this earth, where you might actually prefer to stay (despite

its perils, the perverse machinery of cause and effect embodied in snuffbox goblins and gumdrop poodles), would be finite, yet once you died you'd have no choice but to go on forever and ever. You had only to imagine a door, the door through which you couldn't step, and the next thing you knew that door would be opening and behind it would be . . . another door! And another!

The Marsh King's daughter returns from "a moment" in heaven to find that the stork she was talking to moments earlier hasn't any idea who she is. " 'Yes,' " the stork says, " 'there certainly was a princess in Egypt who came from the Danish land, but she disappeared on her wedding night many hundreds of years ago. You may read all about it on the monument in the garden. There are both storks and swans carved there, and you are at the top yourself, all in white marble.' "

" 'On your very first evening!' " the mother of the winds scolds the Prince. " 'I thought as much. If you were my boy, you should go into the bag!' " To which Death replies, " 'Ah, he shall, soon enough! When he least expects me, I shall come back, lay him in a black coffin, put it on my head, and fly to the skies. The Garden of Paradise blooms there too, and if he is good and holy he shall enter into it. But if his thoughts are wicked and his heart still full of sin, he will sink deeper in his coffin than Paradise sank. And I shall go only once every thousand years to see if he is to sink deeper or rise to the stars—the bright stars up there!' "

The point is ownership. The point is, I believed these were *my* stories. Mine. I didn't think they'd been written for me, Andersen having "had me in mind," or that they conveyed my view of things with unusual precision—no, when I heard these stories I was infused with that shiver of ecstasy that is an unmistakable symptom of the creative act. I felt as if I'd created the stories, as if they had their origin in my imagination, as if they were by definition my *original* work, having "belonged at the beginning to the person in question"—that person being me.

Nor am I referring to plot. In fact plot was the least of it. I'm referring to individual words, phrases. Black as coal. Goblin. Spangle. Snuffbox.

When I was seven years old I didn't have a clue what a snuffbox was, but I knew it was the right name for an object that sprang open unexpectedly to release a goblin. "Snuffbox" dropped straight from God's mouth, where it hadn't yet acquired meaning, and into my brain. Recognizing its aptness, I *participated* in its creation. Later it would come as no surprise that Benny Trimble, who lived down the street from us and was said to use snuff, set fire to his mother's house by smoking in bed.

In the country of Hjørring, high up toward the Skaw in the north of Jutland.

She is in the teapot, and there she may stay.

The storks have a great many stories which they tell their little ones, all about the bogs and the marshes.

Once every thousand years.

Kribble krabble. Skaw. Jutland.

Into the bag! The bright stars up there!

There was nothing passive about this experience. Even now, typing Andersen's sentences, I can feel the ghost of that first ecstatic shiver. It wasn't like being a reader, not even the kind of reader a writer eventually becomes, studying, dismantling, pilfering ("She threw herself on Fleda's neck") from another writer's paragraphs. This was my first taste of the sensation and, not unlike what happened to the doomed Prince in "The Garden of Paradise"—who isn't satisfied merely to dance with the Fairy but must kiss her—it aroused in me a desire for more. Up to a point this desire could be satisfied by more Andersen. But only up to a point—and then, at some crucial moment, Andersen had to be not merely left behind, but denied.

I didn't notice the problem right away. Because I had once loved to read fairy tales I assumed I still loved to read them. Many of my metaphors had their roots in fairy tales. I wrote an entire four-hundred-page novel with a fairy tale at its heart.

But when I tried rereading "The Elder-Tree Mother" (which is relatively short), my eyes refused to fasten on the words; it was as if the story had turned to a block of ice over which my eyes were forced to skid and slide. In fact there was absolutely nothing seductive about the story, though the *idea* of reading it, the fact that it had once played a key role in my life, continued on some level to seduce me. It seemed to me I should have been thoroughly enjoying myself, and instead I was in the grip of that frantic repulsion I feel when someone reads over my shoulder: a sense of another pair of eyes reading at the same moment I am reading them the same words I am reading. Under these circumstances, the eyes become rebellious. Just try and make me read, they say. Take the goddamn newspaper, if you're so hot to read it. I'll read something else. . . .

This never happens with books I first encountered as an adult. Sometimes they'll disappoint on rereading, but they'll never prove impenetrable; more often I'll end up exhilarated.

Nor does it happen with books recommended by friends. Recently I read *The Spoils of Poynton* on a friend's recommendation, and there's no question that my own pleasure in the book was deepened by imagining his reaction to such sentences as "Tall, straight and fair, long-limbed and strangely festooned, she stood there without a look in her eye or any perceptible intention of any sort in any other feature." Though why should this experience have been a pleasing one, and the other anything but? Granted, my friend's eyes had been there *before* mine— still, who wants to find an otherwise trackless waste dotted with bootprints? And while my aversion to "The Elder-Tree Mother" was based on a sense of someone reading over my shoulder, obviously no one was. In fact many people had read it before me, including people I knew. Friends, even.

No, the key difference, I think, stems from the fact that fairy tales (and not Henry James) first shaped my experience as a reader; that it was in profound communion with fairy tales that my status as a reader was first negotiated. Surely my sense that these stories had their origin in me was based on this fact. When I heard them I was very young. I had no other category at my disposal than "mine": whatever I wanted with all my heart I appropriated. To the prevailing view of the helpless reader's imagination held hostage by a piece of fiction, I opposed my own imagination's desire to possess rather than be possessed.

In other words, there was a time in my life when there was absolutely no distinction in me between reader and writer. I was, in every fiber of my being, both, simultaneously; I was becoming an artist. Nor did it hurt that Andersen's tales seemed oddly autobiographical: those breathtaking descriptions of the soul shedding her earthly plumage, strewing it mutely across an essentially shifty landscape where storks and teapots and vaporizers and snuffboxes jabbered on and on. It's no wonder I can't bear the thought of sharing whatever it was that made this possible with someone else, not even with my adult self, who usually seems bent on keeping the two parts separate. Andersen's tales made ideal accomplices. " 'Do not come with me,' " the Fairy warns the Prince, " 'for with every step your longing will grow stronger . . . and if you press a kiss upon my lips, Paradise will sink deep down into the earth . . . The sharp winds of the wilderness will whistle around you. The cold rain will drop from your hair. Sorrow and labor will be your lot.' "

According to the actuarial tables of my childhood, a woman of fifty has twenty years left to go. Nowadays of course we all think we'll live forever, or at least to a hundred. And then?

You can stay by yourself in the dark wilderness of your bedroom, turning pages, all by yourself, utterly utterly alone.

Or you can go to Paradise, a bright and crowded place, where God will insist on reading over your shoulder.

CHITRA BANERJEE DIVAKARUNI

✳ ✳ ✳ ✳ ✳ ✳

The Princess in
the Palace of Snakes

Growing up in Calcutta, I was poor. My aunt, who was not poor, said this was because my mother had married foolishly. You were the best-looking of us all, she'd say to my mother when we went to visit her. If only you hadn't listened to That Man.

That Man was my father, who was never there. I remembered him vaguely as deep laughter and the smell of cologne, as warm hands that threw me up in the air and always caught me. As the empty space in the wide bed in which my mother sometimes wept.

Already my life was surrounded by the basic elements of the fairy tale: beauty and a foolish heart, love and poverty and betrayal. Being a child, I liked that.

During those hot Bengal afternoons while my uncle was at work and my cousins, who were older, were still at school, my mother and aunt sat under the slow-whirring ceiling fan and drank iced lassi and ate fragrant supari and sighed over the past, that magic time when all things had seemed possible. They left me to my own devices. I liked that too. I would go into the office room, which was out of bounds for children, and take from my uncle's table a round glass paperweight in which air bubbles glowed and shimmered. All afternoon I would run down the marble staircase to the ground floor, cool and dim as the bottom of a lake, and slowly climb back up, holding the paperweight in front of me. I was the princess in the underwater palace of snakes, carrying the jewel that allowed me to rise to the surface of the lake.

This is her story:

The princess lives in an underwater palace filled with snakes. We do not know who she is, or how she came there. Do not feel sorry for her. She is happy enough. The snakes are not horrid creatures, as in Western tales, but beautiful, green and yellow and gold. And gentle: they feed her and play with her and sing her to sleep. She has never left the palace, has never wanted to. But then, she does not know that there is more to the world than these sinuous beings, this dim green light, these cool walls built of shell and submarine stone.

As you might guess, there is in the story a prince. And his friend, the minister's son. Wandering in the forest, they happen upon an ajagar, a mythic snake with a jewel on its head. It attacks them; they kill it and take the jewel, and when they bring it to the lake to wash it clean, they are astonished to see the waters parting, a marble staircase appearing. They go down it and find the princess. She falls in love with the prince, of course—innocent and unadvised, what chance does she have—and for a while all three live happily in the palace of snakes. (The snakes, I think, are less happy; but on this the tale does not comment.)

Soon the prince wants to take his bride-to-be back to his

kingdom. He sends his friend to bring an entourage worthy of escorting her—elephants with gold umbrellas, soldiers with silver spears, drummers in turbans of red silk, palanquins of rosewood and sandalwood. And while they wait for the entourage to arrive, he tells the princess stories of the marvelous world above the lake.

The prince must have been a skillful storyteller—too skillful for his own good—for one day, while he is sleeping, the princess decides she cannot wait any longer to see the wonders of this new world. She takes the jewel, the waters part, she walks up the marble stairs.

The story goes on to how she is lured away and captured by an evil king who wants to marry her; how, with her gone, the snakes in the palace turn on the sleeping prince and trap him in their poisonous coils; how, together, she and the faithful minister's son trick the evil king and find their way back to the lake. The prince is rescued, they go to his kingdom, and the tale ends with a sumptuous wedding.

But I am caught by that moment of ascent when the princess saw for the first time the glint of gold light on green mango leaves. When she heard a kokil cry its song from a jasmine bough, when she smelled the sweet red earth, the clean blue sky. I think it was afternoon then. The long jagged shadows of coconut trees must have shivered on the water. Perhaps in the distance, woodcutters, on their way home, were singing a peasant ditty. She breathed in that strange melody and felt it begin to change her, cell by cell. Never again would she be satisfied by the worldless songs of her serpent companions.

This was the moment I played over and over in my aunt's house, not knowing why I was drawn to it.

I didn't know then that the power of the moment lay in the

princess's dual vision, the innocence of child-seeing that creates a world newly, the adult consciousness that compares and understands and remembers. I didn't know that the tragedy of the moment lay in that too: as she stands in the lake, looking up at air, she is part of two worlds but wholly of neither. For the rest of her life she will belong nowhere.

Those Calcutta afternoons, when our visit was over, I would leave my aunt's house reluctantly, gazing back at the marble staircase that rose out of the magic lake. I couldn't wait to come back next week so I could be the princess of the snake palace again.

I didn't know then that I would live her life in earnest soon enough—at least that one heart-breaking, heart-thrilling moment of it—when I left India to come to America.

DEBORAH EISENBERG

✳ ✳ ✳ ✳ ✳ ✳

In a Trance of Self

In the big square the bolder boys used to tie their little sleds to the farm carts and go a long way in this fashion. They had no end of fun over it. Just in the middle of their games, a big sled came along. It was painted white and the occupant wore a white fur coat and cap. The sled drove twice round the square, and Kay quickly tied his sled on behind. Then off they went, faster and faster, into the next street. The driver turned round and nodded to Kay in the most friendly way, just as if they knew each other. Every time Kay wanted to loose his sled, the person nodded again and Kay stayed where he was, and they drove right out through the town gates. Then the snow began to fall so heavily that the little boy could not see a hand before him as they rushed along. He undid the cords and tried to get away from the big sled, but it was no use. His little sled stuck fast, and on they rushed, faster than the wind. He shouted aloud but nobody heard him, and the sled tore on through the snowdrifts. Every now and then it gave a bound, as if they were jumping over hedges and ditches. He was very frightened and he wanted to say his prayers, but he could only remember the multiplication tables.

The snowflakes grew bigger and bigger till at last they looked like big white chickens. All at once they sprang on one side, the big sled stopped, and the person who drove got up, coat and cap smothered in snow. It was a tall and upright lady all shining white, the Snow Queen herself.

"We have come along at a good pace," she said, "but it's cold enough to kill one. Creep inside my bearskin coat."

She took him into the sled by her, wrapped him in her furs, and he felt as if he were sinking into a snowdrift.

"Are you still cold?" she asked and kissed him on the forehead. Ugh! It was colder than ice. It went to his very heart, which was already more than half ice. He felt as if he were dying, but only for a moment, and then it seemed to have done him good. He no longer felt the cold.

"My sled! Don't forget my sled!" He only now remembered it. It was tied to one of the chickens which flew along behind them. The Snow Queen kissed Kay again and then he forgot all about little Gerda, grandmother, and all the others at home.

"Now I mustn't kiss you any more," she said, "or I should kiss you to death!"

Kay looked at her and she was so pretty! A cleverer, more beautiful face could hardly be imagined. She did not seem to be made of ice now, as she was when she waved her hand to him from outside the window. In his eyes she was quite perfect, and he was not a bit afraid of her. He told her that he could do mental arithmetic as far as fractions, and that he knew the number of square miles and the number of inhabitants of the country. She always smiled at him, and he then thought that he surely did not know enough; and he looked up into the wide expanse of heaven, into

*which they rose higher and higher as she flew with him on a dark
cloud, while the storm surged around them, the wind ringing in
their ears like well-known old songs.*

*They flew over woods and lakes, over oceans and islands. The
cold wind whistled down below them, the wolves howled, the black
crows flew screaming over the sparkling snow. But up above, the
moon shone bright and clear—and Kay looked at it all the long,
long winter nights. In the day he slept at the Snow Queen's feet.*[1]

This capture occurs in the second of the seven episodes into
which "The Snow Queen" is divided. But the fact is, little Kay
had glimpsed the Snow Queen once before, when she appeared
to him at bedtime outside the window—lovely and alarming;
restless, glittering. . . . A year, more or less, seems to have
passed since that first premonitory sighting, and during that
time, something significant has happened to Kay.

A mirror (invented by a real *devil*) has fallen to earth and
shattered, and tiny shards of it have been floating about the
world. Naturally, these fragments possess the special properties
of the mirror in its entirety: anything good appears, as reflected, shriveled, grotesque, foolish, or otherwise unsatisfac-
tory, and anything bad appears magnified or intensified.

One summer day—the summer after he has glimpsed the
Snow Queen at the window—Kay is playing with his constant
companion, little Gerda, when he cries out in pain, but his pain
subsides immediately, and Kay proceeds to deride Gerda's tears
of sympathy, saying they make her look ugly.

What has happened, of course, is that Kay has been pierced
by that most dangerous of all substances, and, anesthetized by
his very wounds, he doesn't realize that one splinter of mirror
has penetrated his eye and his vision is now distorted, and that

another splinter has penetrated his heart, which is turning to ice.

Naturally, Kay now sees only the ridiculous and contemptible in everyone and everything around him, and at the same time, he is freed from the constraints of affection. He cleverly mocks the townspeople and even the old grandmother who has lovingly cared for him and little Gerda; he even scorns Gerda herself, and forsakes her to go play in the square with the big boys. His accomplishments are noted and admired—by none more than himself.

This is the condition in which the Snow Queen finds Kay when she arrives to claim him—isolated by disdain, debilitated by self-admiration, and highly susceptible to flattery.

During the days when the Snow Queen remains at home in her glacial palace in Spitzbergen, she sits at the heart of her vast, drifted, windy halls on a frozen lake, which she calls the Mirror of Reason. This mirror, too, is broken into myriad bits, and when the queen is away, Kay plays with the bits, arranging them in the manner of a puzzle, or a game. Although the queen clearly has no intention of letting Kay go, she has promised him that if he manages to form a certain word—*eternity*—with the ice puzzle, the world, and a new pair of skates, shall be his.[2]

While Kay languishes at the place of the Snow Queen, utterly in thrall, Gerda searches for him throughout the world, with the assistance of its various creatures. Her adventures as she roams here and there across the face of the earth are as populous and unpredictable as Kay's sequestration is austere and unvarying. But bizarre, taxing, or even terrifying as some of her experiences are, Gerda never entirely loses heart, though she's once driven to a cross outburst at a narcissus.

Encouraged by the sunshine to believe that Kay is still alive,

Gerda is accompanied by the sparrows as the river carries her to the home of a childless and lonely sorceress, who detains Gerda for a time with her charming garden, where summer is artificially maintained by enchantment. The self-absorbed flowers there tell Gerda their brief, visionary stories, and although the stories reveal much of the vast world, none of the flowers knows—or cares—anything about Kay.

When Gerda is eventually recalled to her search, she discovers that beyond the garden it is autumn, and in the snowy woods she makes the acquaintance of a kindly and independent-minded but rather pedantic crow. Gerda, unlike the old grandmother, doesn't happen to know crow language, but the crow asks her what she's doing there all alone, and she certainly understands *that*.

The two manage to communicate reasonably well, and the crow tells Gerda about his tame (and, as we are to learn, altogether more conventional) sweetheart, who spends a lot of time at a nearby palace, and may have encountered Kay. Evidently the princess who lives in this particular palace is very clever, and, having become fed up with the longueurs of prestige and power, has decided to get married so she'll have someone interesting around to talk to. She's advertised for a husband, but it's turned out that only one boy—out of all those who have applied for the job—a poor out-of-towner, is able to maintain his presence of mind once faced with the grandeur inside the palace and to carry on a decent conversation rather than merely repeating what the princess has just said.

This boy must surely be Kay, Gerda concludes, so the crow and his sweetheart conspire to sneak Gerda up a back stairway, where dreams rush by ahead of them on horseback on their way to take the prince and princess out hunting. Despite a strange feeling that she's doing something wrong, Gerda enters the bedroom, and as she gazes at the sleeping prince's back, she can't restrain herself from calling out Kay's name. But when the boy turns toward her, waking, she sees it is not Kay after all.

Deeply moved by Gerda's story, the prince and the princess equip her with fur boots, a muff, a gold chariot stocked with treats, horses, and various supernumeraries with gold crowns, and Gerda sets off again.

As Gerda and her retinue drive through the dark woods, a band of robbers, maddened by the glare of gold, seize the char- iot and slaughter the horses and all the attendants. And the next episode, the story of the little robber girl, is surely one of the most thrilling, cryptic, and emotionally anarchic scenes in all the literature which, purporting to make itself pleasing to chil- dren, avails itself of direct address to the unconscious.

An old robber woman, with a long beard, draws her glitter- ing knife in anticipation of killing Gerda for a tasty feast, but is prevented from doing so by her indulged and headstrong little daughter, who wants a playmate, as well as Gerda's muff and dress and someone to sleep with.

The robber girl, taking Gerda for a princess, assures her that the robbers won't kill her unless she herself becomes angry with Gerda. But when Gerda recounts her story, the robber girl is so moved she declares that they won't kill Gerda even if she does become angry—no, she'll kill Gerda herself. Then she dries Gerda's tears and appropriates Gerda's muff.

Eventually, after showing Gerda around, the robber girl falls asleep with one arm around her terrified new friend and the other hand clutching her knife. As the girl snores away and her mother rollicks about in the leaping firelight with the rest of the robber band, the robbers' imprisoned pigeons whisperingly inform Gerda that they've actually seen Kay—floating over the trees in the Snow Queen's sled, heading up toward Lapland.

The next day, during one of her mother's drunken snoozes, the robber girl engineers Gerda's escape, and even gives Gerda her favorite pet, a reindeer she loves to torment with her knife, as transportation and guide. She provides Gerda and the reindeer with two loaves and a ham, and returns to Gerda her boots. Then she generously gives her mother's mittens to Gerda—in exchange for the muff, which, naturally, she keeps.

> *Gerda stretched out her hands in the big mittens to the robber girl and said good-by. And then the reindeer darted off over briars and bushes, through the big wood, over swamps and plains, as fast as it could go. The wolves howled and the ravens screamed, while the red lights quivered up in the sky.*
>
> *"There are my old northern lights," said the reindeer. "See how they flash!" And on it rushed faster than ever, day and night. The loaves were eaten, and the ham too, and then they were in Lapland.*

The two travelers stop at the hut of the Lapp woman, who feeds them and listens to their stories. She then writes them an introduction on the material at hand—a dried codfish—to her knowledgeable friend, the Finn woman, who lives up north, not far from the Snow Queen's fortress.

The Finn woman receives Gerda and the reindeer, reads the note on the fish, and puts the fish thriftily into the pot for supper. She seems to be as conversant with the forces of nature as she is unwasteful of nature's resources, and the reindeer implores her to make for Gerda a potion which will give Gerda the strength to overcome the Snow Queen.

The Finn woman pores over some arcane texts with such intensity that she's soon drenched with sweat, and then discloses Kay's dire situation to the reindeer. But, she tells the reindeer, she cannot increase the power Gerda already possesses: Gerda has come through the world on her own bare feet, and, man and beast, bowing to the innocence in her heart, must serve her; no magic exists which can better prepare her to pit herself against the Snow Queen.

Now that the Snow Queen has so entirely captivated Kay, her interest in him seems to have flagged, and fortunately, when the reindeer drops Gerda off, as instructed, at the palace gardens, armed with nothing more than her innocence and the power of prayer, the Snow Queen is off on a junket to Vesuvius and Aetna, and Gerda finds Kay alone.

And what *about* Kay? Has he been pining for Gerda, whose every thought is of him? Has he been dreaming of her all through her arduous journey? Oh, of course not—not at all. By now he is all but the living dead, though the Snow Queen's kisses have prevented him from understanding this. And at Gerda's approach, he remains frozen and immobile, evidently neither seeing nor hearing her when she flings her arms around him and calls his name.

But this time her tears are effective. The scalding flood melts the ice in Kay's heart, and now, recognizing rather than repudiating her, Kay himself bursts into tears.

His own tears wash the grain of mirror from his eye, and he recovers himself, astonished to see where he is and to understand that much, much time has passed. Now it is Gerda's kisses that Kay receives—revivifying kisses that return his color and his very life to him.

Kay and Gerda's joy is so great that even the fragments of the ice mirror dance—and then settle down exactly into the position of the intransigent puzzle's solution, spelling the word *eternity*. And in an astounding literary coup, Andersen brings Kay and Gerda home over the course of the few final paragraphs, with familiar characters and landscapes flowing about them. Lives interweave like garlands, with time passing gracefully at many different rates: the reindeer seems to have acquired a beloved, the Finn woman is just as Gerda left her moments or days earlier, the Lapp woman has made Gerda and Kay some new clothes, the little robber girl, though no less eccentric, acerbic, and vibrant than before, has grown up. In answer to Gerda's inquiries, she announces that the prince and the princess are off in foreign lands, that the crow is dead, and, she adds dismissively, that the crow's tame sweetheart goes about in absurd perpetual mourning.

The earth turns green and blossoms appear wherever Kay and Gerda go, and when they arrive at their destination, the old grandmother is absolutely unchanged, and the clock in the corner is still ticking away. Eternity embraces them as they travel simultaneously backward and forward in time into an adulthood of redeemed innocence.

This is a highly condensed (and inevitably somewhat interpreted) account of "The Snow Queen," but it should be evident that this very *written* story is something quite different from the fairy tales *collected* by Pyle, Perrault, Land, the Brothers Grimm, and others.

Long handling over time and distance has compressed those tales into objects of stonelike smoothness. Their individual markings have worn away, elaborations have broken off. They possess the communicative heft of nonverbal symbols and a bluntly satisfying abstract simplicity. They resound with the impersonal authority of a huge, blended choir; no one voice is responsible, or even detectable. Not only are these stories told *about* fairies, they seem to be told *by* fairies as well.

Many elements of "The Snow Queen" are familiar from those tales: a mirror (as that which reveals—or, in this case, skews—to the interested observer, the nature of what it reflects), transformation, that moment of life at which sexuality becomes an overt determinant in the way one behaves and is treated, the trial-ridden journey toward adulthood, the struggle between goodness and force, the costly victory of innocence over evil, the enlistment of all nature by the character with the pure heart or the passionate quest, the disguised, imprisoned, or narcotized self, the courage which becomes available to the steadfast, wit and enterprise in revolt against autocratic oppression, and so on.

Such elements provide an occasion and a milieu for Andersen's complex—and highly individual—ruminations. In "The Snow Queen," as in Andersen's other stories, the author is everywhere—in the hurtling pace, in the brilliance and abundance of detail, in the stunningly vivid settings and characters, in the intensity of tone and the glamorous prose. . . . Andersen's hand is always apparent, maneuvering the fairy tale archetypes into a labyrinth—quite clearly the labyrinth of a particular psyche—where we are baffled at every turn as we are driven on inward.

It might even be said that the success of the stories lies precisely in the way Andersen brews up ingredients already at hand. Although he disengages them from the contexts which centuries have designed, he not only retains, but actually refreshes their authority and eeriness; he brings out their colors as he presses them into service for his own purposes.

But what exactly *are* Andersen's purposes? "The Snow Queen" seems like a mysterious bell tolling nearby—definitive but inscrutable, full of unearthly meaning. Like any real work of literature, "The Snow Queen" is exactly, of course, what its words say it is. But anyone who's looking for a starting point from which to mull it over will quickly find one—and then plenty of others! In fact, plausible readings tumble out over one another.

Andersen, for example, emphasizes the Snow Queen's "puzzles of reason" and her teasing approbation of Kay's intellect, which causes Kay to forget his prayers but remember his multiplication tables and increases his appetite to show off his skills and erudition; Andersen also emphasizes Gerda's natural comprehension, undamaged by the distortions and reductions of an "informed" point of view, of all the citizens of the earth—human, plant and animal—her ageless innocence; for Gerda, the whole world is Eden. So how can we not understand the story to be a parable about the dangerous illusions of science in contrast to the numinous reality of Christianity?

On the other hand, the story accommodates, with equal comfort, a meditation on the divided self—divided into its male and female, its rational and emotional, its individual and societal, aspects—no one of which can survive without its complement.

Or, we could consider the story to be a barbed commentary on class, in which the Snow Queen appears as the murderous and glittering blight upon the poor, and Gerda appears as the power of endurance and clarity which is the sorrowful and glorious birthright of the poor. And we would then see the sections of the story that concern the realm of the princess—her palace and her courtiers—as well as the ruined castle of the robbers, with its parodic hierarchy, to be elaborations of Andersen's feelings and ideas about worldly society.

Or we could say that Kay's departure from the temporal world, the bleaching away of its splendors in his mind, and his travels with the rarely glimpsed Snow Queen to her strange and beautiful palace, suggest the rigorous apprenticeship of the aesthete, and convey a warning to those who (like Andersen) engage in making art, and a critique of the artistic temperament (like Andersen's).

Similarly, we could say that "The Snow Queen" is an expression of deep anguish, which draws on personal experience of depression and mourns a damaged capacity for love, or that it's a joyful tribute to the richness of the world and the potency of compassion, or even that it's a satirical view of the inaccessible and (as the current cliché has it) "withholding" male.

These, of course, are simply some of the first, general responses of one ordinary reader, and no doubt clinicians and scholars from various disciplines could suggest readings of a much more detailed and arcane nature. Because the story is "good" (by which I mean that everything in it belongs in it, and nothing that isn't in it does) any careful readings are likely to be compatible, and none is likely to be exclusive.

In my experience, in fact, "The Snow Queen" is itself a mirror in which the reader discovers her own preoccupations and embryonic notions of the moment given shape and substance, and different concerns of the story have dominated my experience of it over the years whenever I've happened to pick it up. But what lay at the heart of the story for me throughout my childhood was what I now, as an adult, might consider a description—even, to some extent, an analysis—of the narcissistic personality, a personality in a trance of self, withering away in its encapsulation, becoming increasingly fragile and depleted as it searches for relief in the very source of its imprisonment.

Small wonder it was Kay for whom the Snow Queen came! Small wonder it was Kay whom the mirror's fragments penetrated—Kay, who at such an early age had caught a glimpse of the Snow Queen! Surely Kay had a predisposition, and what appears at first in the story to be an abduction is soon revealed to be a seduction—which has proceeded slowly, preparing itself in privacy and over a long period within the mind and the character of its eager object, until some sort of yielding was inevitable.

Any child who considers herself a candidate for expulsion from the human race is certain to tremble reading about Kay. And though I was brought up in a largely secular, Jewish home, and, as I remember, was always in some way aware that according to any strict interpretation of "The Snow Queen" I was out of luck, I always longed to reach the moment in the story of Gerda's tears, when Kay would be returned to himself.

The notion of compassion as the vehicle of redemption, release and healing runs through Andersen's tales, but nowhere is it expressed more eloquently or persuasively than in those tears of Gerda's which melt the ice in Kay's heart. Kay's release is not only *out* from the Snow Queen's dominion, but *into* the world. His view of himself as special, is, of course, what keeps him incarcerated; his desire that others verify that delusional view only reinforces the bars and locks.

In order to escape, Kay must relinquish his need to see himself as a creature gifted and apart; common sense tells us so. But Andersen adds the mystical insight that empathy—another human's recognition of Kay's anguish—is what will humanize Kay. And in this moment of Kay's release, when he is enabled by Gerda's tears to shed tears of his own, we understand that if only he could have seen himself as simply one among all of earth's beings, he would have secured his own freedom— not by self-pity but by compassion for himself as if for another.[3]

Well, it's a happy ending—the happiest possible: the evil Snow Queen vanquished, eternal peace for little Kay and Gerda, and, by implication, for just about anyone with a modicum of fellow-feeling.

So why is the story so disturbing? Upon finishing it one sets the book aside, exhausted, as if one had just awakened from a long night of urgent and revelatory dreams. And one picks it up over and over again, anxiously, as if the story might turn out some other way, given an altered circumstance or two in one's own life.

The febrile clarity and propulsion, in addition to so rich a concoction of purposes, is accomplished at the expense of the reader's nerves. Especially taxing are the claims on the reader by both Kay *and* Gerda. Who has not, like Gerda, been exiled from the familiar comforts of one's world by the departure or defection of a beloved? And what child has not been confounded by the daily deployment of impossible obstacles and challenges? Who has not been forced to accede to a longing that nothing but its object can allay?

On the other hand, who has not experienced some measure or some element of Kay's despair? Who has not, at one time or another, been paralyzed and estranged as his appetite and affection for life leaches away? Who has not found himself in the grip of a habit of mind experimentally cultivated? Who has not experienced the voluptuous surrender to self-denial? Whose humanity has not atrophied within the snares and evasions of the mirror? Who has not, at least briefly, retreated into a shining hermetic fortress from which the rest of the world appears to be frozen and colorless? Who has not courted an annihilating involvement? Who has not mistaken intensity for significance? What devotee of art has not been denied art's blessing? And who, withholding sympathy from his unworthy self, has not been ennobled by the sympathy of a loving friend?

But not only do we read as the two characters, with an ardent desire for the reunion which is to restore integrity to each, we also read with a vicarious envy on the account of both. We, who are privy to Gerda's splendid, if involuntary, courage, can infer all too vividly and shamingly Kay's gelid resentments: Gerda is the lucky one! But why? What's so special about *Gerda?*

She never even noticed the Snow Queen to begin with! And yet it is stolid, ordinary Gerda—literally the girl next door—and not the refined and sophisticated Kay who is able to feel love, whom yearning draws across the face of the earth, putting her into benign communion with all its constituents—the sunshine, the flowers, sorceresses, royalty, robbers, birds, and animals. While aristocratic Kay, the Snow Queen's elect, who ought to be admired by all, is a prisoner, hollowed out from the inside. Despite Kay's cleverness and daring, it is Gerda who has the strength and the self-confidence never to think of herself at all, always to move forward, accompanied by the affection and assistance of those who encounter her. . . . How desperately unfair it seems!

In fact, one of the most frightening talents of the Snow Queen is that she seems to activate this sort of vicarious self-pity—our self-pity on Kay's account, even though we know perfectly well (because the author makes it clear to us) that no amount of self-pity could release Kay from his fruitless compulsion.

Yet—how strange—we can't help but feel, on Gerda's behalf (though she's certainly above such mean-spiritedness herself), a corresponding self-pity: that it's Kay who's gotten the better part of the bargain. Because it's Kay, after all, who's had the adventure with beauty.

We are told that Andersen (not surprisingly!) was a strange fellow; we are told that his accounts of his life present a frantically romanticized and sanitized version of the fearsome squalor of his childhood, his brutal struggle to become educated and to be recognized as an artist, and the humiliations of his relationships to the socially respectable and even patrician world which extended a (gloved) hand to him. It seems clear that he became encased in the brittle arrogance by which many artists survive exposure to the chilly and changing winds of opinion, and it is said that although he entertained romantic feelings for women as well as men, he never became physically involved with anyone at all.

No one, I think, has outshone Andersen in depicting perdition. Who could ever forget what happened to that uppity girl who trod on a loaf? Or to vain little Karen, with her pretty red shoes?[4] Who could forget the horrible tortures to which their defects consign these children? But Kay virtually swoons into *his* icy hell, and once he is there, the Snow Queen continues to blaze in all her erotic danger.

"The Snow Queen" shimmers with ambivalence and thwarted or suppressed cravings. The author's stance is impeccable: he recommends to us the rewards of equipose or eternity, and purity of soul. And yet what the *story* paints with indelible brilliance is the glamour of immobilization and *aesthetic* purity. What, *really*, are we supposed to feel about Kay's vision? Is it *really* distorted by an alien way of seeing, as the narrator of the story tells us? Or is it actually temporarily *clarified*, as the mirror's impish creator would have us believe?

Andersen appears to be roaming, overwhelmed and dazzled, through the terrain of his own creation, whose features are so hallucinatory they seem to be disclosed to the reader in flashes of lightning. And part of the tremendous vitality of the story no doubt proceeds from the author's struggle to hide from himself exactly what it is he reveals so stunningly to us, and to the severity with which he repudiates the very impulses which generate the narrative; clearly the Snow Queen's allure is so potent it seems that her author himself is in danger of being lost to her.

The occasional censorious tone and didacticism, and the slightly cloying or prissy strains of Andersen's passionate, tormented and highly (I would suppose) idiosyncratic Christian vision only emphasize, by their nervousness, the hazardously volatile nature of his material. He certainly has no trouble at all portraying harmless little Gerda with decorous, and perhaps slightly patronizing, humor and fondness. But when we read of Kay's catastrophic predicament, the Snow Queen herself appears to preempt the author, and only a rapturous sensuality seems adequate to convey her thrilling excesses of coldness. And when Kay, now on solid ground, submits without volition to little Gerda's wholesome and restorative kisses, we can't help but listen for the thrum of the returning sled, in which we once soared through the air and submitted to the dizzying, promise-filled kisses of the Snow Queen.

NOTES

1. Having familiarized myself a bit with four translations of "The Snow Queen" and with the shocking differences between them, I feel fairly comfortable suggesting that the text's resistance to translation is the very measure of its subtlety, precision, and compression. Those passages I quote here are taken from the translation quaintly attributed to Mrs. E. V. Lucas and Mrs. H. B. Paull, in spite of the fact that the other three translations—by Erik Christian Haugaard, by Jean Hersholt, and by Reginald Spink—are all, in certain ways, much better!

There are passages in the Lucas/Paull translation which are vague or incoherent to the point of utter opacity; epigrammatically cast pronouncements, obviously intended as jokes, are often completely bewildering. And at times the reader is haunted by the suspicion that Andersen is counting on us to understand ideas he himself can't be said to.

Any of the other three translations will put the reader at ease in regard to these concerns and dispel various extraneous cloudinesses to reveal the story's brilliant, inherent mystery. The Haugaard, especially, is extremely specific and insightful.

HOWEVER. I find myself unable to set aside the Lucas/Paull translation here. Perhaps it's just an ineradicable sound in my ear from having grown up with it that causes the others to seem like deviations, but I do feel there's something *correct* in its tonalities—its lyricism, its rich sostenutos, and its passages of theatrical breathlessness—and that the few passages I've quoted, show, in their own, somewhat garbled manner, just what the story *is*.

2. To be amazed by the degree to which translation and interpretation are inextricable, please compare:

He went about dragging some sharp flat pieces of ice which he placed in all sorts of patterns, trying to make something out of them, just as when we at home have little tablets of wood, with which we make patterns and call them a "Chinese puzzle."

Kay's patterns were most ingenious, because they were the "Ice Puzzles of Reason." In his eyes they were excellent and of the greatest importance: this was because of the grain of glass still in his eye. He made many patterns forming words, but he could never find the right way to place them for one particular word, a word he was most anxious to make. It was "Eternity."

(LUCAS AND PAULL)

with

He sat arranging and rearranging pieces of ice into patterns. He called this the Game of Reason; and because of the splinters in his eyes, he thought that

what he was doing was of great importance, although it was no different from
playing with wooden blocks, which he had done when he could hardly talk.

He wanted to put the pieces of ice together in such a way that they formed
a certain word, but he could not remember exactly what that word was. The
word that he could not remember was "eternity."

(HAUGAARD)

and

He was shifting some sharp, flat pieces of ice to and fro, trying to fit them
into every possible pattern, for he wanted to make something with them. It
was like the Chinese puzzle game that we play at home, juggling little flat
pieces of wood about into special designs. Kay was cleverly arranging his
pieces in the game of ice-cold reason. To him the patterns were highly re-
markable and of the utmost importance, for the chip of glass in his eye made
him see them that way. He arranged his pieces to spell out many words; but
he could never find the way to make the one word he was so eager to form.
The word was "Eternity."

(HERSHOLT)

and

He was busy dragging about some sharp, flat pieces of ice, laying them in all
manner of ways, bent on getting something out of it all; just as in games we
arrange small wooden pieces to form a pattern. Kay, too, was forming patterns,
the most curious of patterns; for this was the game of icy cold reason. To his
eyes the patterns were very good ones and of the greatest importance; that was
because of the glass splinter in his eye! He made patterns which spelt out a
word, but could never find the one for the word that he really wanted, the word
"eternity."

(SPINK)

3. Another, and more or less contemporaneous, fictional exploration of
   narcissism is "The Sandman" by E. T. A. Hoffmann, whom Andersen

evidently much admired. I don't know if Andersen was familiar with this magnificent story when he wrote "The Snow Queen," but there are a very great number of parallels between the two.

But although Nathaniel, the protagonist of "The Sandman," is plagued by visions which are both delusional and penetrating, the clear-sighted Klara never cries for him. She loves Nathaniel (or at least that persona she considers the "real" Nathaniel) and she speaks about his intermittent affliction with fluency and analytic aplomb, but she more or less tells him to get a grip and cheer up. After Nathaniel is impelled, on what was to have been the eve of their wedding, to hurl himself from the top of a tower, Klara goes off to marry someone more suitable.

4. Shoes (as well as what's underfoot) figure strikingly in a number of Andersen's stories, including "The Snow Queen." Andersen's father, who died when Andersen was eleven, was a shoemaker, and so was Andersen's stepfather.

   . . . *coincidence* . . . ?

MARIA FLOOK

* * * * * *

The Rope Bridge to Sex

A linchpin event of my childhood was when my fourteen-year-old sister ran away. In my family, girls disappeared before their coming of age. Like the story of "Snow White," our mother banished all three of her daughters as soon as we reached our sexual maturity, when our physical assets began to challenge her station. Having once been jilted by her first husband, our mother insisted that she be the sole erotic temptress in her household and she wanted no competition from us. Of course, we had little control over our natural metamorphosis from ivory-skinned girlhood to flesh-toned womanhood. Our father was ineffectual and he made few attempts to protect us. Like a subservient court attendant typical to fairy tales, he did our mother's bidding.

At twelve, I didn't yet recognize the Snow White syndrome, but sensed something was afoot. My mother, Veronica, repeatedly asserted that my older sisters were to blame for their own abrupt exodus and I had better watch my step. The first to be

pushed from the nest was my eldest sister Christine. She enrolled at the University of Delaware at only sixteen, an awkward prodigy. Her freshman year, a college professor knocked
her up and married her unceremoniously. He wasn't a kind alternative to her home life and I noticed how she trembled
when he barked orders, yet she didn't come back to us. Soon
after Christine had left, my fourteen-year-old sister Karen ran
off. She just vanished. The last I saw of her, I was sitting at the
kitchen table writing my detention homework. She paused at
the door and said, "I'm going to the corner shop, do you want
a pack of gum?" She never returned. In one week's time she became an authentic FBI case. The police brought in divers to
check the beaver pool, a little dammed spot upstream from our
house. Someone had seen Karen loitering there. I tried to imagine my sister dead in the beaver pool or in the marsh sedge
along the Delaware River, but each time I pictured my sister's
motionless body in a grassy trench it was as if I'd murdered her
myself.

With my sisters gone, I maintained my neutrality in my
mother's kingdom by acting like a "tomboy" or a stable urchin.
I spent my afternoons mucking stalls at a dilapidated riding
academy and white-washing its sign that said RIDE AT YOUR OWN
RISK in return for my riding privileges. As a saddle bum, I was
masking my gender so as not to be identified as a threat to my
mother. At twelve, I was still welcomed in my mother's house,
but I had to be vigilant. Like my sisters before me, my transformation from girl to sex goddess was quickly approaching,
and soon I would be cast out.

The icy matriarch or jealous guardian is a common theme in
fairy tales, and "Snow White" is its most famous example. Yet, a

more obscure story had even greater implications for me and my sisters. My first introduction to the fairy tale called "The Girl Who Trod on a Loaf" occurred shortly after my sister Karen's disappearance in the winter of 1965. This story became intertwined with events in my household and its pages seemed to spawn *awakenings* in me which would lead me to my eventual flight from home.

One winter night, my mother called me into the sunporch. She presented me with a new book in a faux leather binding, an elaborate edition of Hans Christian Andersen, a volume selection from Book-of-the-Month. My mother asked me to sit down beside her to sample a fairy tale as she read her new Robert Nathan novel. Her invitation was immediately suspect. She didn't often request my company after the yardarm when she had concluded her maternal efforts for the day. Her inclusiveness was highly irregular and I sat down on the edge of a cushioned bamboo chair, ready to pop up again at the slightest wave of her hand.

After dark, the sunporch was a nasty parlor; its huge panes of black glass could never be warmed by the interior lighting. As she faced me, the back of my mother's head was reflected in the window. I saw her hair collected in a tight "chignon." It was a disturbing image, perhaps because I had recently seen the taxidermied skull in the movie *Psycho*.

My mother was a gorgeous beauty, but her chiseled features were harshly exaggerated in the glass room. Reflected in the blank panels, her face looked washed-out and frozen, white as an ice queen. I watched her nurse her gin and tonic and turn the pages of the Robert Nathan romance. Her casual reading hour and even her typical television habits seemed inappropriate when my sister was still lost. How could my mother have her routine entertainments when Karen was still out there in the night, unclaimed?

I sat down in the chilly room and opened the book of fairy tales. I couldn't help myself. Fairy tales described queer tricks and transformations, rites of passage gone awry, innocence tested, robbed, and restored, betrayals between close kin that occurred in the nest, right under a person's own roof. Fairy tale characters were assigned random feats of endurance; they were forced to turn straw into gold or even worse—they were asked to think of three wishes, and often, the last wish must reverse the first!

I recognized how fairy tale characters often flee from their homes to begin unassisted journeys into dark woods or perilous terrain. Fairy tale characters had to decipher antique maps or draw their own itineraries, choose the "high road" or the "low road"; their decisions were crucial and would alter their journey for better or for worse. To reach the safety of new shores, characters might need to ford a river, shinny over a log, scale a wall, dupe trolls at a magic kiosk, edge across a rope bridge, or teeter on insecure stepping-stones.

I recognized how many instances these fairy tales addressed situations like mine. In order for girl children to survive their sexual maturation, they would have to escape from their malevolent matriarchs. My sister Karen had disappeared. From what poison apple had she sampled? What spell had been cast upon her? I imagined benevolent dwarves or much worse; I pictured witches in domestic disguises luring Karen into their bungalows. In fact, my sister Karen simply ran off with a pimp in a detailed Chrysler Newport.

As a child, I read fairy tales searching for portraits of kind surrogates, good fairies and tolerant foster parents who might harbor lost children. I imagined where my sisters had fled— one wed a harsh man who was quite like the archetypal ogre described in many fairy stories; my other sister simply evaporated. Of course, I had not yet learned of her setup with moody grifters and addicted vets. The only reliable bit of information I could synthesize from each case was that both my sisters escaped when they could no longer deny their sexuality.

My mother had secured one chapter of the fairy tale collection with her glass swizzle stick, marking the story called "The Girl Who Trod on a Loaf."

"Read this one first," she told me. Her eyes cold green as a medicine bottle.

I was suspicious of her recommendation and scanned the table of contents, finding more familiar stories, "The Princess and the Pea," "The Little Mermaid," "Thumbelina."

But the title itself, "The Girl Who Trod on a Loaf," with its strange diction, had begun to work on me. I found the verb "trod" slightly archaic, and judging it so provided me with a safety buffer. If the language were *old-fashioned*, its moral couldn't possibly be appropriate for modern-day children and I wouldn't have to "learn a lesson." The word "loaf" also seemed rather absurd in that context. Of course we always had loaves of *sliced* bread, delivered to our house by the Bond bread truck. I often ran to the front door to greet the driver who was always dressed in a starched white jacket and holding a wide basket of fresh bakery items crooked on his arm. I could choose a pecan ring or a jelly roll—a delicious sponge cake scroll smeared with raspberry paste.

I didn't believe that the "loaf" of the fairy tale title referred to the delicacies in the Bond bread truck, but rather the title evoked slabs of coarse bread I had seen pulled apart by hand in movies like *Heidi* and *Ben-Hur*. Imagining these prehistorical loaves of hard bread gave me a feeling of superiority and the distance I needed to enter the fairy tale with my feet firmly planted in the present-day world of Wonder bread.

Sitting beside my mother, I opened the book. The leather jacket creaked like a saddle pommel. Its spine cracked like a pistol snap as I wrested the covers apart. The work within must be significant to merit the same sturdy binding usually reserved for Bibles or Shakespeare sets. I noticed, when I turned the pages, that even the pages *felt* different. Each page had a furry nap and was strangely flecked like blotter paper.

"The Girl Who Trod on a Loaf" introduces a young girl with a "bad streak." "Inger" is "proud and vain" and for her amusement she pulls the wings off flies. Even worse, she impales a "cockchafer" (again an archaic term) on a pin. She holds a leaf up to the insect's feet to watch it try to climb off the skewer, but, of course, it is doomed. "Now the cockchafer's reading," Inger says. "Look how it's turning over the page."

I was immediately smitten by Inger's macabre sense of humor. Her wicked mirth cast a spell on me and I wished she would go even further. In her portrait, I recognized myself. Hadn't I stranded tadpoles on sunny boulders just to watch them struggle to hop back in the water on their half-formed haunches? I collected salamanders, and with my fingertip I poked their spotted flesh, tender as pudding skin. I arranged the salamanders in a line on a Limoges dinner plate and examined them under a hundred-watt table lamp. To my horror their porous bodies dried up in an instant, stranding the lizards in an ornate pattern circling the rim of the dish.

I recognized how Inger and I were similarly distressed by our emerging adolescence. Our bodies were changing and we had no control of the outcome. Could this be why we asserted our power over helpless insects and amphibians?

In the story, we are told that Inger is a *beauty*, and her solipsism is a direct symptom of being cursed with good looks. "She was very pretty and that was her *misfortune*, for otherwise she would have been slapped a good deal oftener than she was."

Beautiful girls under the age of twelve get away with murder. I knew this.

I was littlest, the "cute one," still flat-chested. I could get away with swiping another sweet when my older sisters were banished, first from the table and eventually from home as soon as their bodies had ripened.

Inger's mother understood that it would only get worse between her and her daughter. "You once trod on my apron, you'll end by treading on my heart."

At her menarche, Inger is sent to work as a servant for a rich family where she is dressed in finery. Her mistress's generosity only encourages Inger's vanity and her obsession with fashionable clothes is her sole preoccupation. One day, her mistress asks Inger if she would like to visit her poor mother. Inger reluctantly agrees and starts for home. "So she went, though it was only to show herself off and let them see how fine she had become," but when she enters her village and finds her mother collecting sticks, dressed in tattered rags, Inger fears someone will see her with her poorly attired mother. She decides to ignore her flesh and blood, and she goes back to her mistress.

This is the turning point in the story. The reader knows terrible things shall befall Inger after such a betrayal.

Six months pass and Inger continues to enjoy dressing herself in finery. Again, her thoughtful mistress encourages Inger to visit her mother. She tells Inger, "Take this loaf home to your mother," and she gives to Inger a "fine white loaf." Inger gets dressed in her "best things and her new shoes" and leaves her employers' house to walk to her old home. On her journey she comes to a "marshy place" and worries about soiling her new shoes crossing the water. With no thought of its value to others, she flings the fine loaf of bread into the water to use it as a stepping-stone to get across the bog.

Here, Inger takes her greatest risk, and like the archetypal drawbridge or the rope ladder, her use of the loaf as a stepping-stone leads Inger into her transformation, for better or for worse.

Throughout my childhood, I could choose between two routes to get to my elementary school. I could follow the concrete sidewalk out of my neighborhood and walk two more blocks along a busy road to a crossing guard. The guard wore a silver badge pinned to a yellowed elastic belt which crossed her breast and circled her waist like a truss. The vile harness repelled me and I didn't like being ushered to school in her militaristic routine. I preferred to take a "secret path" through the woods, a dense stand of oak and maple which walled our better neighborhood from the poorer quadrants which flanked the elementary school. The woods were sometimes quite dark, still unlighted from the low angle of the winter sun, but I knew the landmarks—rotten logs or twisted tree trunks—and I tracked the route, enjoying my solitude. I often pretended I was on horseback, maybe a knight or a poacher relishing his trespass into private hunting grounds.

The forest trail opened upon a wide stream, sometimes a torrent and at other times smooth as a sheet of saran. To cross the stream I had to make strategic hops and skips across six jiggling stones that formed a zigzag bridge in the rushing water. Sometimes the water was too high from a recent rain and the stones disappeared below the surface. I would have to hike up to a little dam which formed a pristine beaver pool, the exact spot where the police had searched for my sister. There, I inched across the dam's narrow lip above the spillway where a waterfall forked and cascaded in twinned columns. I couldn't stop thinking of a news story I had read about a drowned girl, years ago, but where had I read it? Salamanders were attracted to the girl's hair and when police towed her body ashore, her head was swarming. Was that in a fairy story I read, or did the FBI tell of it?

Crossing the stream using the stepping-stones was a daily test. The first stone was a square piece of slippery flint the size of a potholder and a full leg span from the shore. My first leap had to be both athletic and agile enough to land me on the little mossed swatch without my tipping off of it. The second stone was larger and more secure, and I could jump directly from the first stone to the second, expending the dangerous extra momentum created by my first leap. Teetering on the second stone, I regained my balance. There I froze for one moment, keeping my knee bent before I lurched to the third stone which spiked the strong current creating a fan of water. I was halfway across. The next three stones were in descending size until the last was almost submerged but for its wobbly crown.

These I danced across without pause and I leapt to the opposite bank.

Safely ashore, there was one more challenge ahead of me. To get to my elementary school, I had to trespass on private property and walk a diagonal across the backyard of an old farmhouse. The house was rented by a couple who had a deformed child. Each morning, the mother put the child in a pen outside her kitchen door. I passed this forlorn scene each day on my approach to school. Every morning I saw the five-year-old boy sitting in his chicken wire enclosure—the kitchen door was propped open with a large fieldstone, quite like ones I had used to ford the stream. Each day I stopped at the corral and reached through the chicken wire. I opened my packet of cheese curls and shook the orange puffs into the boy's lap. I invented the ritual to counter my instantaneous nausea which accompanies the emotional disquiet known as pity. Indeed, more tasking to me than the eerie woods or the tricky stepping-stones was when I had to cross the path of a "freak of nature."

"The Girl Who Trod on a Loaf" was immediately familiar to me because of its stepping-stone ethos. Ever since my sister had disappeared in the vicinity of the stream, I was extra cautious when I crossed the water, jumping from stone to boulder. After my two sisters' predicaments, I felt the strong undercurrent of my female fate. I began to imagine that these stepping-stones could lead to "the erotic life" that our mother coveted and to which my sisters had been banished to face on their own.

Falling off these stepping-stones might actually be more perilous than just the usual trial of spending all day in wet shoes. But it was when I read about Inger, who "trod" on a loaf and sank to the Devil's abyss when crossing a stream—well, that sealed my suspicions.

With a fairy tale's typical swift judgment and a lightning-fast sentence, Inger is immediately dealt a sinister fate for spoiling the loaf and disregarding her mother's well-being. The instant Inger steps on the precious loaf she sinks to the bottom of the marshy bog into the domain of the "marsh-woman." The marsh-woman ran a vile industry, so foul-smelling that "a cesspit is a palatial apartment compared to the marsh-woman's brewery." Here we meet Inger's *foster mother* who will control her metamorphosis, however long it takes.

It just so happens that the Devil and his grandmother are visiting the marsh brewery when Inger arrives, and the Devil's grandmother wants to take Inger home to use her as a statue for her great-grandson's entrance hall. "In this way Inger came to hell in a round-about way."

Once there, Inger sees all the disquiet souls: "Among them was the miser who had lost the key to his safe and now remembers he had left it in the lock." Spiders built webs to imprison Inger with her horrible peers and these permanent webs "cut into the feet like screws and clamped them like copper chains."

" 'This comes of taking care to keep your shoes clean,' " Inger said to herself. " 'They should have corrected me more often and cured me of my bad ways *if* I had any. Now I dare say they have something to talk about up there—ooh, how I am tormented!' "

When Inger is hungry she tries to break off a piece of the loaf still stuck to her shoe, but she can't bend her back. She's been turned into a statue to decorate the entranceway of hell. Inger is removed from the human world and is forced to reside in the underworld of the marsh-woman and the Devil. Snakes entwine in her hair and Inger is somehow able to hear what people say about her. "She heard that a whole ballad about her had been brought out—*The proud young girl who trod on the loaf to save her pretty shoes*—and it was sung all over the country."

An "innocent child" in the village hears the ballad written about Inger and she asks if Inger might "ever come up again."

The adults say, "If she will ask to be forgiven and promise never to do it again . . . but she won't ask to be forgiven."

The innocent child says, "I'll give her my dollhouse if they let her come up. It's so horrible for poor Inger."

I recognized the girl's plea, for hadn't I begged for my sister Karen to return? I had even prayed to God, promising him that if Karen came home I would give her my tea set, my china horses, I would barter anything to have her back.

Well, Inger felt a strange tug when she understood that the little girl cared for her. "It gave her a queer feeling that she would like to have cried herself, but *she couldn't cry*, and that too was a torment."

I often wondered if my sister knew of my despair at her leaving—and if she did, wasn't she cold-hearted not to contact me from her new hideout? It took many years for me to understand that my sister couldn't worry about me; I soon learned that in my household it was "everyone for herself."

For almost a century, Inger resides in the marsh brewery, hearing people speak of her with remorse and wonder. One day, she hears someone sigh and it is her own mother's last breath. She even hears her old mistress discuss her without criticism but there is no one who can rescue her until she recognizes her soulless actions.

My identification with Inger came not only from my sisters' disappearances, but of course I recognized my *mother* in Inger, my mother trapped in her realm of petty lust and vanity. The portrait of Inger illustrated to me how someone can be completely unaware and untormented by her remarkable solipsism. There wasn't much chance that Veronica would sink in a bog and have her comeuppance. Veronica would never have to get her feet wet and would forever remain safely above the water-line of self-discovery. It was up to me, like it had been up to my sisters, to flee from her example.

A full year passed and my sister Karen was still missing.

That spring, Christine left her abusive professor and came home with her three young children. Her husband had struck her with his open hand and I thought I saw his palmprint on her cheek, a rosy glove. Her eyes looked sunken from years of psychological browbeating. She was searching for a house to rent near the university, where she wanted to return to finish her degree after her disastrous hiatus from her college program. There were few houses available in her price range, but one night she took me with her to go look at a split-level in Newark, near the University of Delaware.

I walked through the empty split-level, tugging along my two toddler nephews as Christine cradled the baby in her arms. The house itself wasn't that bad, but for some ungodly reason the whole place had been carpeted wall-to-wall in blinding lemon-lime sculpted broadloom. The walls were painted a slick lizard green. The stinging, sliced-citrus scheme was so hideous, it was hard to imagine that a single mother and her three red-headed babes could survive it. The split-level was like a sinister lair described in Grimms or Andersen; every room was the color of a Venus's-flytrap. "It must be some sort of joke,"

Christine whispered as she pulled my sleeve and we ran out to the car. We were certain that if we stayed another minute, the house might have swallowed us up in bad fortune. Christine put her face in her hands and wept. Her escape from her ogre husband was going to be more difficult than she had thought.

This episode was one of the first times I understood that a moment in the "real world" could take on the surreal proportions of a sinister fairy tale. I patted my big sister's arm and told her we'd look in the paper again for another rental.

On the way back to our mother's house we drove through rural farmland, through the endless black velvet fields of low soybeans. In one instant, our headlights washed over a parked car on the shoulder, just as a man pitched a cardboard box out the window of his station wagon. We saw the box hit the ground and spill a mother cat and her litter of kittens. The car sped away, throwing gravel. The cats had landed in an empty field across an irrigation ditch. Christine pulled off the road and told me we should rescue the little family and bring it to the ASPCA.

I was fond of cats, but I saw that the cat family was on the other side of a murky canal where the man had heaved the carton. It would be impossible to retrieve the mother cat and her mewling offspring.

A full moon behind a cowl of yellow mist offered just enough light to see the reflective eyes of the tabby mother, distressed by her sudden station as abandoned pet. She was nosing her babies and yowling to us for assistance. Christine stayed with her children, so it was up to me to cross the mucky irrigation ditch and collect the castaways. I stood at the lip of the ditch and once again the fairy tale about Inger electrified me. I edged along the muddy hem and studied my options. The water was of an indeterminate depth but the ditch was too wide to jump across. There weren't any fieldstones to arrange, no discarded plank or pine log to use as a bridge. I would have to wade across to reach the cats.

I listened to the excitement of my niece and nephews as they anticipated holding the kittens. Their innocent bliss was an encouragement and I plunged into the water which was immediately waist-deep. Then it was as high as my bra elastic, as high as my nipples which began to sting and tighten from the icy assault.

I remembered a scene from *Psycho*, when Tony Perkins rolls a car into a swamp, his murder victim locked in the trunk. In this scene the soundtrack delivers a prolonged sonata of corresponding sucking effects.

I scrambled to the other side of the ditch.

As I stumbled up the bank, I roused a nest of field rats. The rodents leapt into the air, waist-high, in a spirograph of red eyes. I screamed. Everything was becoming too much for me. I screamed because of the rats, because of *Psycho*, and most of all, I yelped just as Inger must have protested when the loaf sank under her feet.

My screams chased the mother cat across the field.

I looked down to see her newborn orphans at my feet.

I collected the six blind kittens and placed them in the box. I called for the mother cat but I couldn't see in the dark. Was it she who prowled toward me, her tail lifted, or was it just a tuft of grass? The cat had disappeared from sight. My human screams were all she had needed to disown her tribe. She never came back.

Christine drove us to the pound to deliver our booty, but without their mother to nurse them, the attendant explained, the kittens were doomed to be gassed. The pound didn't have staff to feed the tiny newborns with an eyedropper. In an instant, our good deed had gone awry.

After many years as a floor piece in the Devil's entranceway, Inger begins to feel her first swoons of contrition. Her change of heart occurs when the little girl, who had long ago shown compassion for Inger's plight, is herself an old woman on her deathbed. This sweet soul's last thoughts return to Inger and she begs God to show compassion for the imprisoned girl. Inger is impressed by the dying woman's compassion, "To think that an angel of God should be weeping for her!" Inger's moment of awe is transforming and she is suddenly freed from her frozen perch. "Inger's stiffened, stony form evaporated; a little bird soared like forked lightning up towards the world of men. . . . The idea of a good deed had awakened."

In her transformation, Inger flies about and collects crumbs to share with less fortunate sparrows and others who need nurturing. She collects so many crumbs that the "weight of them all would have equalled that of the whole loaf Inger had trodden on so as not to dirty her shoes."

With her good deed completed, the little "bird's grey wings turned white."

One morning I crossed the stepping-stones on my way to school. It was the very last time I would take this route. As I passed the farmhouse, I saw that the "mongoloid" boy wasn't yet placed in his pen. I wondered if perhaps he was sick from a cold. I had often seen him remove his parka and peel off his socks until he sat naked as a capon. No wonder he had caught cold. As I passed by the house, long grey plumes of car exhaust leaked from the seams of the garage door. I had never seen nor heard of that particular enactment of a mortal crime, and I didn't think twice about it.

Later that day, the neighborhood was stunned to learn that the mother who had lived in the farmhouse had put her child beside her in their Rambler station wagon. She had closed the garage door and turned on the ignition.

The next morning, my mother forbade me to walk to school through the woods. She had never before shown any concern about my route to school, even when the police had suggested that my sister Karen might have met foul play at the beaver pool. My mother shrugged in amusement and had told the officers, "You'll never find Karen in that water. She's in someone's arms, getting a head start on a honeymoon."

But the tragedy at the farmhouse awakened my mother's fears. She was distressed by the news of a mother's impulse to murder her own child. It might have seemed like a tangible concept to Veronica. Did she recognize how simple it might be? Could she, herself, turn that corner?

She told me, "I don't want you to walk through those woods again."

My sister Karen resurfaced after two years. She was working a peep window in Virginia Beach, earning money as a child prostitute. She lived in a trailer park with a couple who managed an adult theater near Naval Base Norfolk. Our mother didn't want her coming back, and my parents put Karen in a mental hospital until she reached the age of majority. As soon as she was released, she was back in the Life again.

I still had two more years left of high school when I took off from home. Like my sisters before me, my erotic education seemed paramount to my college prep regimen. I have come to recognize that my maternal example is the toxic taproot of my vision, a sexual consciousness that drives my flight and my flight to art.

In "The Girl Who Trod on a Loaf," Inger is my mother in her nascent form. Neither Inger nor my mother shall be held accountable. For even when Inger expresses sorrow for her misdeeds and repays the world for the bread she took, Inger isn't excused. The loaf is symbolic of a neutral sustenance which might have preserved her innocence, but Inger's hunger was greater. In the story she can't be forgiven until she rejects her human form, the source of her carnal vanity. In her final transformation she *escapes* her mortal world, her sexual life, and forfeits any chance of connecting with us.

In the last lines of the fairy tale Inger turns into a burning speck. "The bird was so dazzling white that there was no chance of seeing what became of it. They said that it flew straight into the sun."

PATRICIA FOSTER

✳ ✳ ✳ ✳ ✳ ✳

Little Red Cap

At age twelve, I'm still loyal to girlhood, riding my bike, alone and unencumbered, down the red dirt road to Magnolia Springs. I set my course in the middle of the road, away from the ruts and the wide-gullied ditches where dandelions and blackberries grow up the steep sides into the fields. Thick, drowsy heat swells around me, and I dream of lying face-down in the deep end of the springs, seeing for myself the subterranean life of its private depth: tadpoles and minnows and the blind, slippery eels. No one I know has ever been to the bottom. Even walking across the moss-covered rocks I hold my breath until I'm safely on the opposite bank, staring into the cold, murky water and eating my peanut butter sandwich. Beyond this idyll is the frightening territory of adolescence, the roar of change and diminishment, of awkward, treacherous growth. Hair sprouts in damp, indecent places and there's a new shame that lingers in the air, tempers the way girls act around boys as if it's not just boys' fists and bristly hair that's

different, but something restless and secretly compelling. I'm
not sure I want to be a part of this. At first I pretend not to notice how the other girls' breasts are swelling—pushing out of
their blouses like overturned teacups—while I fold my arms
over the empty front of my blouse.

When I look in the mirror, I fuss and frown, then run outside. Just as I do one early spring day in Mrs. Andreason's class,
relieved to be through with arithmetic and the study of
seventh-grade astronomy. I'm tired of worrying about the plan-
ets, especially Pluto, which seems so far away, so forlorn and irrelevant, like the tiniest knot on the end of a kite. Waves of heat
hit my body as I run down the steps into the steamy grass. Tar
bubbles up on the blacktop, and the leaves on the trees are
wilted and droopy. I want to spin around, to create a rift of air,
but kids rush by so fast, I can't let myself stop. David Spivey is
chasing Rita Lorenzo, lunging for her collar and tagging her in
a game I don't understand. She spits at him, then smiles, rubs
the spot on her collar he touched, then rushes at him with her
pocketbook. Behind us Mrs. Andreason stands watch in the
doorway, hands on her hips like a general, her gaze hawklike,
scowling, even her shadow a looming presence. We're all running to the canteen to buy Cokes and candy, anything cold and
sweet to hold us until three.

After buying my Coke, I wander with Joanie, my new best
friend, to the field behind the basketball courts and the volleyball net. Here we all congregate beneath the shade of an oak
tree, its limbs extending clear to the stadium fence. Each day a
gang of us try to balance on the tree's massive roots, though
there's not enough room for everyone. When I've finished my
Coke, I wander beyond the tree to the Cyclone fence. I like to

poke my fingers through the holes, feel the sudden prickle of heat when my fingers accidentally bump the wire. It's like touching the stove, a sudden sting. I don't know why I become engrossed in this, involved in this small competition with myself, but I'm startled when Billy Simms whispers behind me, "Hey, you wanna see a monkey?" I don't think before I turn to him, surprised to see him so near, his smiling mouth, his brilliant blue eyes. It's as if we're caught together in a bubble, the two of us standing in the stillness of a bright afternoon sun, the sounds of screaming kids as far away as Pluto.

"Sure," I say, not daring to move, suddenly aware of the sluggish feel of my tongue. I've never really looked at Billy before, never considered him as separate and distinct from all the other boys in this class, boys who snap bra straps, who punch girls in the stomach, who think crying is stupid. But now I notice the beads of sweat above his lip, the way his blond hair lightens to white at the very tip of his bangs. His blue pants have a tear in the knee, the lace of one sneaker is undone, the edges frayed. His eyes move over me with the same entranced gaze as if we're magnets, attracted by an inexplicable force. The intimacy is eerie, almost unbearable. I know he has something important to show me, something that will change me, making me indifferent to trees and sky and heat.

But to my surprise, he whips out a mirror. *See a monkey see a monkey see a monkey*, he whispers, thrusting the mirror up close to my face.

I feel light-headed, dizzy, a deep hole opening up inside my body. The hole becomes darker, larger, a void sucking me in, enfolding me so that I'm no longer standing in the sunlight staring at Billy but hidden inside a terrible wound. I want to push the mirror away, but before I can protest, Billy runs back to a group of boys, whooping with triumph, his wild laughter shattering the air.

Late afternoon. My room is dim, the lights turned off, the drapes pulled tight so that not even a glimmer of sunlight can penetrate the darkness. I see again the whiteness of the sun above my head, the way it glints off Billy's front teeth, his eyes resting quickly on mine, coaxing something out of me, a desire that slips and slides beyond my control. But then I see the flash of the mirror, stupidity draped over my face like a ridiculous mask. I imagine myself growing uglier and uglier, my monkey self exploding through pale, freckled skin, lips thickening, teeth as yellow as urine. My monkey self has a cap of red-blond hair, the frizz starting at my temples, streaking to the ends so that I look electrified. The pimples on my chin and nose spread like wildfire, creeping from the little nest of blackheads to the dimple on one cheek. Worse, I have no breasts. And yet what's most troubling is that I can't quit staring into the mirror, can't quit blinking and smiling. I know it would be smarter to remain invisible, to hide in the background of girlhood, irrelevant and silent, but something dangerous battles inside, this desire to be noticed, this desire to crash through that mirror with my fist.

I plan my revenge. Though I've never thought much about Billy, now I think of him constantly: Billy wrestling with Tommy Schneeflock, their faces flushed, hands punching hard, bodies tangled in a human knot; Billy drawing airplanes that look like startled birds when he's supposed to be doing an arithmetic problem; Billy going to the bathroom, his little spiggot aimed at the toilet rim, his mind lost to bomber jets and home runs.

As I sit in the car on the way home from school, I see the exact slit of my mouth, the hard marbles of my eyes, the clench of my jaw when I meet Billy at school and say the worst possible things to him: *Hick, moron, you've got weeds in your brain.*

But for the next three days I don't see Billy. Each morning I look around at his desk, empty, deserted, and feel surprisingly relieved. On the third afternoon I'm doing the Mashed Potato with Joanie, twisting and stomping and yelling in a frenzy just like the teenagers on *American Bandstand*, forgetting all about Billy, about my monkey self, about the power of revenge. I hop from foot to foot, arms pumping, hips jerking. In this moment I'm a wild passionate princess lost in the snow, led barefoot and hungry to this lonely spot in Alabama. Here I hide in a twelve-year-old's body, a girl afraid of snakes and roaches, a girl who screams when she sees sharks on TV, their mouths wide open, ready to eat.

I think that I might tell Joanie about Billy as we walk through the high grass to her four-room house, and onto the street where the boys play baseball, but before I can decide we're already at her door, then inside the living room, giggling at the sound of her father's snores. Her mother, pinched and frazzled, signals to us, a finger to her mouth, already shushing us before we make much noise. When her father sleeps before the night shift, we're unable to breathe, but sit together, knees touching on the plastic-wrapped sofa, watching the flashing images on a silent TV. The smell is always of sleep, of hair oil and shaving cream, the scent of lemon-waxed floors and warm, stale beer. Beyond us in the kitchen, her mother washes dishes as if acting out a pantomime, her hand slipping deep into the water, finding a dish, then washing it and rinsing it almost without sound. When we can't stand it anymore, we rush into the bathroom, turn on the cold water and break into silent hysteria, laughing so hard we have to pee. But it's here in the bathroom that I catch a glimpse of myself in the mirror. Joanie is sitting on the ledge of the tub, her legs braced against the tile while I'm washing my hands in the lavatory. I look up quickly, too quickly, alarmed to see my pug nose growing larger, the nostrils flaring, lips twitching like a monkey's. My hands go limp underwater.

"Hurry," Joanie whispers, motioning for me to sit on the toilet and talk to her, but the fury is back. Instead, I rush out of the bathroom, not saying good-bye, streaking through the tall grass until I'm safe inside the darkness of my room.

It's exactly a week later that Billy comes up to me at recess while I'm standing at the edge of the oak tree, trying to hot-dog it across a gnarled root in my new Bass Weejuns. I don't see him at first, but all week I've been expecting him. I'm ready. I have a mirror of my own. This afternoon is an afternoon like any other, so ordinary it's superfluous: the air is thick with humidity and our clothes stick to our backs; there is the smell of azaleas and mown grass; a covey of blackbirds flies up from the mimosa tree in a cloud of darkness. It's now that Billy leaves the boys throwing rocks at the stadium wall and starts toward me. The same unruly hair falls across his forehead, his eyes brilliant blue, but I pretend to be looking beyond him to the senior girls in their gym shorts playing volleyball. I see him only as a speck taking up more and more space as he comes closer and closer. Nothing moves in the air, not even the leaves. He looks down at his feet as if he doesn't see me either, as if he's standing in complete isolation from the world. And then, before I can prepare myself, he blurts, "Wanna go to the dance with me?" his

voice raspy, almost a hiss. It's such an unexpected proposal, I
stare stupidly at him, then turn on my heels and run, the mirror still clutched tight in my hand.

Even today I can see Billy's face, the blond hair falling across
his forehead, his cheeks flushed with heat, his nostrils quivering
when he said, "Hey, wanna see a monkey?" But most of all I remember the way our eyes locked together as if we were traveling in a singular orbit. In that moment it seemed that I knew
him, knew the secrets inside his brain, saw the small house he
lived in with his mother, his single bed with the comic books
stacked underneath and the picture of the palomino above his
bed, its dark mane flowing in the wind. In my mind his face
grows shrewd and calculating, the wolf no longer friendly, but
cunning, sneering, a change so obvious I'm warned, alerted to
disaster. But in reality he smiled and I held that smile as if we
were bound to each other, the small desolations deep in our
hearts absolved. And then the mirror came out, flashing beams
of terror beneath a frozen sun.

     Small moments define us, dig deep into our psyches to lay
their spotty eggs. When Billy Simms showed me the mirror and
suggested I looked like a monkey, I believed him though I can't
say why that particular moment remains in my memory. Surely,
it was a fairy tale moment, a paradigm of gender, beauty, and
danger, the heroine trapped by her own naïveté, by the temptation to uncover secrets that might truly transform her. Like
the easily deceived Little Red Cap, I too fell into the seducer's
trap. But craftily, I internalized the model, carrying that mirror
like a flash card inside my head. No longer would I need Billy's
critique; from now on, I would monitor myself.

———

It must have been a year and a half after the incident with Billy Simms that my brother was invited to Tulane by the Athletic Department at Tulane University, and as a family we went for a weekend to New Orleans. It's early winter, the days warm enough for shirt-sleeves, the nights cool and damp, the fishy smell of Lake Pontchartrain drifting into the air. We know how cruel the weather can be, turning suddenly into a freezing rain, the wind whipping through the streets in thunderous squalls, awnings flapping, trash blowing up from the gutters. The streets in New Orleans are narrow and dark, the sun slanting through gaps between buildings, brightening the balconies that jut out into the street.

After we've had a tour of the campus, my mother, sister and I leave the men to their talk about football and sports and head downtown to Maison Blanche. Thrilled to be in a city, to be going to a major department store (something I've been to only a few times in my life), I watch as Creoles and Cajuns, people with dark curly hair and flashing eyes swirl around me, intense and confident, ignoring me, going about their daily lives. Women, dressed in elegant coats with matching pillbox hats like the one Jackie Kennedy wore at the inauguration, slide through the doors of Maison Blanche, oblivious, absorbed, moving through the crowds as if to a choreographed script, stopping occasionally to touch a pair of gloves, a scarf, picking it up, examining it, moving on. We are on our way to the Foundation Department where my sister and I will buy our first padded bras. The resentment over boys and their disruption of our lives has been subtly replaced by the desire to look like other girls. More than anything, that look demands breasts. My mother and all her sisters have full, beautiful breasts that provide an ample cleavage in the cocktail dresses they wear to parties and in the bathing suits they pretend to hate because they're afraid of water. Their breasts spill out of the tops of their slips, droop downward in their nightgowns, jiggly and soft. I know because I always look. I stare at them with absolute adoration. I want them too, for breasts are what boys look at in a girl and what girls look at in each other, comparing themselves as they shower after gym class.

I'm ashamed about a lot of things today as the elevator lurches upward, leaving us inside a serene peach room with dainty chairs grouped in conversational pairs as though women might sit together and discuss slips and girdles. Weeks earlier my algebra teacher, Mr. McDuffy, stopped me after class while I was gathering my books, stuffing my pencil in my purse, thinking about nothing more significant than the day's equations. "Patricia." Mr. McDuffy looked at me with an air of amused scrutiny. I came closer to his desk. "Your hair looks like a pickaninny's," he said, standing before me, his arms crossed against his chest. He was not laughing, but a creepy smirk played across his face as if he, like Billy, had played a good joke. Embarrassed and furious, I went home crying, arms over my head, covering my frizzy curls. Though it seemed to me just one more testimony to my inappropriateness in the Female Department, I planned my revenge. "I can tell him he's getting bald," I told my mother, "and that he needs to lose twenty pounds." But my father cut that desire to the quick. "You will not be *controversial*," he ordered, shaking his head, a standard comment in our house when it came to challenging teachers, coaches, or the status quo. Defeated, I shut myself in the bathroom, staring at myself in the mirror. There seemed no other escape than to divert the anger into destroying my hair: bleach-

ing it, straightening it, rolling it so tight on orange juice cans
the pins dug deep into my scalp. The only pleasure came in that
one moment of transformation when the rollers were removed
and my hair looked smooth and bouffant like the other girls'.

"We'd like to look at your brassieres," Mother says to the well-
dressed woman who stands like a sentinel behind the glass
counter. Her stare is bold and hard.

"What size?" she asks, narrowing her eyes as if calculating
just how developed we are.

My sister and I gaze around the room, knowing she'll be disappointed in us. We're embarrassed at the few lacy foundations
so blatantly displayed. The female body is not something either
of us expects to make friends with; we're wary, though deeply
enthralled. We watch our mother tug on her girdle each morning, stomach and hips resisting, then finally the flesh succumb-
ing to its stiff formal shape. Once a woman is suited up, there's
only a small space of rib cage between the brassiere and the girdle that's free. The space needed to breathe.

When the fitter shows us to a dressing room, I'm surprised
that she comes in with us, intending to be part of our per-
formance. I hoped it would be private and familial, just the
three of us together, my sister and I used to each other's bodies
and not yet embarrassed. Now that the "fitter" is here, we're
uncomfortable, awkward. I take off my dress and hang it on the
gold hook beside the mirror while she watches, her eyes disap-
proving as if she's not overly fond of the female body, or perhaps, of the human race. Much later I realize she was probably
bored, a minor employee, a woman in her forties stuck in the
Foundation Department of a large department store. Where

can she go? But at the time she seems to have too much authority and keeps telling my mother that "fit is important . . . a girl's posture can be ruined by improper fit!"

"Now you must lean over into it, dear," she says as she hands me the first bra, and I become confused because there's nothing to lean over into it with. I think that's why we're buying padded ones, but I know to speak about such things would be superfluous, humiliating. We're counterfeiters, deceivers, and this woman has our number. As she tugs at a strap, showing us how to adjust it, I turn to the mirror and face myself. For a chilling moment I remember that my body is no longer my own. Others have written their desires upon it, desires tangling with and deflecting my own. More than anything I long to return to girlhood, *squatting in the dirt to pick blackberries, leaning my knees into the soil as I try to pull the berries free from thorns. A hard white sun boils above my head. Insects shiver with motion. Occasionally, a car drones by, the sound of its carburetor echoing in the distance. I push my elbows into the dirt, reach into the brambles. I jump ditches, high-step through stickers, watching for snakes. Then, with my bucket full, I sink into the grass, my body langorous, stretched out in the sun. I turn over on my stomach and cram blackberries into my mouth.*

And yet back at the hotel I'm ecstatic. Secretly I dream about looking like a woman, and now with the new bra, my clothes will suggest that I am. Here in our hotel that looks out over the street, where people bustle about, where fancy cars drive up and deposit groups of flamboyantly dressed women, where street life trots and staggers, I've already forgotten about the fitter. There's so much here to see, particularly the women who don't quite look like women, their shoulders too broad, hips too narrow, necks too muscular. These women wear an edge of masculine hardness beneath their painted gloss though they try to cover it with caps and jewelry and wild, tousled hair that never moves. It will be much later that I understand these are drag queens, their lives as much a masquerade as my own. At the time I simply feel sorry for them. I think only that they aren't quite succeeding. Their monkey selves have escaped, lewd and preening, and like me, they'll have to work much harder to hold the line.

My childhood had no cohesive narrative, no sense of a beginning, a middle, an end, only a host of vague longings, a fear of devouring surprises. "Oooooh," I shuddered at any attention devoted to my looks, but by then a part of me had surrendered to the cultural code of beauty's demands. Life was a collage of such surprises, and growing up I felt unprepared while believing defiantly in preparedness, in the possibility that I would eventually be safe and protected. I decided it was all a matter of appearances, of perfecting myself. "I have to get my waist really *tiny*," I'd announce, "so the belt fits on the very last hole." I demanded specific clothes—tank tops, black suede hip-huggers, A-line dresses, a red Eisenhower jacket. Clothes became my deflections, my deferment. I understood that with the right body, you could turn insults into compliments (girls hooted and booed in seventh grade were often ogled and pandered to the summer after eighth, when they appeared at the beach in leopard-skin bikinis), and second best would be to have clothes that seemed to suggest such a body, even if that body had been "fixed" and "distorted" to conform.

The summer after our trip to New Orleans, I stand in front of our full-length mirror admiring myself. With the madras dress buttoned over the waist cinch and padded bra, I feel in control, thrilled at my image. From the side and front I look like a girl in *Seventeen*, and it's this likeness I covet. Of course, there will be no laziness now, no slouching, no flopping down on chairs or couches to read *Jane Eyre* or to find the sex scenes in *Exodus*. In this getup, I'll never spread-eagle across the bed, my stomach full of strawberry shortcake, my eyes wandering over the pages of a book.

At night the red welts striate my stomach, and there's a startling freedom once the waist cinch is removed. When I throw it onto the bed, my stomach gooshes out into little ripples of flesh. The skin is puckered and soft like dough, and I squeeze it together with my hands. This freedom makes me so giddy, I jump up on my bed, shimmying in front of the mirror. The girl I see there is transfixed, all her deep longings hidden beneath the rhetoric of improvement. *You can fix everything*, she thinks. *All stories need a happy ending.* Surely changing the body is merely a private act of coercion.

But greediness, even masochistic greed, is seldom fulfilled. And as you might expect, my story fragments, slips out of my grasp. Twelve years later, at age twenty-four, I rush through the Atlanta airport at midnight on my way home to Alabama. My face is downcast, an attempt to hide the acne on my forehead while my bald head is hidden beneath a blue bandanna. In jeans and a T-shirt, I try to look anonymous, invisible, a generic student, and yet as I rush past two young men, I hear one say, "Jesus, look at *that!*" I never turn to match a face with a voice but stride quickly into the ladies' room, hiding for five minutes inside a stall. I stare at the tile above the toilet paper holder: gray with greenish flecks, dirt ridged between the grooves.

With impatience I take toilet paper and scrub the soiled area clean. But deep inside me, I have learned a difficult lesson: I cannot will my body into acceptance. The body, like the mind, is too messy, too curious to bend itself to such intimidation. It will be years before I understand that my hair fell out and my face broke out as a result of starvation and stress. What fairy tale creature had I trained myself to become?

I stand on a mountaintop in Ireland. I am forty-two years old. I feel the wind through my hair, smell the scent of woods and dirt. I am alone, triumphant, wanting to be nowhere else. I wear baggy clothes, jeans, a sweater, a frumpy coat. My hair is curly, my body loose. Great clouds of mist swirl around me, enveloping me in a fog. I stand there for a long time. When the mist clears, I see the valleys below me, the heather growing up the mountain, the paths winding up and down where other travelers have trod. This day is really many years. Days and months of shifting my gaze, opening my eyes just a bit wider until I think of walking out of the old plot, setting out on a fairy tale of my own. What if I don't go to Grandmother's house at all? What if I strike out alone? There are no siren calls, no dreams, no tea leaves or tarot cards daring me to go. I simply look up one day, one month, at a painting on my wall. It's a painting of women sweeping, women in long blue dresses against a background of searing yellow sky. Their brooms seem to make musical swishes across the floor. The women are all looking down, following the pattern of their task. But in my mind they wake up this day as if a magic clock has been struck. Surprised, they stare out at the round yellow sun. The next thing I know, they drop their brooms and rush out toward that bright yellow light, lifting their faces to its warmth. I think of how the sunlight might call, how it might feel on my skin, my chin tilted upward, my mind opened to its heat. In that moment, my body straightens, then allows itself to slouch. I feel my stomach, the soft curve of it, something I haven't allowed myself to feel in years. Even without the waist cinch, I've become guarded, careful, bound in a conceptual harness. But this day, this year, brooms clatter to the floor, a waist cinch falls from latticed skin, and a woman turns her face to sun and wind.

When I look back down the mountain's path, I see my new husband, a tiny dot below me as he sits on a ledge, reading a book. Turning back to the wind, I can't help but think how easy it now seems to slit open the old life, to slide free of the wolf's devouring body, but how hard, how tentative, that first decisive cut.

VIVIAN GORNICK

✳ ✳ ✳ ✳ ✳ ✳

Taking a Long Hard Look at
"The Princess and the Pea"

I learned early that life was either Chekhovian or
Shakespearean. In our house there was no contest. My
mother lay on a couch, in a half-darkened room, one arm flung
across her forehead, the other pressed against her breast. "I'm
lonely!" she cried, and from every quarter of the tenement
women, and men also, flapped about, trying to assuage an anguish of the soul they took to be superior. But she turned away,
her eyes closed in frantic dissatisfaction. She wanted a solace of
the spirit none of them could provide. They were not the right
people. No one around her was the right person. There had
been only one right person, and now he was dead.

She had elevated love to the status of the holy grail. To find
love was not simply to have sexual happiness, it was to achieve
a place in the universe. When she married my father, she told
me, a cloud of obscurity lifted from her soul. That's how she
put it: a cloud of obscurity. Papa was magic: his look, his touch,

148

his understanding. She leaned forward when she got to the end of this sentence. Understanding was the talismanic word. To be understood was everything. Without understanding, she said, she didn't know she was alive; with understanding she felt centered and in the world. In my father's presence she responded with a depth she hadn't known she possessed to poetry, politics, music, sex: everything. She closed her eyes dramatically. Everything. When he died, she said, "everything" went with him. The cloud over her soul returned, blacker than ever: now it blotted out the earth. She refused, absolutely refused, to live in the world without understanding.

Papa's understanding was like having the glass slipper fit. The glamour of recognition was magically: bestowed. Smart, flirtatious, impassioned, all she had to do was stand there and be adored. The pleasure her intelligent welcome gave my hardworking father when he walked through the door at six in the evening transformed a Bronx tenement apartment into a rich and royal background. His appreciating response brought largeness into the room. Without ever having to leave the kitchen, my mother could impact upon the world.

When my father died she went into a sentimental decline, suffering like a character in a nineteenth-century novel the loss of the man (never-to-be-replaced) who had understood her. His presence had made her life significant. His absence now returned her to sackcloth and ashes. The depression was profound and, apparently, non-negotiable, persisting undiminished and undiluted for years on end. She could not forget her distinguished loss, her wounded existence, the absolute *rightness* of what had once been hers. Whatever was now being offered, it would not do. Refusal took on a life of its own. Nothing was ever exactly the right thing. No one was ever exactly the right one.

I became my mother's daughter. "I'm lonely!" I cried at twelve; at seventeen; at twenty-eight. A pity, really, as I was compulsively sociable. All I ever wanted to do was talk. Heaven on earth was me in a voluble state of free association. But very young I grew anxious. I was not able to find myself interesting without intelligent response. I required the company of minds attuned to my own. No one around gave me back the words I needed to hear. The ones I *did* get back isolated me. I was forever telling the children on the block a story that had grown out of something that had just happened at school, in the grocery store, in the building. I'd give them the narration, then I'd sum up, giving them the sentence that delivered the meaning of the story. After that I wanted someone to speak a sentence that would let me know my own had been received. Instead, eager looks evaporated, expressions turned puzzled or hostile and, inevitably, someone said, "Whaddaya mean by that?"

I grew agitated, restless and insulting, permanently aggrieved. "How can you say that!" I cried long before I could vote. "That's the stupidest thing I ever heard." I was beside myself with my mother's sense of deprivation. It was as though I'd been cheated at birth of the Ideal Friend, and now all I could do was register the insufficiency of the one at hand.

I was never going to know what Keats knew before he was twenty-five, that "any set of people is as good as any other." Now *there* was a Shakespearean life. Keats occupied his own experience to such a remarkable degree he needed only the barest of human exchanges to connect with an inner clarity he had himself achieved. For that, almost anyone would do. He lived inside the heaven of a mind absorbed by its own conversation.

I would wander for the rest of my life in the purgatory of self-exile, always looking for the right person to talk to.

It was transcendence I was after: the authority of a principled imagination: the redemption of high seriousness. But how was I to get from here to there? I hadn't a clue. This dead end led quickly into high-minded moralizing. I became the only girl on the block who pronounced regularly on the meaning and nature of Love. Real love, true love, right love; love that was passionate and madly sympathetic, providing communion of the deepest sort. You knew *instantly*, I declared categorically, when you were in the presence of love. If you didn't know, it wasn't love. And if it *was*, you were to give yourself over to it without question—whatever the obstacles—because love was the supreme intensity, the significant exaltation. It was the certainty with which I rehearsed this litany—again and again—that marked me forever.

At the same time that I was pontificating about Love, I was a girl who continually daydreamed herself Emma Goldman. In my imagination I was forever up on the stage of a great auditorium, or on a platform out in the street, addressing a crowd of thousands, urging them to revolution. The conviction that one day I would have the eloquence and the vision to move people to such action was my secret thrill. Sometimes I'd feel puzzled about how I would manage life both as an agent of revolution and as a devotee of Love. Inevitably, then, a picture formed itself in the air before me of myself on the stage, my face glowing with purpose, and an adoring man in the audience waiting for me to come down into his arms. That seemed to account adequately for all necessities.

As I passed into adolescence and then into my late teens, this image in my head of myself leading the revolution began, mysteriously, to complicate itself. I knew, of course, that a significant life included real work—work done out in the world—but now I seemed to imagine that an Ideal Partner was necessary in order to do the work. With the right man at my side, I posited, I could do it all. With*out* the right man . . . But no, that was unthinkable. There would *be* no without the right man. I would have to make certain of that. The emphasis began to shift away from doing the work to finding the right man in *order* to do the work. Slowly but surely, finding the right man seemed to become the work.

In college, the girls who were my friends were literary. Every one of them identified either with George Eliot's Dorothea Brooke, who takes a pedant for a man of intellect, or with Henry James's Isobel Archer, who sees the evil-hearted Osmond as a man of cultivation. Those who identified with Dorothea were impressed by her prideful devotion to "standards," those who didn't thought her a provincial prig. Those who identified with Isobel adored her for the largeness of her emotional ambition, those who didn't thought her dangerously naive. Either way, my friends and I saw ourselves as variations of one or the other. The seriousness of our concerns lay in our preoccupation with these two fictional women. Their destinies were prototypes of what we imagined our own to be.

None of us questioned the essential situation. The problem in each book was: what happens when the protagonist—beautiful, intelligent, sensitive—mistakes the wrong man for the right man. As a problem, the situation seemed eminently reasonable to all of us. We saw it happening every day of the week.

Among ourselves were young women of grace, talent, and beauty attached, or becoming attached, to men—dull in mind or coarse in spirit—who were bound to drag them down. The prospect of such a fate haunted all of us. We each shuddered to think that we might become such women, and fall into the hell of a life bound either to a Casaubon or an Osmond. That's how we thought of it: as falling into a life; having to evade something out there, waiting to ensnare us.

Not me, I determined. If I couldn't find the right man, I swore boldly, I'd do without.

For ten years after college I knocked about, in pursuit of the holy grail: Love with a capital L, Work with a capital W. I read, I wrote, I fell into bed. I was married to an artist for ten minutes, I smoked marijuana for five. Lively and animated, I roamed the streets of New York and Europe. Somehow, nothing quite suited. I couldn't figure out how to get down to work, and needless to say I couldn't stumble on the right man. Repeatedly, I'd determine on a course of action; repeatedly, I'd fall back. In time, a great lassitude overcame me. It was as though I'd fallen asleep on my feet, and needed to be awakened.

In my thirties I married a scientist, a man of melancholy temperament. It had taken him eighteen years to complete his dissertation. His difficulty made him poetic in my eyes. He, of course, was remarkably sensitive to my own divided will. During our courtship we walked together by the hour while I discoursed passionately, and with eloquence, on why I could not get to Moscow. His eyes flashed with emotion as I spoke.

"My dear girl!" he would exclaim. "My beautiful, marvelous girl. You are life itself!"

I became the interesting, conflicted personage, and he the intelligent, responsive wife. The arrangement made us both happy. It felt like comradeship. At last, I thought, I had an Ideal Friend.

Gerald was the most understanding man I had ever known. Every day I poured out at him a torrent of dramatic narrative, and every day he nodded along beside me, saying, "In other words . . ." giving me back myself twice as good as I'd given it to him. Hearing my own words come back at me through his ever-enlarging rhetoric rescued me repeatedly from an irresoluteness I could not conquer. Talking with my husband was as good as sitting down at the typewriter. Better. In conversation with Gerald my thoughts seemed full and consequential. The flow came easily. I opened my mouth to speak and soon everything I had to say was: there. I'd smile at him. If it wasn't for you, my smile said, I'd never have had this delightful turn of mind.

Cocooned inside our endless talk, from time to time I'd think, When will you act? Then Gerald and I would go for a walk. I'd take his arm and say, "I've been thinking . . ." He'd turn eagerly toward me. "Yes, dearheart?" his expression said. "What delightful thing have you been thinking?" I'd open my mouth and begin to talk.

Life seemed sweet, larger than it had before. Alone, I had been cramped up inside, now I felt myself breathing freely. I was glad to wake up with my husband beside me. I experienced comfort of the soul, and a way to embrace existence I'd not known before. In this mood we thought it a fine thing to roam about, leave the city, discover the country. We traveled west, and when we reached the California coast rented a bungalow. I remember the first moment I saw that glittering circle of sand,

sky, rock, and water, and all those glamorous houses gleaming
up and down the brilliant mountainside. A wonderful piece of
laughter began to grow in me. The world was lovely, radiant,
entertaining. I could be happy here. All this deliciousness, and I
had a friend in the house.

One morning I woke up desolate. Why, I could not tell.
Nothing had changed. He was the same, I was the same. Just a
few weeks before I'd awakened feeling festive. Now I stood in
the shower stricken, spots of grief dancing in the air before my
eyes, the old loneliness seeping back in.

Who is he? I thought.

He's not the right one, I thought.

If only I had the right one, I thought.

A year later we were divorced.

I was still my mother's daughter. Now she was the negative
and I the print, but there we both were. Alone, at last, with not
the right one.

I did not understand, until years after I'd left Gerald, that I was
born to find the wrong man, as were Dorothea and Isobel.
That's what we were in business for. If this had not been the
case, we'd have all—privileged women that we were—found
some useful work to do and long forgotten the whole question
of the right man. But we did not forget it. We never forgot it.
The elusive right man became our obsessive preoccupation.
Not finding him was the defining experience.

It is the same with the princess on the pea. She's not after the
prince, she's after the pea. That moment when she feels the pea
beneath the twenty mattresses, that is *her* moment of defini-

tion. It is the very meaning of her journey, why she has traveled so far, what she has come to declare: the dissatisfaction that will keep her life at bay.

So it was with my mother who spent most of her life sighing for the absent right one. And so it was with me.

We were in thrall to passive longing, all of us—Dorothea and Isobel, me and my mother, the fairy tale princess. Longing is what attracted us, what compelled our deepest attention. The essence, indeed, of a Chekhovian life. Think of all those Natashas sighing through three long acts for what is not, and can never be. While one (wrong) man after another listens sympathetically to the recital of a dilemma for which there is no solution.

Gerald and I were the Doctor and Natasha walking in the woods, forever talking, talking, talking. Behind Natasha's eloquent and enchanting conversation lies a passivity of monumental proportion—for which the doctor is the perfect foil. His endless listening provides her with necessary illusion, makes her think she's on the move, going somewhere. But it's only a quick fix; after the high comes a great weariness. Inevitably, Natasha and the Doctor must part. They have only been keeping each other company, wasting their equally insufficient intent together. Yet Natasha turns away in a mood to accuse. The problem, she tells herself angrily, is that he wasn't the right one. I am not such a fool that I will say he was, when he wasn't. If he had *been* the right one, then I should think and act, be and do.

What we all wanted—me and Natasha, Dorothea and Isobel, my mother and the princess—was to think and act, be and do. But we didn't want it enough. Not wanting it enough, we fell into a petulance that mimicked the act of thinking. We narrowed our eyes and spotted the flaw: pursed our lips and announced imperfection: folded our arms and passed judgment. Judgment always encourages the critical intelligence to dwell on that which is missing, but *passing* judgment makes that which is missing a permanent irritation. Soon enough, through the painful logic of inborn grievance, the irritation becomes a wound, an infliction: a devotion and a destiny.

LUCY GREALY

✳ ✳ ✳ ✳ ✳ ✳

Girl

Giiirrrl, you do look fine."

In truth, Lisa does not look fine. Black half moons shine dimly beneath her eyes, and the foundation she has wiped thick as salve upon them has only made it worse. It brings to mind those Band-Aids that pretend to be the color of skin. The black circles weren't bruises, no one had hit her or anything; they were simply the aftermath of her life as she'd lived it, tick by tick, up until that very moment. Deb knows that Lisa does not look fine, but still, the response is part of the rote, and as Lisa steps into the living room in her black minidress, she looks at us expectantly.

"Girl, you sure do look fine," Carl agrees with Deb. Carl is not in drag, but still has the accent. Why do all the drag queens I meet speak with this accent? Is cross-dressing a place you have to live in, a region with its own colloquial vowels?

When I am in England, which I visit often because of

London-dwelling siblings, I avoid speaking for as long as possible while in public places. Not just because I fear being found out as an alien, but also there is the very real possibility of suddenly blurting out a half-assed English accent myself. Nothing is more mortifying. I've seen it happen to others. The rhythms just soak into you; you can't help it.

Here, I avoid speaking as well. Not that these people are about to mistake me for one of their own. It's the early eighties and I am in college and, so far, have successfully avoided sex my entire life. And even as I wear my hair very short, avoid any clothing remotely feminine, and run when my friends turn to me with their bottles of makeup, I do take a certain quiet pride in being the genuine article, the thing they are all imitating. I think. I mean, it's not that I wear rubber minidresses, or even wish to. I'm not a femme fatale, or at least not yet, and even then will never be as good as they are.

"Come here and let me touch that dress," Carl says, blowing a straight, hurried line of smoke out his mouth. Carl isn't going out tonight because he's leaving for Florida on the early flight. A job interview, I think, but I'm not sure. In the kitchen, earlier that evening, he told me about the flight in a tone of voice that let me know I was supposed to already understand these details. I nodded my head and dodged my ignorance with an offering of the tale of my first and definitely last visit to Disney World in Orlando. A lot of ear paraphernalia, I explained.

Lisa walks over and permits Carl to finger the material.

"Is this Dior, or De Or?"

"Same to you, sweetie," Lisa replies with a smile. The joke has something to do with a hybrid of New Yorkese "dese, dose, and dem" lingo, and a play on the idea that the dress is other, or "Or," than an actual Christian Dior. I think. I try to pick things up as I go along. Cynicism, I do know, is the basic grammar.

Soon enough, Lisa and Deb leave for the club near Forty-Third Street. Carl goes home to pack. I go home alone, declining offers from both sides. Somehow I know either place would ultimately depress me.

I hang out with drag queens because I think they are exotic. Their exoticism transfers a title of cool upon me without my actually having to do very much except sit around on endless couches in cramped apartments and offer ignored opinions on clothes, hair, and makeup. I feel safe there. Hanging out with mall shoppers from Westchester—the other breed of female whose ludicrous ideas of what it was to be female once held out threats simply because I came of age among them—is something I consider beneath me, so instead, and in revenge, I hang with their evil twins, the drag queens of Manhattan. Both consume equal amounts of hair spray and mascara. Both live out an interpretation of what it is to be female that has nothing to do with me, the so-called genuine article.

I hated fairy tales as a child because they had nothing to do with reality. Not because they spoke of goblins and elves and giants, not because of such obvious unreality. It had more to do with their neatly packaged morals. Mostly, I hated the notion that you got what you deserved. As I understood life, you rarely got what you deserved, and if you did, you'd better start looking over your shoulder. How could anyone hold such a romantic, naive idea about the world that outlined such a ludicrous notion?

Of course, I'm speaking of the sterilized version of fairy tales most of America's youth are subjected to. The flat-chested Snow White and her clownish dwarves, the gnomish Rumpelstiltskin, whose evilness is de facto because of his ugliness. It never occurred to me to wonder what desperate loneliness drove Rumpelstiltskin to so covet a firstborn child of his own, or what brand of cultural and personal narcissism fueled Cinderella's belief that the reward for perseverance through hardship was material wealth. I just somehow understood they were wrong.

If I'd been allowed to read the unabridged versions, the Grimms' tales of ambiguous rewards and even the darkly punishing tales of Hans Christian Andersen—magic shoes that dance your feet to bloody stubs, mermaids who give up everything magical for an unrequited and lackluster reality—I might have later understood better the lives of my perverted friends. As it was, I spent time with Deb and Lisa and Carl, a.k.a. Carol, because they glittered, and because I wanted to walk away with some of that glitter upon me without ever actually having to take responsibility for it. I could imagine myself a femme fatale all evening, an underground literary curiosity, but still wake up intact in the morning. No midnight-pumpkin curfews for me, no regrets that perhaps that frog hadn't been a prince after all. I could take of all their feminine desires, all their fairy tale beliefs that it was just a matter of trying and primping hard enough, and walk away clean.

Four o'clock in the morning: a loud banging on my dormitory door. I'm dreaming about sailing—I hate sailing—and the captain's menacing orders, the waves banging, the storm approaching, all blend into one and arrive at my door.

"Let me in! It's an emergency!" I recognize Deb's voice.

Seriously doubting it's an emergency, because it never is, I get up and unlock the door.

"I must have money," Deb announces, sitting down on my bed. Typically, almost cartoonishly, she opens her purse and takes out her compact and lipstick.

"What do you need money for?" I ask, taking the bait.

Deb launches into a story about how Lisa has been arrested for soliciting, and she, Deb, is raising bail money. I tell her I don't have any, which is the truth. Almost the truth. I have a hundred-dollar bill hidden in a book, John Berryman's *The Dream Songs*, on my shelf. I feel guilty for not telling Deb, but I also know from experience I'd never see that money again if I did tell her. It's not that she's dishonest, she just doesn't seem to keep tabs on things the way most people do. Still, I feel guilty. Lisa's been arrested before, I tell myself, and she always gets out of it. It's not like we're that close or anything. It's the only money I've got, I tell myself. Deb walks away with the sixteen dollars I had in my wallet.

Lisa's arrest will be only one more minor diversion on the road to who she "really is." She works the streets once in a while both because she likes having that power over men, and because the money is good. Her taste in clothes is expensive, as are all of her friends'. I'm a regular ragamuffin next to them. To them, what they desire constitutes accurate projections of who they really are. In this way, they're no different from hardly anyone else. If they can refine their desires to recognize only the best, that is proof enough that they themselves are the best.

"I'm going to get me a Porsche, honey, and then you'll be sorry."

"Porsche, girl, you *are* just new-money trash. Got to have a Jaguar. Only way to go."

"You're all wrong: a Mercedes convertible, two door, forest green."

At this point in my life I put up with this metaphysical foolishness because my own sexual life is so hidden and tortured. It's a tradeoff: I get to watch them in all their fabricated glory, and they get to be watched. My friends have enough sexuality to go around, and I lap it up, knowing I can do so at my own pace. This isn't true around "real" women, because they offer the image of what I am not, and it isn't true around "real" men, because all they offer is what I can't have.

Despite all the sterilized, Disneyfied versions of fairy tales that presented themselves to me throughout my childhood, one original story, in all its oddness, did find its way to my doorstep. Hans Christian Andersen's "The Girl Who Trod on a Loaf."

Basically, it's the tale of a girl who was a rather horrid little girl: she loved to pull the wings off flies, and was so vain that rather than ruin her shoes, she preferred to throw down a loaf of bread on the ground and use it as a stepping-stone. The loaf was intended for her hungry mother, and when the girl stepped on the now-ruined and muddy loaf, she sank down into the lair of the Marsh Woman. There, she was traded off to the Bogeyman's mother, who wanted to use her as a statue in her own home. The girl who trod on the loaf was doomed then to stand motionless, hungry and unhappy, in the cold, dark chamber.

Three things struck me most about this tale: one, once a statue, the girl was tormented by flies who crawled all over her and could not fly away because their wings had been plucked off them. Two, that the girl could actually hear all the tales and songs written about her fate up above, in the land she'd once inhabited. Three, that she herself never actually escaped: eventually, she transformed into a bird which flew up to the world and did its own version of good, but she herself, as an actual little girl, was gone forever.

There's no easy way to interpret this story. I do know that the author's subtle touch regarding the flies chilled me to the bone. Up until that moment in life I'd embarked on a good amount of insect torture of my own. This story stopped me dead in my tracks. It had nothing to do with my having been turned into a "good" person: simply, I was afraid I'd suffer the same fate. Transformation of the inner self not through good intent, but morbid fear.

That the girl could hear the stories and songs made up about her plight touched me in a far less precise way. How often we want to be the heroes of our own stories, at whatever cost. And then to go through all that, only to transform into something which, while beautiful and airy, could not possibly fully enjoy the freedom in exactly the way the girl had desired it. Or could she? Does the thing we are always trying to transform into, the thing we most desire to be, *have* to cast off what it once was, or is that the whole point?

Though there wasn't anything *overtly* sexual in this or any of the other fairy tales I read, there was something *deeply* sexual about them, an underground-troll kind of sexuality that lived beneath the bridge you had to walk over on your way to the rest of your life. At any moment, it could grab you. As an adolescent, my deep fear of sex could be matched only by my deeper interest. I thought that sex, once undertaken, was the thing which transformed you forever and ever and ever. There wouldn't be any coming back, any godmothers to uncast the spell. Because I was too afraid to cross that bridge for myself until I was into my twenties, I watched my friends cross it for me. These particular friends not only crossed it, they jumped into the river.

Lisa wants me to write something about her. That's the hitch to being a writer among theatrical people: they are all looking for good parts.

"I got a million stories, sweetie, and they could be yours," Lisa winks at me. She thinks the way it works is that I will pay her for her stories.

"Who do you want to play you when they make the movie?" Carol asks.

"Oh, lord, who else but Dolly Parton?" Lisa says, adjusting her breasts.

"She's not an actress, she's a singer," Carol rejoins, but it's too late, Lisa is already singing "Nine to Five" and shimmying up against the doorway. All of my favorite drag queens love doorways. Their lives center around entrances and exits, and when you absolutely must stick around, they tell me, try and do it in a doorway. Life as an eternal passage.

My own femininity is lurking in another doorway. Once in a while, if I turn quickly enough, I can almost see myself as I will be in only a year or two's time; loitering suggestively in a short black dress. You see, soon I'll graduate, go to the Midwest to earn yet another degree, and change into an entirely different person. I'll abandon one version of myself, only to throw my-self with abandon into the next self. I'll make up for lost time. I'll grow my hair long and learn the fangledness of garter belts. And jealousy. And the unabridged versions of the old-time sad-nesses—the stories I thought would disappear. Though I'll never get to the point of false eyelashes, for a few years I will wear my new sexuality as carefully and protectively as I once wore my asexuality. I will learn to style my hair and dance in high heels. The transformation will be so complete that my old friends will almost not recognize me when I return for a visit. Much later, two of them will be dead from AIDS.

But for now, of course, none of us know just how the story will turn out.

"Well, isn't it just little Miss Cinderella!" Deb declares as I walk into the apartment in a tight little dress, a whole summer later.

"Girl, I hear you been getting it till you're raw!" Lisa screams, much to my embarrassment. It's true, I'd recently, fi-nally, lost my virginity.

"Tell us all about him," Deb asks.

Though in truth the guy is a loser, they're all looking at me expectantly, pulling out their packs of cigarettes in anticipa-tion. So I tell a version of the tale anyway; not exactly the true tale, but a small true part of the tale, a version in which I get what I want, and what I want turns out to be exactly who I am. My friends coo, over all of us, long into the night.

BELL HOOKS

✳ ✳ ✳ ✳ ✳ ✳

To Love Justice

Fairy tales were the refuge of my troubled childhood. Despite all the lessons contained in them about being a dutiful daughter, a good girl, which I internalized to some extent, I was most obsessed with the idea of justice—the insistence in most tales that the righteous would prevail. The evocation of a just world, where right would prevail over wrong, was a balm to my wounded spirits during my childhood. It was a source of hope. In the end I could believe that no matter the injustices I suffered, truth would come to light and I would be redeemed. Indeed, the message of redemptive love shared in so many beloved fairy tales sustained me.

One of my favorite stories from the Brothers Grimm is "The Goose Girl." As a child, this story appealed to me, like many others, because it was situated in a world where nature was presented as both benevolent and threatening. Like any girl growing up in the fifties in southern small-town rural America, I was always fascinated by nature. Since my father's father,

Daddy Gus, was a farmer who worked as a sharecropper, there was always a focus on the natural environment. Weather was an everyday obsession. Taking care of crops required patience and diligence. I can close my eyes and see myself as a little girl walking behind my grandfather, the sun on our backs, straw hats on our heads, checking tomato plants. I can remember how hard it was to walk straight down the neat rows, to not let my feet crush plants.

Oftentimes in the rural world I was raised in as a small child, huge fields would be hidden by borders of plants. Honeysuckle and wild asparagus would grow on the other side. Following the right path could lead one to a magical world, to a world of mysterious shapes, of growing things, a paradise of hidden delights. In *An Unspoken Hunger*, naturalist Terry Tempest Williams describes moments of transformation as she revels in nature: "In these moments I felt innocent and wild, privy to secrets and gifts exchanged only in nature. . . . Hands on the earth, I closed my eyes and remembered where the source of my power lies. My connection to the natural world is my connection to self—erotic, mysterious, and whole." The ecstasy and sense of enchantment I felt in the natural world was never talked about by grown-ups, but it was there in the stories I read.

Fairy tales were the manuals that instructed me how to confront and cope with that world. They sanctioned the merger of fantasy and dreaming with concrete reality. They sanctioned all that was taboo in the family. Fantasy was often seen by Christian folks as dangerous, as potentially Satanic. My love of fairy tales was accepted as long as it was not much talked about. I liked to lie in a dark room and daydream my favorite stories, making self the center of the drama.

In "The Goose Girl" the princess who has no name (I always

thought that these unnamed girls were without identification so that we as readers could easily insert ourselves into the princess role) has a talking horse, Falada. In the Kentucky world of my childhood, horses were essential to life. I longed to ride, to have my own horse. Daily dreaming of my imaginary horse that I would ride everywhere and look at the world from a high place, I was primed to embrace Falada, the goose girl's faithful stead.

Again and again in fairy tales daughters are sent away from loving, protective mothers to find their way in the world. Usually, they are journeying to unfamiliar places to marry. In "The Goose Girl" the mother is old and widowed, and while she cannot journey with her daughter to "that far land," where she will marry a king's son, she loves her "from the bottom of her heart" and sends her off with a young maid and the talking horse, Falada. Before they journey, the mother goes to her bed-chamber and there she cuts her finger with a knife and lets "three drops of blood fall on it." This blood has magical power.

In the Christian church of my childhood we learned that the blood of Christ was shed for our redemption, that it was the ultimate expression of love, the most profound gift. Writing about the redemptive power of blood in an essay "The Radiance of Red: Blood Work," I emphasize that at communion "we drink the symbolic blood to be one with God, to acknowledge the sacrifice of blood that makes growth and new life possible." In this case it is the mother's blood that has the power to comfort and protect. Feminist poet Judy Grahn extolls the power of the mother's blood in her book *Blood, Bread, and Roses: How Menstruation Created the World*, reminding us "that women's blood was held in awe and terror" because "women bled and did not die." Even though the goose girl is given the legacy of power from her mother by the gift of blood, she has the task to guard her gift.

Significantly, the goose girl proceeds on a transformative journey where she must become fully aware to learn how to live in the world. Undergoing a rite of passage, she must learn both awareness and mindfulness. The "raging thirst" that she feels on her journey is symbolic of her quest for life. When the chambermaid accompanying her rebels, she dismounts to drink at the river; quenching her thirst, uttering the words "God! God!" Evoking the divine, the goose girl is reminded that she has not been left without comfort, and yet the three drops of blood comfort her with the warning: "If the mother only knew, her heart would surely break in two." As a girl I often pondered why the mother's heart would break if she knew. Then and now I think she would be brokenhearted because the daughter has so quickly forgotten the lesson of survival her mother taught her.

The goose girl fails to heed her mother's warning because she is a "humble creature." This failure leads to her distress. When her position is challenged and the familiar world that she has known is disrupted, it caused her great sorrow. Her grief about change makes it impossible for her to notice that "the little rag with the blood floated away on the water without her ever noticing it." Without the remembrance of her past, symbolized by the mother's gift, the goose girl loses her identity and with it her power.

Choosing to exploit this loss of power, the chambermaid forces the princess to change places with her. When they arrive at the palace, the young prince is unable to tell who is his true bride. He judges only from appearance. It is the older, wiser king whose gaze is fixated on the "delicate and beautiful" girl who had accompanied the bride. In many fairy tales, disguises are never so complete that they suppress true identity. In this marvelous moment of reversal and intrigue, we see that the value of the princess is there not because of outer garments but because of the quality of her soul. She radiates that quality despite her apparent disenfranchised circumstance.

When the "true bride" goes to work with the lad who attends the geese, her humility is tested and she stands strong. Writing in her book *Holy Daring* about the life of St. Teresa of Avila, Tessa Bielecki offers the insight that the courage to bear great trials is part of the spiritual practice that enables us to reach a life of ecstasy: "Teresa tells us over and over again that we must have a great deal of resolute determination to persevere until reaching the end, whatever work is involved, whatever criticism arises, whether we arrive or whether we die in the process, even if we don't have courage for the trials that come our way, even if the world collapses around us, we've got to keep going." The goose girl shows this courage. She does not bemoan her fate. As a troubled child, I identified with the anguish of this girl. Feeling misunderstood, like an outsider in my own family, I was inspired by her patience.

It made my heart glad that she had enough fortitude to make sure that the knacker hired by the impostor to kill the faithful horse, Falada, would keep the horse's head so that she could still converse with this creature who symbolized her all-knowing unconscious. It is in the pastures, during her sojourn with nature, that the princess regains her inner strength and her intuitive powers. She exercises those powers to ward off the unwanted sexual overtures of the lad. This image of the female empowered by the strength of her will to protect herself from unwanted advances was especially enchanting to me as a girl. When she will not do his bidding, the lad tires of her company and complains to the king. Embedded in this story is a sharp critique of patriarchy—of female resistance and the disempowerment of the male who would seize control over the female body and dominate.

Once the lad reports on the goose girl's behavior to the king, not even this royal patriarch can get her to betray her confidences. She tells him, "I may not tell you, and I may not tell any man my sorrow, for thus have I sworn under the wide heavens, else had I been killed." Significantly, the goose girl can tell her story to the iron stove. The placement of this stove in the story moved me because I grew up in a world of wood-burning stoves. It was such a comforting experience to sit by the fire. As a girl, I could see myself there in front of the stove, able to tell my trials. The princes gets inside the stove and begins "to weep and wail." Symbolically, this stove is a womb, a warm place where she enters and is reborn. The tie to her past and her mother is restored and with it her true identity.

I especially like the fact that the goose girl regains her power through the art and act of storytelling. It is this coming to voice that feminist writers wholeheartedly proclaim is essential for the claiming of our power. In her work *The Fruitful Darkness: Reconnecting with the Body of the Earth*, Joan Halifax reminds us that our lives can undergo profound changes when we reach a threshold during a rite of passage where we are "beaten apart by grief." It is fascinating that the goose girl has been so stoical and yet the moment when she speaks the unspeakable, her trauma, she is overcome with intense grief.

Halifax describes the final phase of the rites of passage as the Return, the going back to a place of home or centeredness that we have never really left: "After we are born, we sustain a wound when this cord is cut and we are separated from the maternal organism. We also have a social umbilicus, which ties us to society. This cord is cut in the process of the wounding of initiation. But there is another cord that cannot be cut. . . . It is a life cord or net that connects us to the womb of creation. . . . This is what we return to, this life thread that sews together the fabric of our world." When the goose girl finds her voice, she is reconnected to everything that she has lost. Healing happens. She has been initiated and is now ready to take her place in the world. Her beauty has deepened as there is now a unity between outer form and inner strength.

Again it is the king in the role of benevolent wise elder who witnesses this transformation and reveals her true identity to the prince. Her virtue is rewarded. Importantly, her new "look" is so radiant and powerful that she can sit at the table with the false bride and not be recognized. There in the face of a community of witnesses the chambermaid is exposed. Responding to a story about betrayal, the maid offers a severe judgment which is then meted out to her. The maid is not the victim of the harsh judgment of male onlookers. It is she who decrees her fate. This is yet another example in this story of female agency. What she has decreed she must suffer.

This story of justice, of the sustaining power of redemptive love, inspires. The bride and groom govern their kingdom with "peace and happiness." Having successfully endured her trials and faced her destiny with dignity and grace, the princess is able to know joy. For me, this remains a story that offers hope. It tells any child who is unjustly wounded and broken in spirit that there is a witness to their pain, that one day they will be able to tell their story and be whole again.

FANNY HOWE

✳ ✳ ✳ ✳ ✳ ✳

Fairies

Everything I know about fairies comes from Oscar Wilde's mother, Francesca Speranza—or Lady Wilde. She wrote *Legends of Ancient Ireland*, which was published in England in 1902. She gathered her evidence from "oral communications with the peasantry" and from history texts, where she begins: "From the beautiful Eden-land at the head of the Persian Gulf, where creeds and cultures rose to life, the first migrations emanated," including flocks of fairies traveling from Iran to Erin.

Of those fairies—the *Sidhe* of Ireland, she writes: "Their voices were heard in the mountain echo, and their forms seen in the purple and golden mountain mist; they whispered amidst the perfumed hawthorn branches; the rush of the autumn leaves was the scamper of little elves—red, yellow, and brown—wind-elven, and dancing in their glee; and the bending of the waving barley was caused by the flight of the Elf King and his Court across the fields. They danced with soundless feet, and their step was so light that the drops of dew they danced on only trembled but did not break. . . ."

Lady Wilde's collection of Irish folklore often refers to its primary sources—Christianity and Sublime Pantheism—but, once in motion, the volume becomes a storybook, a collection of herbal medicines, and accounts of the saints and their eccentricities, fakirs (the sacred fraternity of beggars), and a discussion of antiquities and early Irish art.

It is a learned book, written with respect, humor, and curiosity. One would not mind being stuck with it, and it alone, for a year or so. Fairies are described as fallen angels, but not birds who are the angels' angels, according to Dante, and a lost paradise is implicit in their existence. Nondualistic, but moody instead, fairies build spiderly bridges between emotions, and there is linkage rather than a leap between good and evil.

Fairies are scary and to this day many people won't tamper with their rings on the drumlins. Now, how did fairy tales come to be called fairy tales, since they often have nothing to do with fairies? Perhaps fairies themselves whispered these stories into kitchens and beds around the world. The pantheistic, the pagan, the petrifying truths conveyed in fairy tales do have something resonant of a world that recently included paradise. (Read

Edmund Spenser's "Faerie Queene.") No need for an afterlife in such a world. The other world is the earth and our air a holy halo around it. Or else: This *is* the afterlife, the trace and effect of every gesture that comes before the one being made right now. "The bending of the waving barley was caused by the flight of the Elf King and his Court across the fields."

According to Lady Wilde, the *Feadh-Ree* (fairy) is a riff on the word *Peri*, the Persian mystic race that flew about the gulf invisibly. They live in a land of perpetual youth, but are fated to perish utterly on Chastisement Day. They drink nectar from flowers and wear their yellow hair long to the ground. They have too much pride and their population exceeds ours. Many fairy stories are about babies, lovers, dying people, and their corpses, those liminal happenings effected by spells and fairy music.

In my new little novel, *Nod*, I provide some information on fairies. They love music, for one thing, and if you feel you are entering a dangerous situation, play some music so the fairies will be enamored of the sound and forget their naughty business. They especially love to dance on May Day when they mimic the two circling revolutions of sun and moon. If you put your ear to the ground, you can hear fairy music, believe it or not. Approaching a dolmen in Ireland in some wild meadow, don't get confused—or do!—by how small the door is leading inside, because humans were much smaller in stature in megalithic times. The true "little people" dig holes in the ground, like gophers, and use snapdragons for crockery. Draw a red thread across the door and tie it fast to prevent a fairy from coming in the night. The children of fairies and mortal women are good at music but have moody fits when they are excessively moved. No one ever saw an intoxicated fairy, they are very careful in this regard, but they like to have a little of everything; so don't be stingy or they will get back at you.

When I was a child in Killiney, south of Dublin, I saw a fairy on a stone wall—a tiny fellow in green and brown—but my mother, close by, didn't see him or believe me. We were on our way to visit the Druid chair that faces the rising sun under some sacred oak trees (now encircled by suburban housing, but left alone) to make parting wishes before our return to America. Years later, my son—a little boy drunk on too much reading in *The Crock of Gold* and *Gnomes*—saw elves galavanting in a field in Stonington, Connecticut. His sisters and I believed him, but nonetheless I hid his fairy books away for a long while.

I myself have always been gullible. Consequently, my life is errant and my stories are a defense of belief. My choice of vocabulary—when I was losing belief—saved me, because I chose literally my mother tongue: Anglo-Irishly steeped in poetry and exaggerated narratives. But I am skeptical before all other believers and appeal to reason when they get too airy. When people write for children, they must defend belief, but it is harder to do so when you are writing for adults. Littleness makes belief a necessity. And it makes business a necessity too!

———

Lady Wilde writes: "The Leprechauns are merry, industrious, tricky little sprites, who do all the shoemaker's work and the tailor's and the cobbler's for the fairy gentry, and are often seen at sunset under the hedge singing and stitching." It is the littleness of these creatures that puts them deep into nature, not as spirits of nature, but as human-minded participants in foliage and riverbend. While Thoreau was leaning over his windowsill watching the war of the red ants versus the black, it was only his imagination that could enter their littleness, not any part of his body. But Leprechauns could twist a shoe into shape under a dock leaf. Tininess and fairy life go together. Still, fairies can also cure a sick cow and cut paths through human houses because they change form, size, and meaning at will.

William Blake described seeing the following in his garden in Sussex: "There was a great stillness among the branches and flowers, and more than common sweetness in the air; I heard a low and pleasant sound and I knew not whence it came. At last I saw the broad leaf of a flower move, and underneath I saw a procession of creatures, of the color and size of green and grey grasshoppers, bearing a body laid out on a rose-leaf, which they buried with songs, and then disappeared. It was a fairy funeral."

Lady Wilde was Anglo-Irish. Her family came from Wexford. She had masses of hair, was very large, and she named herself Speranza. She was a major intellectual figure in Dublin, devoted to her son Oscar through his trials just as she stood by her

husband through his trial for rape. She was relentless in her loy-
alties and in her research into Irish folklore. She was super-
stitious and, though a Protestant, a lover of Catholicism. My
own mother is Anglo-Irish, her paternal family—Fitzmaurice
Mannings—dating back to the sixteenth century, from County
Kerry, and from a long line of crooked men. The male Bennetts
in her maternal family she refers to as "the flopsy Bennetts," but
the women like Speranza were often political activists, nation-
alists, and scholars. When we were children, my mother played
a record of Orson Welles (who had studied with her at the Gate
Theater in Dublin) reading "The Happy Prince" by Oscar
Wilde.

This reading reduced me to sobs every time, and remains with
me as one of the most spellbinding fairy tales ever written. Far
more in the tradition of Hans Andersen than the Grimms, one
feels deeply the links between the Celtic imagination and
the Scandinavian in this sorrowful story of altruism. Orson
Welles—as artificial in much of his "theater" as Wilde was in
his life—read the story in melodious, deep-throated tones:
"Swallow, swallow, little swallow, will you not stay with me one
night longer?" being the refrain. In the story the good ones die
and the vain and foolish survive as philistines of progress. But
as with Andersen, Wilde's story ends on a Christian note—
written and uttered with such genuine belief that the story did
establish a little theological hope in me. I was eight. My
mother's skeptical nature and my father's despairing postwar
atheism both melted a little over the sound of Orson Welles
reading "The Happy Prince." Both of them forgave him and
Hans Andersen their sentimentality, though to this day I don't

know why except that these fairy tales restored their own hope
for a while.

In Michael MacLiammoir's introduction to Wilde's fairy tales,
he writes that Wilde's "son Vyvyan Holland, in a delightful book
called *Son of Oscar Wilde*, tells us how, when his father was tired
of playing with him and his brother Cyril, he would keep them
quiet by telling them fairy stories. 'There was one,' Mr. Holland
says, 'about the fairies who lived in the great bottles of coloured
water that the chemists used to put in their windows, with
lights behind them that made them take on all kinds of different shapes. The fairies came down from their bottles at night
and played and danced and made pills in the empty shop.' Cyril
once asked his father why he had tears in his eyes when he told
us the story of the Selfish Giant, and he replied that 'really
beautiful things always made him cry.' "

At the end of "The Happy Prince" he wrote (and must have
been weeping when he wrote it):

> "Bring me the two most precious things in the city," said God to
> one of His Angels; and the Angel brought Him the leaden heart
> and the dead bird.
>
> "You have rightly chosen," said God, "for in my garden of
> Paradise this little bird shall sing for evermore, and in my city of
> gold the Happy Prince shall praise me."

Wilde also wrote a little story called "The Fisherman and His
Soul" that tells the story of a handsome young fisherman who

sells his soul for the love of a mermaid. He does so despite the warnings of a priest: "Accursed be the Fauns of the woodland, and accursed be the singers of the sea! I have seen them at night-time, and they have sought to lure me from my beads. They tap at the window and laugh. They whisper into my ears the tale of their perilous joys. They tempt me with temptations, and when I would pray they make mouths at me. They are lost, I tell thee, they are lost. For them there is no heaven nor hell, and in neither shall they praise God's name." This tale concerns itself less with the fisherman than with the experience of his soul—void of a heart—roaming the earth. Immoral, voyeuristic, this shadow (like the shadow soul in Andersen's tales) becomes a Satanic spirit. The fisherman, on the other hand, is absolved ultimately of sin because of the purity of his love for the mermaid.

This fairy tale, read in the light of its author's personal life and his last prose work—*De Profundis*—hints at later, more "out" contemporary fairy tales. ("To regret one's own experiences is to arrest one's own development. To deny one's own experiences is to put a lie into the lips of one's own life. It's no less than a denial of the soul.") In Wilde's dandyism laced with his strong maternal influence—her learning, her love of Ireland— a sublime pantheism—a preadolescent *belief* in an earth comfortably populated by aliens (fairies, angels) was allowed to thrive. The potential for flight to these airy regions, away from the indoctrinations of fictions we have come to model our lives after, rests on a kind of tiptoe tilt, the one that the very young assume before bending back to ground. Fairies, winged and poised to spring, have that posture too. Do they come from outer space and yearn to return there? Or do they only wish for a different kind of tale—not the dreadful ones we have learned about winners and losers—but one about a plenteous universe—and long to fly free to it?

Because of these questions it is impossible for me to write a story that does not include a child. In fact the older I get the more my writing becomes child-identified. The presence of a child or children in literature, either as readers or as characters, helps to establish a common ground—one that is innocent because it is both general to all people and involuntary. None of us asks to be born, chooses our parents, or plans to be raised where we are as children, but we all experience these facts of childhood as a given, a necessity in that sense. Childhood is the ultimate experience of helplessness, being at the mercy of others more powerful. Children in literature in this way serve the function of reminding everyone of injustice, bad luck, good luck, and chance. (Likewise characters in literature also represent the ultimate and primary experience of helplessness, in the hands of their writer.) The turning point on which the beliefs of children often flutter and fail is the moment of forgetfulness, when the gate slams on childhood and its memory is absolutely closed to them. The propagation of fairy-faith is located at this threshold, where the forever forgotten is sealed away.

So it would seem that an important relationship to both time and memory is involved in the existence of fairies: the animation of the invisible, and the way it runs ahead of us—and we seem, as humans, to be discarded by a future that is chasing us from behind. Into all of this drops the tale. The effort at stabilizing time, of imprinting little figures on sheets of paper and packing them tight, is obviously related to the pretend games children play. Toy soldiers, dollhouses, "the world of counterpane"—it is this activity that generates written fiction. The writer (like the child) is hunched over the page, controlling little signs and symbols that replicate a population he or she is manipulating. The littleness of letters makes this a breeze. With a one-two-three-start-middle-end, the characters are controlled. As MacLiammoir goes on to say about Wilde, "The poet turns now and then to look back over his shoulder . . . and then, remembering a little the moods of childhood, he needs must weep." His weeping over the traces of a lost landscape (beauty incarnate) is his literal method for writing about childhood. His ink is salt, his figures manageable. Like the instruction by Blake to himself regarding the form of one of his pictures: "Angels to be very small as small as the letters that they may not interfere with the subject at bottom which is to be stormy sky and rain separated from the angels by clouds."

Angels, like fairies, flew on their own power. The capacity to fly was built into their bodies. This capacity, like a piece of useless punctuation, has been erased from the writer's imagination. Instead, technically proficient UFOs and aliens from outer space occupy a respectable literary genre, and conveniently these images of creatures from outer space, with their devious plans and devices—like characters in conventional realistic fiction—affirm the interests of nation, state, and law by obeying the lowest (most familiar) human characteristics in their air-craft. We imagine aliens performing violent acts and sell-out gestures, betrayals and lies. The fact is, the technology given to creatures from outer space automatically inserts them into a masculine, science-based tradition. Fairies, like dragonflies and butterflies, are prettified on their way to extinction, because what they had came naturally.

Yet children continue to "believe in" them, given the chance. The mad applause for Tinker Bell in the middle of the per-formance of *Peter Pan* is like a reenactment of the storming of the Winter Palace. It's a protection of children's rights to be-lieve in something other than what oppressive reason allows. And that is bewilderment. A society for the protection of fairies would really be a society for the protection of bewil-derment.

It is the job of the storyteller to inspire questions and aston-ishment, not to set out a series of predetermined results based on old fictions about social relations. It was the "fairy" in the tale that used to throw logic off its trajectory.

There is a kind of story—one kind that interests me—that draws on the fairy tale model in order to contain and study rad-ical bewilderment. An Austrian writer in the mid-nineteenth century, Adalbert Stifter, wrote a collection of stories called

Colored Stones in which he provides ecstatic depictions of mountain life and the children who inhabit them. One story especially, called "Rock Crystal" and translated by Marianne Moore, is a fairy tale that exists in a real place and time. (Not in a "once-upon-a-time" as in "hovering over" transcendentally.) This is a real mountain village that the author has known, yet the story is laden with the sublime pantheism of the true fairy tale. Correspondences between the soul and the earth are carefully, painstakingly "painted in words" by Stifter in this haunting novella.

It is a story of a brother and sister who get lost. (The sibling tie, by its very nature founded on the mutual tragedy of birth to the same parents, already represents a sin that is innocent.) It is Christmas Eve. They are sent out through a mountain pass to visit their grandmother. On their way home they become lost in a snowstorm in the mountains, take shelter in an icy chasm overnight, and in the night sky before dawn, when it seems sure that they will die of cold, this is what they see:

The children sat, open-eyed, gazing up at the small stars. Something now began to happen as they watched. While they sat thus, a faint light bloomed amid the stars, describing upon the heavens a delicate arc. The faint green luminescence traveled slowly downward. But the arc grew brighter and brighter until the stars paled away, while a shudder of light, invading other parts of the firmament—taking on an emerald tinge—vibrated and flooded the stellar spaces. Then from the highest point of the arc sheaves radiated like points of a crown, all aglow. Adjacent

horizons caught the brightening flush; it flickered and spread in
faint quivers through the vastness round about. . . .

and Stifter suggests the scientific source for this, but then lets it
go, and in minute detail describes the fading of the phenome-
non and its replacement by daybreak.

Partly because of the obvious echoes in the story of a brother
and sister becoming lost, but also because of the sublime pantheism of this story, it drinks at the same stream as the fairy
tale. However, unlike Wilde's sentimental ending, Stifter's
conclusion as in all his stories is an absolutely cold one. The
children's rescue and return to their village is a triumph of
communal human effort, a reaffirmation of the importance of
national identity. The children erred and were set right again.
This social issue is in the end the subject of the story, but it
is suffused with ambivalence and irony. While there are no
fairies in his stories, the fleeing figure of cosmic love is drawn
in the night skies, a hope that is liberated from cause and effect. As in the story of Pandora, when hope is released from
her treasure-box with all the sins of the world, Stifter in his
fine odd stories lets us know everything else is there, too, including prejudiced villagers and a grandmother whose love is
"morbid."

A contemporary and much more sorrowful version of
the same story is the film *Landscape in the Mist* by Theo
Angelopoulos. Again, two children—brother and sister—set
off by themselves and become lost. They are searching for their

father, who abandoned them and went to Germany. Dismal train rides, lonely highways, urban squalor and cruelty—all these become allegorical stations in their search for the father.

The film is short on speech but poetic when voices emerge, and the ecstatic ending of the film—a vision redolent of Paradise—brings one face-to-face with the irreduceable fact of hope in the midst of a poisoned landscape. The soft children's voice-overs become little haunts from a fairy-haunted past.

Fictions like these, while they are based in the science of motion and emotion, develop a structure of thought that opens out to a cosmic unknown. Isn't this what fairy tales do too?

Once, when I was nervous beyond belief, I pretended that all the people on the street were elves, and what had before looked like a firing squad now was reduced to a riotous mob of little people. I felt much better. However, there is no lasting fantasy escape from the reality of malign powers that drive us all along. While that one got me home safely on the bus, the use-value of the vision would soon enough grow weak. Fiction seeks the immortal archetype, but rarely finds the one that speaks for a dispersed, alienated, unsuccessful people. William Blake described her like this in *Thel*:

> *O thou little virgin of the peaceful valley.*
> *Giving to those that cannot crave, the voiceless, the o'ertired.*
> *Thy breath doth nourish the innocent lamb, he smells thy milky*
>   *garments.*

Fairies explain as well as anything else the estrangement we feel about a conventional, realistic life—given the weird arrival of suffering seemingly out of nowhere.

Lady Wilde wrote: "A farmer who had lost one son by heart disease (always a mysterious malady to the peasants) and another by gradual decay, consulted a wise fairy woman as to what should be done, for his wife also had become delicate and weak. The woman told him that on November Eve the fairies had made a road through the house, and were going back and forward ever since, and whatever they looked upon was doomed. The only remedy was to build up the old door and open another entrance. This the man did, and when the witch-women came as usual in the morning to beg for water or milk or meal they found no door, and were obliged to turn back. After this the spell was taken off the household, and they all prospered without fear of the fairies."

But fairies can't be blamed for everything. An early Irish poem concludes:

I that brought winter in
And the windy glistening sky,
I that brought sorrow and sin,
Hell and pain and terror, I.

The subject of the poem is Eve but it is also Everyone. The world that we can sense is the one we have invented too. It is the invisible world—the interior life—what people now call "spirituality"—that remains the unexplorable sector of our being. What you can't remember (almost everything) stays free. It is in this free zone that the fairies, pagan in their allegiance to a rustic earth with blowing red and yellow leaves and blue waters, but always unseen, still stand nonetheless on the side of hope.

FERN KUPFER

✳ ✳ ✳ ✳ ✳ ✳

Trust

My daughter was about three years old when a close friend of mine suddenly died of a heart attack. Gabi was in the kitchen with me when I answered the phone and heard the news; she watched, wide-eyed, as I leaned against the doorway and began to cry. I took her into my arms for my comfort as much as hers. I said: "I feel sad because George died." Only a few weeks before, we had eaten dinner with George and Judy; Gabi had played with their children in the backyard.

Gabi patted my shoulder and then, with perfect three-year-old logic she attempted to console: "Well, Judy is still your friend and she didn't *dive*."

And so began our first talk about death, about what it means for the living. I would have preferred my young daughter's introduction to the subject to be less traumatic—perhaps the loss of a goldfish or a baby bird—not the father of one of her friends. Gabi, even at three, understood that George's "dive" was surely the end of something. Looking intensely into my eyes, my daughter pleaded for reassurance: "But you will never dive, will you?"

I told her that every living thing, everyone does die, but what happened to George as a young man was something unusual. That probably I would die when she was all grown up with children of her own. Did she understand?

Now, two decades later, I still recall the set of her chin, her firm resolve when she answered: "Mommy, I would *never* want to live in a world without you."

It is the story of a child in the world without a mother, without resource or protection, that haunted me so in the fairy tales I read as a girl. Of abused Cinderella, isolated Rapunzel, of motherless Snow White living off in the woods and having to pick up after all those little men. I remember the books I read growing up in the Bronx in the early fifties. *The Green Fairy Book. The Red Fairy Book. The Blue Fairy Book*. I don't recall that they had a particular organization except for color. Every three or four pages there were wispy, black-and-white sketches. And words. Lots of words with elegant sentence construction and an occasionally arcane vocabulary.

I can't say that it was my favorite, but the one fairy tale that I found most provoking as a child, and one that has new meaning for me in my life today, is "Hansel and Gretel." I just reread it the other day and I guess I was surprised at how I had remembered it differently. How, to my mind, Gretel was the hero, the enterprising one. But in the original Grimms'—and that was most likely the one I read forty years ago—Gretel is actually a bit of a whiner. It is Hansel who assuages her fear, Hansel who devises the plan to find their way out of the woods with the bread crumbs. And once trapped by the wicked witch, it is Hansel's idea to put a bone out to fool the myopic crone lest she think he is fat enough to eat. So where did I ever get the idea that Gretel was the brains of that outfit?

But the core of the story—that Hansel and Gretel were motherless children, living with a woman who didn't love them and a wimp of a father who wouldn't protect them—must be the source of every child's most primal nightmare.

Seven years ago, I married for the second time. Joe had custody of his two daughters—Megan, thirteen, and Katie, ten—and had lived alone with them for most of their lives. Right before I married Joe, my mother had sent me an article stating that ten and thirteen were the worst ages for children to adjust in a second marriage. Thanks, Ma, I said. I also began to rethink the role when the wicked stepmother herself *c'est moi*.

We had an outdoor wedding on the most beautiful day in June where everything was just bursting into bloom. The Unitarian minister (I am Jewish; my Lebanese husband was raised a serious Catholic) read a poem about marriage being a rose garden "where squash is fond to grow." We included the children in the ceremony. Joe and I made vows to each other and to our girls ("because you are the daughter of the one I love . . ."); we all exchanged rings. There wasn't a dry eye in the crowd.

I was nervous, of course. The Valium I had taken along with a few sips of champagne after the ceremony made me appear a little cockeyed in the wedding video. I loved Joe for his gentleness, his loyalty, his humor. But I also had *qualms*. The notion of living with someone else's children is enough to give anyone qualms. *Especially* if you've had a child yourself and know the commitment needed to turn out a reasonably successful human being. To say nothing of the hours of carpooling.

As a columnist, I frequently wrote about my blended family. I wrote about how stepfamilies are many things, and complicated is one of them. I wrote about how being a stepmother was one of the most difficult things I'd ever done. One of my articles was actually a defense of Hansel and Gretel's stepmother. I'd asked: Did anyone think that perhaps Hansel and Gretel's stepmother was not such a terrible person? She sent the kids off into the woods because she wanted a little time alone with her husband—so was that such a crime?

The fall after Joe and I married, Gabi was off to college. Megan and Katie's mother was living in another state, saw the girls infrequently, and disappointed them often. I have sometimes thought that in a way, her chosen absence from their lives was just as painful as a death. Then, of course, there *I* was. The girls did not choose me. Their father did. And they were expected to be good sports and come along for the ride.

Megan, who was older, was not pleased. She was the woman of the house and had her father to herself. "Don't take it personally, Fern," she told me. "I just wouldn't want him to marry anyone." When we all went to movies, Megan edged ahead to get a seat next to her father. In restaurants she did the same. Then she commanded his full attention during the meal: "Will I like these potatoes? Is this chicken too spicy for me, Dad?"

Katie, at ten, was thrilled to have what she called a "real Donna Reed family." But Katie was so eager to please that the pressure of being agreeable (this was before her much less agreeable teenage persona kicked in) caused her a lot of stress. She knew that a real mom would love her no matter what. But getting another woman—a stepmother—to love her, well, that would take some wooing. Under her nervous eye, I found myself putting off signs of displeasure with her father. Katie was always taking our emotional temperatures—sure that any disagreement would spell divorce.

I think that initially, both the girls were nervous that if they were not around constantly to monitor the family, they wouldn't know what was going on. They didn't want to ever leave us. On vacations, they also didn't want to leave their friends. I was straight about why I wanted them to visit their mother. I told them that taking care of children was often hard work. Their father and I wanted a break. I also said that they were too young to make that decision for themselves. And if they *never* visited their mother, they would feel guilty later on in life and have too much to explain to the therapist. Believe me, I'm doing you kids a favor, I said.

There was an image I used to conjure up when I first married Joe and I felt overwhelmed by the responsibility of my new parenting role and underwhelmed by the children's appreciation of my efforts. Then I would picture my own daughter living with her father and some other woman, the stepmother. Gabi coming home from school and being asked about her day by another woman; Gabi sitting at the table eating a meal prepared by another woman; Gabi feeling sad and having to talk over her problems with another woman.

This image opened my heart. I asked myself: "If I were not around, how would I want my own daughter to be treated by another woman?" And, of course, I knew. For this imagining has guided me always to try to be the kind of stepmother I would want my own child to live with were I not there to care for her.

Now after seven years, I think we've all done pretty well in this family we've created. Gabi still has her pink bedroom in our house and considers coming to visit "going home." Megan is still her daddy's girl, but she respects me and seeks my counsel about money and school and friends. She knows that I have her best interests at heart. Katie, going through a moody and tempestuous teenhood, shows me her poetry and shares confidences about boys. All the girls are secure in the knowledge that the life Joe and I have made together is one of commitment and care and love. And although I am a stepmother to Joe's girls, they know that I am a woman they can trust.

Katie, seventeen now, is wise beyond her years. The other day, as we sat in the sunny kitchen having a cup of tea, we talked about those first years together. "Megan and I were really very young," she said. "I didn't think that at the time. I didn't understand. But you really took on a lot when you married Dad." Katie looked at me, woman-to-woman, across the kitchen table. "I don't know if I would ever do all that for a man," she said.

"Well . . ." I began. Then shrugged. How could I explain that without making her feel as if the complications of our life were *her* fault? The most difficult thing I've ever done? Were she and her sister *really* so terrible? No, I'd say. Well, sometimes. She could understand someday only if she were a stepmother herself.

"Because you are the daughter of the one I love . . ." I went in with my eyes open. What those little girls would need from me. What they would want, but what possibly I couldn't give. Being a stepmother is not for sissies. I went in with my eyes open and there were still surprises. I did my best, and most days that was good enough. It is not always easy to be fair, to be unselfish, to be responsible, to be kind. But I loved Joe and

knew that he trusted me enough to do right by his girls. And so
I did.

W ell, we're back to Hansel and Gretel, I guess. Because in
the past few weeks I've been thinking about the *father* in that
fairy tale—that poor sap of a man whose children almost died
because he wasn't strong enough to stop his wife's evil plan. It's
not as though Hansel and Gretel's father didn't care about
them, you know. He is quite happy when they return alive and
well to the cottage in the woods. He hugs them and is appropriately tearful at the reunion.

But he *let* them go into those woods. He knew what the
stepmother was doing and didn't even try to stop her! What
kind of father is that anyway? Not *mine* . . . the child's voice
echoes in my middle-aged head. Certainly not mine.

Oh, my father, what a guy! Two weeks before my father's
brain tumor had been diagnosed, he was playing tennis in the
Florida sun. He had been the oldest person to work in the
Florida school system—he retired the year before when he was
seventy-eight to care for my mother, who had cancer. They had
been happily together for fifty-six years. On their last anniversary, I had called: "How's the marriage doing?" I asked. "We're
still working on it," my father replied without missing a beat.

I spent this last summer going back and forth from my home
in Iowa to West Palm Beach. My brother and Gabi, who just finished her first year of law school and had an internship for the
summer, also helped out. I wasn't teaching in the summer, so
for two months I was on the phone with airlines and doctors
and HMOs and interviewing people who could help take care
of my dad. I was to start school again in September just when

my father had finished the last of the radiation. But the prognosis was not good. Three to six months from the discovery of the tumor, the doctors said.

In September I decided not to return to work and took a semester's leave without pay. As soon as I made the decision, it felt right. I know it sounds kind of corny and new age, but my *body* felt right. Peaceful and centered.

I had remembered reading something that Barbara Bush said to a graduating college class at some East Coast women's college. The choice of Mrs. Bush as a graduation speaker had been criticized by the students at the college. What did she ever *do* except marry someone who became president? the students complained. Who *was* she, after all, except George's wife? As a feminist myself, I was sympathetic with these views.

What Barbara Bush said addressed these concerns. Probably some zippy speechwriter had written her talk, but no matter, the words stayed with me. Mrs. Bush said—I'm paraphrasing here—that of course it was good for women to have careers, life goals, to be able to make their own way in the world. *But*, she added, addressing those new, shiny-faced grads: As you grow older you will realize that while you may easily be replaceable in your job, no one will ever be able to replace you as the mother of your children. No one will ever be able to replace you as a daughter you are to your parents.

And whosever words they be, I found them to be true. It took about an hour for the chair of the English department to find people who would take over my courses for the rest of the semester. It took another New York minute for me to send out an e-mail and resign from all the committees I was supposed to be on. The next day I was on a plane back to Florida to care for my father. And to reflect on the years that he had cared for me.

From my parents' friends I received a lot of praise for being the good daughter. But what I sensed was that being able to care for my father at the end of his life would be not a duty, but a blessing.

My father was a wonderful man whom I adored. With all that is talked about, written, and analyzed with regard to family relationships, my father's relationship to his family was pure and uncomplicated. He was simply *there* for us always; confident, loving, dependable as the dawn.

At fifty years old, I am part of a generation who mostly had "good enough" fathers. A good enough father made a living, came home on time, didn't drink or hit. Fathers to my generation came home from work and read the paper while the women took over the emotional needs of the children.

Funny that I never realized, growing up, how unusual it was for my father to know all the names of my teachers in junior high; or come home from work in the city at four in the afternoon so he could watch my brother play ball. How both my brother and I felt always the presence of our father's steady and affirming gaze throughout our lives.

There was a certain confidence that my father had with regard to being a father—a knowledge that without having read a single parenting book or ever having visited a therapist, he knew what to do. I don't recall a lot of negotiation and explaining, and he said no with a surety that is not heard frequently from today's fathers. There were catchphrases that pretty much summed up what really was his moral stance: Some things were simply "not necessary"; and you didn't take "more than you need"; some behavior was not permitted be-cause "it isn't even nice."

Maybe it was the confidence that rubbed off. He was good. And we were a part of him, so we were also good. With my father, I have always felt loved and taken care of. Safe. I didn't know until I went to college and met friends whose fathers were indifferent or cruel that not everyone had a father who could be trusted. And I didn't know until I was an adult that men could sometimes be unfaithful or selfish or violent.

When my father came home from work every day, he kissed my mother, then asked, "Where are the kids?" My brother and I were always home for dinner at six o'clock, but my father asked anyway. Whenever I walked into a room and my father was reading the newspaper, he put it down.

Once I told a friend that my father often woke me in the morning when I was a little girl by standing in the doorway of my bedroom and calling my name, and when I looked up from the pillow, he would say: "Oy, you are such a *mieskeit* that I can't even stand to look at you in the morning!" Then he would pre-tend to call to my mother, who was busy in the kitchen making breakfast, to come up and see me, to look at what a *mieskeit* her daughter was in the morning. When I told my friend what *mieskeit* meant—it is Yiddish for ugly face—she was appalled.

"*That's* what your father used to call you?" she asked.

"Well, he was just teasing," I quickly explained. "He didn't really mean that I had an ugly face."

She shook her head. "But didn't you feel bad?" she asked. "I think that's so mean—to call a child ugly. To say that you can't stand to look at her?"

I was astonished. Telling the story, seeing it through another

person's eyes, I guess I could understand how my father's teasing could be interpreted. But why, then, in my entire life, did I
always know that what my father meant those mornings when I
lifted my face from the pillow was: "You are so beautiful and I
love you so much that I can hardly bear to look at you."

Taking care of a dying person is a little like taking care of a newborn. The day is organized around feedings, cleaning up, sleep,
bodily functions. For weeks I wore the same cotton shorts and
a T-shirt. I never put on makeup. I witnessed my father's decline—so quick to anyone who saw him from day to day, and yet
in slow motion all the same. I couldn't concentrate to read a
book. But I began to keep a journal. One day I filled up a page by
just writing the same line over and over again, repeating it also
in my head like a mantra: *I can do this because I love him. . . . I can
do this because I love him. . . . I can do this because I love him. . . .*

The hospital bed was set up on the enclosed porch of my
parents' condominium. Through the windows you could see
the blue sky, the palm trees, the pink hibiscus. The oxygen tank,
the wheelchair, the commode, lined one wall. I learned how to
lift my father in the bed and to administer morphine. I fed him
chocolate ice cream, his favorite. I went to the grocery store
and to the mailbox. Once I went out for a manicure. As the girl
put a sandy blush on my nails, I thought: My father is dying.

During the last weeks of his life, my father's concern for his
family remained strong and fast. "Did you give Mommy breakfast?" he would ask me first thing in the morning, though he was
too weak to eat himself. And even slipping in and out of consciousness, he would turn to me: "Fernie, you got enough
money?"

My brother came down two days before Dad passed. We all walked around the small apartment, listening to his ragged breath. My father seemed to struggle so. The hospice nurse had told us my father could still hear us and we could talk to him, give him permission to die. My brother and I stood on either side of the bed, unpracticed and awkward with this speech. "You can go now, Dad . . ." I began. My brother started to cry. "I can't do this," he told me, fleeing the room.

The next morning I woke early, made a strong cup of coffee, and went out to the porch. I held my father's hand and told him how lucky I was to be his daughter. How I always felt so secure in his love. Then I told him he could go. I told him I was married to a good man now. I had a good job. And yes, I had enough money. I told him I would take care of Mom.

I told him to go. I was forceful, even. I said I *wanted* him to go. I said things I didn't even believe. About going toward the tunnel. Following the light. I told him his own mother was waiting for him.

I felt myself almost pushing him out of this life. "You go now, Dad," I repeated. It was a good thing my brother was still sleeping. I think it would have creeped him out.

At eight o'clock Beverly, the nurse we had hired to help at the end, came in. "It's almost time," she said. "Wake your mother and brother."

There were three last breaths—three noisy rattles that I thought were the last. But my father's final breath was actually a gentle poof—as soft as a baby's sigh.

I had started this essay before my father was even sick. Now going back to it after his death, I've been thinking how the stepmother in Hansel and Gretel looms less ominous. But the passive, weak-willed father seems a much more significant figure. How could he not have protected his own? How could he have failed his children so?

Death doesn't end a relationship. It just changes the harmony of things. My father is still in my life. His love and humor; his steadfastness and competence and strength. A father you could trust. That is the legacy that he has given me.

I had a remarkably happy childhood. A friend of mine says that I grew up in the only really functional family she can think of. I don't know if this prepared me for the often terrible losses and hurts I experienced as an adult. I like to think it did—that as Eskimos are padded with layers of fat to protect them from the cold, I was cushioned in childhood by layers of love to help me through some bitter times.

My father, a businessman, was a very practical person. He listened to news rather than music on the radio. Except for the *Times* and the *Wall Street Journal*, he was not a reader. I don't recall that I ever saw him read a single novel. Yet he was very proud of my vocation and had read every word I ever wrote (he was only critical of the occasional sex scene, which he considered "not necessary"). At the end of his life he gave me Power of Attorney and the key to the vault and told my brother and me where the stocks and bonds were. He told me to put air in the tires of the car. He told us he wanted his body to be cremated. He also asked me, a week before his death, to write something about him. And so I did.

URSULA K. LE GUIN

✳ ✳ ✳ ✳ ✳ ✳

The Wilderness Within

Influence—The anxiety of influence—It's enough to give you influenza. I've come to dread the well-intended question, "What writer or writers influenced you as a writer?"

What writer or writers didn't? How can I name Woolf or Dickens or Tolstoy or Shelley without implying that a hundred, a thousand other "influences" didn't matter?

I evade: telling the questioners they really don't want to hear about my compulsive reading disorder, or changing the playing field—"Schubert and Beethoven and Springsteen have had a great influence on my writing"—or, "Well, that would take all night, but I'll tell you what I'm reading right now," an answer I learned from being asked the question. A useful question, which leads to conversation.

Then there was the book, *The Anxiety of Influence*. Yes, I know who's afraid of Virginia Woolf. Still I'm faintly incredulous when I hear that phrase used seriously. The book came out at the same time that a lot of us were energetically rejoicing in the rediscovery and reprinting of earlier woman writers, the rich inheritance that had been withheld from all writers by the macho literary canon. While these guys were over there being paranoid about influence, we were over here celebrating it.

If acknowledging the influence of great writers makes some authors feel threatened, what about *fairy tales?* That should bring on a regular panic attack.

That the accepted notion of literary influence is appallingly simplistic is shown, I think, by the fact that it overlooks—ignores—disdains the effect of "pre-literature"—oral stories, folk tales, fairy tales, picture books—on the tender mind of the pre-writer.

Of course, such deep imprints may be harder to trace than the effect of reading a novel or a poem in one's teens or twenties. The person affected may not be conscious of such early influences, overlaid and obscured by everything learned since. A tale we heard at four years old may have a deep and abiding effect on our mind and spirit, but we aren't likely to be clearly aware of it as adults—unless asked to think about it seriously. And if seriousness is limited to the discourse of canonical Literature, we might well be embarrassed to mention something that was read to us after we'd got into bed in our jammies with a few stuffed animals.

I have absolutely no idea of when I first heard or read the tale of the Sleeping Beauty. I don't even remember (as I do for some stories) the illustrations, or the language, of a certain edition. I certainly read it for myself as a child in several collections, and again in various forms when I was reading aloud to my own children. One of those versions was a charming Czech-made book, an early example of the pop-up genre; it was good magic, the way the thorny rose-hedge leapt up around the little paper castle. And at the end everybody in the castle woke, just as they ought to, and got right up off the page. But when did I first learn that that was what they ought to do?

The Sleeping Beauty, then, is one of the stories that I've "always known," just as it's one of the stories that "we all know." Are not such stories part of our literary inheritance? Do they not influence us? Does that make us anxious?

Francine Prose's essay on the Sleeping Beauty in this book elegantly demonstrates, by the way, that we *don't* know the stories we think we've always known. I had the twelfth fairy and the whole spindle business clear in my mind, but all that after-the-marriage hanky-panky was news to me. As I knew it, as most Americans know it, the story ends with the prince's kiss and everybody getting ready for the wedding.

And I wasn't aware that it held any particular meaning or fascination for me, that it had "had any influence" on me, until, along in my sixties, I came on Sylvia Townsend Warner's evocation of the tale in a tiny poem (it is in her *Collected Poems*):

The Sleeping Beauty woke:
The spit began to turn,
The woodmen cleared the brake,
The gardener mowed the lawn.
Woe's me! And must one kiss
Revoke the silent house, the birdsong wilderness?

As poetry will do, those words took me far beyond themselves, straight through the hedge of thorns, into the secret place.

For all its sweet brevity, the question asked in the last two lines is a total "revisioning" of the story, a subversion of it. Almost, it revokes it.

The pall of sleep that lies upon the house and grounds is supposedly the effect of a malicious spell, a curse; the prince's kiss that breaks the spell is supposed to provide a happy ending. Townsend Warner asks, was it a curse, after all? The thorn-hedge broken, the cooks growling at their porridge-pots, the peasants laboring again at their sowing or harvesting, the cat leaping upon the mouse, Father yawning and scratching his head, Mother jumping up sure that the servants have been misbehaving while she was asleep, Beauty staring in some confusion at the smiling young man who is going to carry her off and make her a wife—Everything back to normal, everyday, commonplace, ordinary life. The silence, the peace, the magic, gone.

Really, it is a grand, deep question the poet asks. It takes me into the story as no Freudian or Jungian or Bettelheimian reduction of it does. It let me see what *I* think the story is about.

I think the story is about that still center: "the silent house, the birdsong wilderness."

That is the image we retain. The unmoving smoke above the chimney top. The spindle fallen from the motionless hand. The cat asleep near the sleeping mouse. No noise, no bustle, no busyness. Utter peace. Nothing moving but the slow, subtle growth of the thorn bushes, ever thicker and higher all about the boundary, and the birds who fly over the high hedge, singing, and pass on.

It is the secret garden; it is Eden; it is the dream of utter, sun-lit safety; it is the changeless kingdom.

Childhood, yes. Celibacy, virginity, yes. A glimpse of adolescence: a place hidden in the heart and mind of a girl of twelve or fifteen. There she is alone, all by herself, content, and nobody knows her. She is thinking: *Don't wake me. Don't know me. Let me be. . . .*

At the same time she is probably shouting out of the windows of other corners of her being, *Here I am, do come, oh do hurry up and come!* And she lets down her hair, and the prince comes thundering up, and they get married, and the world goes on. Which it wouldn't do if she stayed in the hidden corner and renounced love marriage childbearing motherhood and all that.

But at least she had a little while by herself, in the house that was hers, the garden of silence. Too many Beauties never even know there is such a place.

Townsend Warner's lines haunted my mind for some while before I realised that her question had led me not only into the folktale of the Sleeping Beauty but into a story I had to write about it. In this case, the influence was almost direct. I am not anxious about it in any way. I am cheerfully grateful.

My story is called "The Poacher" (it is in the collection *Unlocking the Air*). Its title describes exactly what I, the author, was doing: poaching on the folk tale's domain. Trespassing, thieving. Hunting. Tracking down something that happened in the place where nothing happens.

In my story a peasant boy lives at the edge of a forest where he poaches and gathers a very poor living for himself, a nasty father, and a gentle stepmother (I find reversing stereotypes a simple but inexhaustible pleasure. The stepmother is not much older than he is, and there is a sexual yearning between them that can find no solace). He discovers the great hedge where it cuts across a far part of the forest. This impenetrable, thorny, living wall fascinates him. He keeps going back to it, exploring along it. When he realises that it forms a circle, a complete defense of something within it, some *other place*, he resolves to get through it.

As we know from the tale, the magic hedge is yards thick, yards high, and regrows two razor-thorned shoots for every one you cut, so anybody trying to get through it gives up pretty soon. The twelfth fairy's spell decreed that it would stand for a hundred years. Only when the hundred years are up will a certain prince appear with a certain sword which will cut through the monstrous tangle like a hot knife through butter.

Our peasant boy doesn't know that, of course. He doesn't really know anything. He is dirt poor and ignorant. He has no way out of his life. There is no way out of his life. He starts trying to cut through the hedge.

And he keeps it up for years, with the poor tools he has, slowly, slowly defeating the ever-regrowing vitality of the thorn trees, pushing a narrow, choked opening through the trunks and branches and endless shoots and tangles, doggedly returning and returning; until at last he gets through.

He does not break the spell (as the prince will). He has broken *into* the spell. He has entered it.

It is not he who will revoke it. Instead, he will do what the prince cannot do. He will enjoy it.

He wanders about the fields and gardens inside the great hedge wall, and sees the bee sleeping on the flower, and the sheep and cattle sleeping, and the guardians asleep by the gate. He enters the castle (for in the tale as I knew it, Beauty's father is the king of the realm). He wanders among the sleeping people. My poacher says then, "I knew already that they were all asleep. It was very strange, and I thought I should be afraid; but I could not feel any fear." He says, "I knew I trespassed, but I could not see the harm."

He's hungry, as he has been all his life. "The venison pastry that the chief cook had just taken out of the oven smelled so delicious that hungry flesh could not endure it. I arranged the chief cook in a more comfortable position on the slate floor of the kitchen, with his hat crumpled up for a pillow; and then I attacked the great pie, breaking off a corner with my hands and cramming it in my mouth. It was still warm, savoury, succulent. Next time I came through the kitchen, the pastry was whole, unbroken. The enchantment held. Was it that, as a dream, I could change nothing of this deep reality of sleep?"

So he stays there. He has always been alone, that is nothing new; and now he is not hungry. Not even sexually, for he shares a sleeping peasant girl with her sleeping lover, and she smiles with pleasure in her sleep, and there is no harm in it, for the spell holds: nothing can be changed, or broken, or hurt. What more can he desire?

Speech, perhaps, which he never had much of in his old life either. Here there is no one to answer if he speaks; but he has vast leisure, time without end, and so he teaches himself to read. He reads the princess's book of fairy tales. He knows then where he is. Perhaps he knows what more there is to desire.

He knows who the princess is. "I knew that she, she alone in all the castle, might wake at any moment. I knew that she, alone of all of them, all of us, was dreaming. I knew that if I spoke in that tower room, she would hear me: maybe not waken, but hear me in her sleep, and her dreams would change." He knows that to break the spell, all he need do is move the spindle in her hand so that its tip does not prick into her thumb. "If I did that, if I moved the spindle, a drop of red blood would well up slowly on the delicate little cushion of flesh above the joint. And her eyes would open. Her eyes would open slowly; she would look at me. And the enchantment would be broken, the dream at an end."

My story, like Townsend Warner's poem, merely asks a question. It does not alter anything. All will go on as told. The prince will come; his kiss will wake his virgin bride. I and my poacher had no desire to change the story. We were both just glad to get into it. To be there, awake.

Thinking about it now, I believe that the tale is as impregnable and unassailable as its hedge of thorns. We can play variations round about it, imagine peasant trespassers, or rapist princes, happy or unhappy endings, as we please. We can define it; we can defile it. We can retell it to improve its morality, or try to use it to deliver a "message." When we're done, it will still be there: the place within the thorn-hedge. The silence, the sunlight, the sleepers. The place where nothing changes. Mothers and fathers will read the tale to their children, and it will have an influence upon those children.

The story is, itself, a spell. Why would we want to break it?

CAROLE MASO

✳ ✳ ✳ ✳ ✳ ✳

Exquisite Hour

Is that you snow ghost? Is that you candy gram? Strange visitations . . .

White moves in no particular order. Or patterned on things we can have little idea of—cancelling the landscape, negating the landscape, isolation. Is that you? A sky so white . . . delirious . . .

This is your Exquisite Hour.

You are the isolate, beautiful like that, with your indolence, waywardness—desultory—clutching a snow globe and a rabbit. Fugitive.

The avalanche of your touch, as we fall into your blizzard. Is it safe there?

Don't make me laugh.

And remembering is like falling some. Yes, you were the noviate, the fugitive—exquisite. Oh yes.

And he leads her through the stages of her remoteness hoping, hoping, out of selfishness perhaps, that she'll come back now if only for a moment. Her white out. Her blur. She flickers on. Flickers off. Is that you snow ghost . . . Sucking on a candy numb. Falling. He rose beneath her tongue.

Voice 3, although it has forgotten almost everything, recognizes things as Voice 4 relates them. Voice 4 doesn't tell it anything it didn't know before. There was a time when it too knew the story very well . . .

. . . tell me about the pearls again.

She liked to place a few pearls in his condom.

really did she?

and later one by one—she strung them.

oh?

Mindlessly even now as she listens she slips one or two into her dreamy mouth, trying to remember. O forgetfulness, as the snow . . .

She whispers *maitre*. She's no match for him. And he says *angel eyes*, as the drug sucks the world back from her.

Must have been an angel . . .

The eerie glow of the snow. She strung them. Sweet and numb—beneath her tongue.

She slips.

And the world dims.

And the world low-lit.

Until you can scarcely remember

scarcely—scarcely

And you let that place open in you—like a blinding white bloom—gardenia, behind the ear of that woman, that—

God that velvet voice astray—

astride you now—

You swerve with her into forgetfulness or carelessness—or something—

In our ice house. God, it's gorgeous here as you watch space enter you, take you now in its embrace—let everything slide. Is that you—fill up with white—How everything—

irreversible you've heard—a distant world fills up with white.

The eerie glow of the snow. White moves in no particular order. And in the light, you, gloating. Such lips. Sucking on emptiness. Until the lips and tongue are numb, until . . .

Yes, in the pleasure gardens, a beautiful music mindlessly she still slips a pearl from time to time into her dreamy mouth.

And she clutches her icy writing tablets. Her hand abstracting—every word you make dissolves now. In our ice house whispering *scarcely, scarcely*. You are driving into last late white—your Escape Club, it's lovely, *n'est-ce pas?*

And the blue tablet, once black, slips away, slides from you, *sans souci*. You're no match for it.

One hardly remembers such snow. Such silence.

A full feeling—a fulled up feeling. The white lit way. Your cloudy, luminous eyes, your cup of moon spilled night.

And she shakes her snow globe and puts it on the mantel. And she smiles wreathed in freezing fog. How soft now the edges are. How like smoke the trees have become.

And you love what is far. And you love what is far why not? And the snow with its induction into sleep. I know . . .

And you are hip high in snow. White world. I know you're hurting. I know a lot of things.

Her bleak atmospherics. And the remoteness calls her: *lover, beauty*. And the remoteness whispers *wrap yourself around me. Give it up*. And she retreats easily and she gives in easily. It comes naturally now. Licking the last flakes off the pane.

They say: follow your star.

Ming, is that you? Her gray cat. And doesn't it look exactly like snow has fallen on his furry paws? They say . . .

She fingers her books: slim, bleak, appreciated by only a few. The white paper before her dissolving now—every word you write—in a kind of tearing and oblivion.

And she slips into the white of herself—into the white—her life snowing. A muffled, peaceful sound and she feels could it be? slightly aroused by the white, by the taking away finally of everything as she falls into some infinite. Voice 3 said something about pearls once. And the little girls danced all night—remember? Until their shoes were thin.

A little bit.

And she makes love to the distance as it opens inside her and she's falling. The space opening now wider and wide until it seems—and she is straddling it, and she is pulling it up inside of her or it is—the vortex swirling. The suck of the void. I know you're dizzy honey. I know.

And a voice long dead sings, *Il neige*.

You are licking the last flakes—hip high

Look, you're no match for it.

And the white moves in. Oh, *il neige* all right—your cracked snow globe left on some mantel by the sea, fuck.

You've forgotten it.

Ovoid, lunate, opalescent life—fuck.

You miss your mouth almost entirely now.

Over forty varieties of lipstick . . .

You did, you used to put pearls. A shadow self. Disaffected now. Few friends and no interests. Aimlessness.

"Why you wonder all of a sudden—why should I be—the only person to whom happiness—is absolutely forbidden?"

And when she lifts her bleary head she sees, out the window—her weird atmospherics: strange last fires of the city. *Hey*. Walking against its inferno lit up. By bonfires. Through drifts and drifts of snow and cold now hide. She lifts her notebook to her chest.

In the delirious, walled city, the voice of 3 is whispering. Fire. The fencing master in white calling *Anna, Anna, Anna* and she tiny and freezing and wrapped in the pelts of rabbits, against the fire glow. Hide.

Pushed up against the fire glow. Mouthing Anna. Offering his hand in the demolished city. Smouldering. And she is just a girl in boarding school reading by firelight. Huddled around the fire of the alphabet trembling—sure, look I know you thought it could save you—And the pages burn.

And where are they when he comes to rescue in his extinguishing whites?

Off in Zurich or Saint-Tropez, remember?

No, not really.

She's been left in the very best. The very best of boarding schools. With her French and Latin lessons very best. Her ballroom dancing. Her fencing instruction.

Her very. Yes. So why so glomy then? Phantom daughter of snow. Clutching a box of very dark chocolates from Switzerland. A demented, bittersweet waltz step.

1—2,3 1—2,3 1—2,3

You'll try to hide in the fire garden, but he'll only find you idiot. He bellowing *Anna, Anna* for hours it seems. But it takes 43 seconds.

How does she know that?

He seems to care. Chanting *Anna, Anna,* wafting like that having detected defection, dissonance—wayward angel, little fugitive, *jardin*, come to me. And I shall tell you the story once more:

Once upon a time there was a king who had twelve daughters each more beautiful than the other.

Now the other story:

He whispers, and it's like a fairy tale: could you tell me that story once more? *My father's father's father*. Bringing silk and tea and spices. And he holds up his bleary chalice, cup of doomed universe, pale stare—silk and tea and other things. What is this Paradise he offers?

". . . The East India Company. The Early Trade at Canton . . ."

". . . like candy . . ."

". . . come on . . ."

Staggering. Staggered in her subzero. In her negative numbers. The landscape cancelled. In the avalanche of his touch.

Avalanche. And doesn't the word come from the French? *Avaler*. To fall. If she could find her French dictionary. If you could find it. Once more. One more time . . .

Fuck.

The snow took our animated, vivacious friends, all.

One hardly remembers such silence. Or such snow. And she in a kind of perfection falls into drift and darkly luminous dream falling. Falling, fallen, or is it fell? The language of the other life. I look up from the page onto a field filled with newly fallen snow.

Come with me, we'll get our wings tonight.

Falling, falling snow but not yet fallen—still, unfallen but about to—it took 43 seconds to fall . . .

. . . wings tonight. Contiguous with the abyss. Brush me a thousand, thousand times.

To gifted Arab doctors eventually fell the medical legacy of the classical world, and with the inheritance came knowledge of the drug opium.

The slur of your touch. Her eyes a glacial blue. The opium of your touch. Pill box. Tiny jewel box. Candy gram. Sweet and numb. Now you suck on the stamen of a poppy. More than contented—oh yes . . . Lapsed. Tiny, ashen bridegroom in white. Tiny magi. Magic. They say: *follow your star*. They always say: *star*. All the processions. He followed her into the fire garden.

The luminous white, the gloomy torso. The glare of the torso of the fencing vest.

A white flower—desire—powder—target in the night. What the insomniac saw. The child saw. In the snow, a fire alphabet. Huddled there.

Strange last fires of the city. Walking against it, lit up by bonfires she runs for protection, remember? into the walled garden on fire where she lifts her writing tablet, wrapped in the pelts of rabbits.

No not really.

I'll make you a star, he whispers.

Champion, he whispers . . .

Masterpiece, the master whispers.

You see his whites even from this distance—and the torso's weird glow. Even from here. What one would call a mesh over the face, a kind of electric wiring through white. And a soft glove . . .

In the mirrored room he said, *bend your knees*. In the mirrored room he said, *en garde*. Hips level and shoulders. Arm away from the body. Hold the position. And he whispers delirious, *I'd like to break you in* . . . soft glove. Target.

Now beat, now beat again, now counterbeat, extend and

lunge. In the luminous, duplicated white. *Champion. Star. Give me your arm:*

She sucks on the rose between bouts, swollen with a kind of—oh yes you do—you like it, don't you—a kind of white rain. Oh yeah, it's nice sucking like this.

I'll make you a champion. Put you in the winner's circle little girl.

You're just twelve. He feeds you something very white from his hand. A strange force enters you and you black out. Driven there. The avalanche of his touch. *Riposte*, he says and the world slips. Contiguous with the abyss. And doesn't avalanche in French—*avaler*—

Riposte, he says, but she can't seem to—the world slips—the known vocabulary—the actions that once accompanied such commands.

Long before the golden age of Muslim civilization at Baghdad, Sabean seamen were piloting their lantern-rigged craft into remote corners of the eastern seas, making regular calls at ports along the Malabar Coast and as early as 300 AD, a colony of Arab traders seems to have been established at Canton.

His father's father's father.

And you slip into the white blur of yourself—into the white—your life snowing. You lift your arm to shield yourself from the glare. Turn away. Away again.

The drift of insomnia and snow . . . Someone took our pretty, vivacious friends, all.

The fencing master leading a white horse who balks to the fire garden . . . The flare of nostrils . . . "Blindfold it." The bridle and bit, of the drug, the suck of the drug—muzzle it—"fuck"—"a tranquilizer." The use of the mute. And he forces the horse into the fire. I'd like to break you in.

Calling *Anna, Anna, Anna*. In the fugitive garden on fire. Whispering *princess, princess*.

She's crossing the river valleys—the Cardamom Hills—She's quite mad.

Bright, so bright. Shiny. Trinkets.

You are light as a feather,
as stiff as a board.
As light as a feather . . .
As stiff as a board . . .

Ming is that you? Sitting on her school books. The cat smuggled in—against the rules.

She enjoyed sex only once, as a school girl with another girl, one voice reminds the other now. Oh yes, that she still seems to remember . . .

Anna, Anna, Anna!

three times she feints.

Three times she deceives the fencing master

Who whispers—whispering—no matter how she closes her ears to it—whispering, *destiny, destiny, masterpiece.*

Three times she escapes him.

Whispering, *princess,*

forty-three seconds my star.

Three times she denies him.

The fourth time she falters, falling. And in the target garden he finds her. In his whites. And weren't you just asking for it? Of course you were. Of course you must have been. O recklessness.

You thought you could hide behind your writing tablet poor child. The burning light of the alphabet. Studious, obedient one.

And now what have you spent your whole life crossing out in white—what?

Not all the opium in China . . .

Not all the love in the world . . .

"The heroin makes one's eyes beautiful. There is no doubt that I am attractive. I watched myself in the glass for a long time, which gave me pleasure."

This is your Exquisite Hour. A blotter of wings. Deranged waltz step—your very off-glissade. Under your tongue. Your oh so very— 1—2,3 1—2,3 1—2,3 1—2,3 . . .

And you dance out of any grasp. They say: *destiny* and *follow your star*, the last landscape neutralized. At last all the things that could never work, they say: *at last*. The Chinese puzzle box of the world—solvable, then solved at last. As of late. Snow ridden—

Snow collecting in the high walled garden. The fire finally out. In a haze of belladonna. In the burnt garden. The garden of char. The black rose of blood rising *wings tonight* and falling in the syringe. Clutching that pathetic rabbit and candy box.

The drift to the needle. *Oh yeah—*

A strange paradise enters her, invades her bloodstream, and she turns away from nostalgia, from sentiment, from fear of any kind. She turns away from his never. Taking in wings and forgetfulness—she opens inside. Falling.

His father's father:

After the bomb was released forty-three seconds passed before it found earth. Can you see it floating and falling in those last moments—not quite one minute left—my love, love. Not quite one minute left my dear. That demented, that lilting free fall—

And the bomb fell like a flower floating

for forty-three seconds

A black bloom under the tongue

forty-three seconds

a kind of slow motion . . .

last exquisite minute.

She watches August descend like a black veil. The month she shall perish she's sure. She shakes her snowy globe—a kind of slow motion—the writing tablet slips; the world embraced by ice. Wings tonight.

She's looking for the syringe and she is wafting and floating and waffling. On her mantel—the cup of mysterious universe, perfect universe, paradise. And I too now, desirous of the night—The fluttering hand. How the hand flutters.

She opens her mouth and devours wings. Light. Under her tongue a dissolving universe—bright—a blotter of world, before everything is obliterated—under her tongue like an x ray revealing finally who she is and where she must go—slow— like a map, like a petal, under her tongue. Hold it there. Hold still. There now. Shhhhhh—As the forever moves in.

Does she remember the time—a blotter of wings, the pattern the petals made—the time she made a print of the penis in vegetable dye?

No.

That odd split head. A tattoo. A lovely pattern . . . Or the day—does she remember stuffing butterfly wings into her mouth, imagining motion, eating—as if she might eat motion . . . Move again.

Parry riposte.

It is not winter as one might expect at the asylum, at the retreat for the cessation of the abuse of narcotics; but a kind of perpetual spring—a wide expanse of green. Making her—it always made her nauseous and dizzy—the hilly, the color she roams, homeless there. Is that you? Withdrawal?

All night you wear a gleaming pelt. Claws. It's terrifying crawling around on all fours biting. Snout to the earth. Trying to get free. All day you type a letter, go to group therapy, walk with an escort across the green.

All day you try, in vain, to subtract his image from the mirror,

The fencing master mouthing *masterpiece*.

To take his image from the mirror.

All night you wear a pelt again—and those strange marbleized eyes . . .

Look, she's no match for it.

The gorgeous dissonance of her body now as she faces and then voluntarily walks back toward the white. God, she's dying, begging for it. Wings tonight. A woman rocking on the rockaby.

Brush me a thousand, thousand times.

Never let me go.

A drug-induced abortion. "What a miserable waste." Stop the child. Stop the child. No bigger than your thumb. "What a miserable waste of happiness."

Brush me a thousand strokes. Never let me go.

"A drug-induced abortion," they whisper.

"What a miserable waste . . ." Is that you snow ghost? Insomniac child.

". . . bringing back a series of exotic fevers . . . and a white powder . . ."

". . . she fell in love with the horsey set . . ." (clinking of glasses)

". . . have you heard lately from Mary Burns?"

"Isn't she a little old for that dress?"

(useless chatter)

". . . That's not Dr. Gisella Brigitte Oppenheim over there is it?"

A clinking of blue glasses sparkling.

As a child she liked to go ice skating. As a child she dreamed of going to the Ice Capades with her mother.

"Poor dear, her mother! Oh! She loathed just the *idea* of the child . . . dumping her in boarding school . . . Never going to fetch her . . ."

(useless chatter)

". . . Dietrich Fischer-Dieskau"

You close your eyes to *Winterreise*. It's too much, too much. And he sings *A stranger I arrived, a stranger I depart again*. You yawn.

And he sings *I do not want to breathe again until the towers are out of sight*. And you disintegrate a little.

Yen, dope fiend, hop head. Tincture of—

The drift to the needle.

"have some fun."

Oh what a party.

And there's the diplomat again . . . "quite handsome."

In another life she'd like to suck him off—in another world . . .

She's still capable of surprising herself.

(A glacial smile)

". . . acting like school girls."

Peaches in the voice and falling. It's like peaches . . . numb. Catching the peach, lifting her buttocks once—holding her cheeks in your hands and lifting. A falling feeling—schoolgirls . . .

. . . the use of the mute.

(glasses clinking, shards of civility)

Correct me if I'm mistaken but that seems to be, that looks an awful lot like Mr. Brilliant Chang. Eliza Bright. Professor Dog Head turning the corner now all the world lit up again. Highest purity. Their gorgeous charms and powders. Their glitter. Exquisite. Charms tonight.

Nothing but snow and ice.

The snow made us left-hearted, slowed up the ventricles. We ploughed through perfect remotelessness. We ploughed through fields—warped. Through irresistible drifts. Drifts of—we're lost.

Protected from all harm. All harm dissolved in white—hip high. As you fall from what seems now an incredible height . . . unharmed. Last flakes on the pane. Precious disappearing things. For forty-three seconds they say. To reach its target.

His father's father

You are as light as a feather.

Her mouth now smeared across the wall.

". . . she's lovely, remote, rather serene, don't you think? smiling . . ."

"she wrote books once, you know . . ."

"really?"

"white opium smokers . . ."

". . . the early trade at Canton . . ."

". . . pleasure users"

The First Opium War 1839–42.

You wrap yourself around the void. The vortex swirling. A blossoming under the tongue. The snow opening. I know you're hurting badly, he says. I know you're dizzy baby, he says removing his mask. I know a lot of things.

A stranger I arrived and a stranger I depart again.

And she'd like to stuff a sock soaked with ether into the yowling mouth of Dietrich Fischer-Dieskau.

Correct me if I'm wrong but that looks exactly like . . . That seems to be—blurring, a flurry of—There were sparkles, a sparkling—glowing—a high walled garden—forty-three seconds—with fire.

The bridle. The mute.

What was I saying?

In the sensuous lexicon of falling, where I write, where I like to write, more and more often now. Charting a motion and its many permutations, its many fallings into desire, language—waywardness, hope . . .

How you just wanted to be taken away. Taken out—to become silent because there wasn't any language for this. Look you're no match. You're no match for it.

Once.

Once you walked off so far away from the person you had been. You staggered and forgot how to get back. Lost the way back.

Dancing till your shoes were thin—all the fathers watching . . . trying to catch you at it.

When you look up it's still called the earth sure. Although everything is changed. You're still called your name strange OK, OK. Dizzy, clutching a black book.

And I am drowned in smoke this time. Having left the flue closed (deliberately, then?) and I think of you Anna—trying to navigate your way through snow—looking up, the countryside suddenly wreathed in smoke and snow. Staring as if seeing fire permanently in the mind, in the eye, mesmerized by heat, by light. Delirious. And I rest my blurry pen. . . . Must have been an angel. . . .

And you are listening to a woman singing only slightly out of phase. Her voice perfected in its exhaustion, its decadance as it falls away arriving late to the party—wafting and falling. Velvet, like velvet. Wings.

"You're my thrill, you do something to me."

"he's a diplomat's diplomat . . ."

". . . bringing silks . . ."

"You send chills right through me."

Silken—the woman with the velvet voice. Exquisite. Salvation. Lady Day.

Halo. Aureole. I lift my arm to the glare. Useless. And we're lost in her squalls—her luxurious, her gorgeous darks— *"where's my will?"* singing only slightly out of phase. And her moody accomplice holding the mute. I know you're hurtin' darlin' . . . I know you're kind of blue. Here:

Bright, So bright. Shiny. Junked up. And you move into the swerve and drag of her voice. Gardenia floating, gardenia falling. Drug and voice and flooding down are dripping. A strange paradise enters. The woman singing.

You're my thrill. Yeah, you do something to me all right.

See how they cook the opium into pearls . . .

And you bring up the woman's voice now. Push the score. So as not to get lost, not yet, oh—in the garbled warp her—God, it's beautiful here. The pier collapsing.

And the velvet woman remembers the effect of key don't change it. And he doesn't change it. His mouth on her—don't change anything oh—

But that was long ago.

She watches snow fall on the lovers in miniature now as she shakes her globe. Large, hopeless, gloating, outside.

And she watches the tiny figure put pearls—

She smiles.

At first we didn't see the movement, the beginnings of movement. But it begins at the first note of "India Song." The woman in black and the man sitting near her begin to stir. Emerge from death. Their footsteps make no sound.

They are standing up.

They are close together.

What are they doing?

They are dancing.

They are merged together in the dance, almost motionless. Now quite motionless.

Voice 2: Why are you crying?

No answer. Silence.

Once upon a time there was a king who had twelve daughters, each more beautiful than the other. They slept together in a hall where their beds stood close to one another. At night when they had gone to bed the King locked the door and bolted it. When he unlocked it in the morning, he noticed that their shoes had been danced to pieces, and nobody could explain how it happened.

And she carries her blur and releases it just before he—before—in immaculate whites. It's dangerous here. Everything on fire. She holds her rabbit pelt and book to her.

1—2,3 1—2,3

So the king sent a proclamation saying that anyone who could discover where his daughters did their dancing might choose one of them to be his wife and reign after his death.

Merged together in a dance, almost motionless.

And we savor the distance. And we savor the forest. Tasting its many darknesses. And we love what is far. And we are called to the river's eternity. The black pomegrante on the table. Our pupils dilated: *look, look, oh look!*

In which I am standing in my father's dark house
In which I am standing in my father's dark house
counting beads—before the flood—
before the deluge—a girl of twelve years.
You are as light as a feather.
Dizzy (1—2,3) now. One—two, three—

When the King put the question, "Where did my daughters dance their shoes to pieces in the night?" he answered, "dancing with twelve princes in an underground castle."

And you walk out of all enclosures, all that has confined you—

She is walking with walking stick dressed in white toward the bridge when you beg to be excused from your father's dark house

I want to go further into those mountains—though Kashmir is closed. I want fistfuls of moonstones. I want now my mother's maroon silk sari with the silver border. Her hair smelling of coconut oil. I hope to be standing soon in the flower festival north of Katmandu.

Only bells, only charms as you walk away. As I walk away from all that has kept me in place. Afraid.

Wearing on our hands our frayed dancing shoes. Discarding at last the fencing plastron, and the pelts of rabbits. The father's dark house redolent with arches. We say, *at last.*

Snow falls like music and you escape. They always say: *follow your star*. Independent, indifferent—spectral visions of the fencing master. A blur of blades. There now—there—*touché*. She finds the brilliant opening—*touché*, and walks away from his never . . .

You must have been an angel . . . All harm dissolved in white—the effect of key don't change it—hip high. Let it melt under your tongue like snow—forgetfulness . . .

I'd like a little nighttime language. I'd like a little night language—music. I need a little night now.

(Mozart playing)

". . . the loafing class"

The glare of the snow. "Hello." You squint. You lift your arm to it.

". . . like the awful smirks on the faces of child prostitutes."

And weren't they just asking for it?

Clutching her heart-shaped box.

Hiding in the smirking garden. Is that you snow ghost?

While he does a demented step, a kind of *flèche*, 1—2,3 1—2,3 1—2,3 1—2,3

"Oh let the child have her Ming. Poor thing."

Never

"How quickly she is out of jumper and togs. How quickly the pigtails I loved to pull—as she bent her knees then opened— now coiffed for her senior dance. She is tall, slim, high-heeled—no longer adorable. Her improbable bosom. Turning back, I remember that night when I finally found her in the fire garden . . . And though I hear it is a sin, a crime, what I do, and wish and feel for you still—my flower, my fawn—I would never have hurt you, never harm you, *never, never* . . .

"My princess.

"She was my masterpiece once," the fencing master says. "Princess. Star."

In tights. Magnificent innocence in your whites. In white with mesh and mask over the face whispering *maitre*, on your knees.

"How vague now you have become, how unrecognizable with your blue vial, your crazy cat—I would never have hurt you."

Drugged into a kind of adulthood. Junked up and falling in slow motion. Saying *never, never*, and you will *never tell anyone ever:*

You are the isolate. With your vial of pure ice. Your pink mouth smeared across the wall. No match for the master.

The fencing master mouthing *masterpiece*.

One scarcely can remember such silence—Unbearable.

And from the house redolent with arches the famous bearded doctor announces: "Either she is speaking the truth and all the fathers are vile, or she is a liar and the patriarchal order is safe."

And she doesn't stand a ghost of a chance.

". . . a vivid imagination."

". . . a flawed moral character."

The bomb like a flower opening for forty-three seconds . . . The bomb falling like a kind of never.

Suspended in a kind of bluish liquid.

 . . . The target garden on fire.

She did, she did, she tried to hide.

Not a ghost of a chance . . .

Not all the opium in China . . .
Not all the love in the world . . .

Who knows what might have been—had things been different—early on—from the beginning even.

In another world in another time long ago you dreamt.
Dreamt of dancing all night. Until your shoes were worn—

Without the surveillance of the fathers.

"This afternoon a curious thing happened to me. The reality of
everything began to recede. I felt lonely and inaccessible and
forgotten, and had a number of illusions, sometimes vivid and
sometimes unreal. There were two sisters, one of whom talked
about a river."

The river glistening . . . this is your exquisite.

But oh how now she slips out of last sociabilities—surprisingly effortlessly—surprisingly free of regrets—last impedi-
ments. Falling, falling into forgetfulness,

and she wraps herself around the voluptuous—takes it in.

Sucking on the stamen of a poppy smile. Correct me if I'm
wrong but that seems to be . . .

She carries her blur and releases it just before he. In the target garden.

. . . that seems to be . . .

The fencing master was arrested and disappeared, as it
proved, forever.

You look up. At last you see—at last—someone in the mirror you think you recognize.

You are as light as a feather, as stiff as a board.

"Champion," you say.

"You're a winner."

"The winner's circle . . ."

And then nothing. *Enfin*.

One scarcely remembers such snow—or such silence. The white-lit way. The world low-lit. How soft the edges are. How like smoke the trees have become. Every word you make dissolves now. Look:

The Herbalist's Treasury from the tenth century smile. The poppy, the shield that confers immortality. Brilliant—brilliant—that color. You lift a hand to shield you from the glare and smile. Moving into her with more force now—*Hey—oh—it's good that way*.

Is that you Ming? The cat smuggled in poor child they looked the other way. School girl rituals and levitations. Devouring butterfly wings. Floating. As light as a feather. Letting go now of the candy box—sweet and numb. As stiff as a board. And the globe.

How slowly and yet how quickly—and with such little effort now—eternity, oblivion . . . At last you subtract your image from the mirror. This is your Exquisite Hour.

And the snow says: *Hey*.

The space now wider and wide until it seems—and she is straddling it—sucking on a string of pearls.

At last you see—at last—someone in the mirror you think you recognize. And I am happier than I have ever felt, she thinks. I am more or less happy in my life . . . as if I belong here.

And so perhaps for the first, for the first time. For the first time she looks into the mirror and she likes what she sees. For the first time.

Licking the last flakes from the pane. The demented waltz step and smiles. A row of girls holding hands out for a stroll—strange—vanishing in the snow.

JANE MILLER

✳ ✳ ✳ ✳ ✳ ✳

Midnights

It is midnight when we arrive in the city, having an argument. I want her to be more communicative and she wants me to be less manipulative. We are weary leaving the train and its oily windows, and it is only when we are outside the station, where the steps splay out like a peacock displaying its feathers, the drizzled stone slick and iridescent, and we glide, not lifting our feet because of the heavy bags and because of our brooding, toward the mysterious water's edge, that we look out toward the watery castles and floating glass mirages and see the whole moat lit by shimmering headlamps. As if on cue from some dead, watery conductor, I hear the muffled engines of cruising boats and the four, five, and then six varieties of hen- and chicken-sounding "k" and "ch" and "qu" consonants of the dozen citizens boarding the local bubbling taxi: Stazione, Venice.

———

It is always midnight inhabiting a strange place. It makes no difference to me that we are at the port at three in the afternoon, at the height of summer. There isn't a breath. The air is stony, the high stone walls dusty, the dust still, gritty, sandy; the sand very warm. Two women in black, shelling peas, very tight to the white wall, on short stools. Bleary-eyed fishermen knitting the tears in their nets. I buy an American magazine at the kiosk, and walk glumly to the bus stop. Everything in *Newsweek* leaks green and pink and yellow, and the speech is stiff, familiar, horrible. In the street, everything slips into photographic negative, innocent, violent, neutral, distant, pressing, primary. I read every ad on the uncomfortable bus. My clothes are very soft, I have washed them a hundred times since my arrival. I am completely at home, lost, empty. I can't speak a word of Greek, and I have married one: lover, whom I have had to drop off at the port, whose father is dying. I return to my room, my mule. I have six tomatoes in the shade, in the heat. Thank God I have a lemon tree outside the window (broken) so that when I turn off the light at dusk to avoid the mosquitoes another hour, the honey-lime scent drips intravenously into the room, where I am studying the capital letters of the alphabet in the child's notebook. The child's eyes are always at the door, two huge dark almonds, staring in at the traveler: Faros, Sifnos.

I fall off a balcony and see life on the stars as they go by, painfully slowly, strange iron trees breathing, and bodies with two, three heads like melons, eyeless, hairless. It is the night of a thousand nights, buildings leaning, gardens on the roofs, fish in the seas staring, gulping the air, falling. Off the thin body of Tomales Bay the mist rises, hangs in the air, darkens. The sharks at the mouth of the bay surface and, with a wicked flick, slice the foam off the water. Life on earth floats up the space through which I fall, and away; the objects of my desire, the landscape of my youth (of forgotten algaic ponds of summer), narrow and disappear. Another star approaches, twinkling, its lit arms dangling, poised with heads for hands, X-ray branches for legs, mocking the bishop pines, creature neither of the sea nor land, rupturing space. It is midnight in a dream: Inverness, California.

Like horses thrown into the water, the young girls leap, squealing, into the cold lake at dawn. We must make it to the other side or, failing, float there until the rescue. We slap back our hair each mistaken stroke, our necks breaking. One, I see, has made it, but I see her from so far that I know I shall never find the end of this dark water. It is midnight when I begin to cry, a young pink cry, a baby pig's. The horses' skinny legs are snapping all around me, black haunch fills the sky. Why must I swim sadly forever? Each piece of the night sky is glass, and shatters around me with each stroke. Some on the shore are already giggling. I hear their tinkling flutes, their baggy drums. My lungs fill and empty; I fill the sky with stars and swallow them, in, out. The heart is dark, darker than a thought. It works to save me, to propel me. If my eyes are closed, there are flares in the night. If I open them underwater, there are clear tadpoles wiggling in the dark. I swim to the end of the night, and I miss my mother: Stormville, New York.

———

Wherever the traveler goes in a quest for beauty and knowledge, if the place responds like a peacock displaying its iridescence, we have the stuff legends are made of. Imagery explodes and creates a derangement of the senses. Those who have already gone and returned no longer remember it that way, or remember the place fondly, or inexactly. But during the ritual visit itself, the unfamiliar and disoriented prevail, requiring that we notice things in their entirety, which we must do to "get anywhere" in the confrontation with the new. To see a thing entire is to see its otherworldliness, to see the stripes and the fangs and the sausagelike intestines, working the analogical possibilities to experience it ("it" is, by now, a monstrous thing).

Having given it our full attention, a meditation, what follows is often revelatory. The spirit of a place, a person, or a thing exchanges freely with the stranger's spirit. When I first read the poet Federico García Lorca's legends, I understood that there is no story, there are only moments. And I broke from narrative finally, and felt that precipitous falling that is dangerous only as long as one believes in gravity. In every other world, in art, in dreams, in childhood, in love, it is natural to fall up, or simply float. My experience in the language is the experience of the poet suspended in the earthy matter. Lorca's "narraciones" use stock imagery, familiar signs and seasons, but nothing is as expected. The scenic is turned on its head, time scatters, the program is off speed, the matter questioned, the dialogue nervy, the magic easily comprehended. Here is a summary of one of his accounts or, loosely, legends, "Santa Lucía and San Lázaro": "At midnight I arrived in the city. . . . There was nothing to do but get in bed. I lay down. . . . In the courtyard, the innkeeper and his wife sang a duet. . . . [Next day] It was the height of activity in the market. . . . I wanted to eat and asked the way. . . . That night was the night of the fiesta. . . ."

All this seems basic, logical, timely. But, in the interstices, Lorca is wild, superhuman, transformative. Let him fill you in, reader:

> At midnight I arrived in the city. The frost danced on one foot. "A girl can be brunette, she can be blond, but she cannot be blind." This is what the proprietor at the inn told a man brutally sectioned in two by a waistband.

> In the courtyard, the innkeeper and his wife sang a duet of thistle and violet. Their dark voices, like two moles in flight, stumbled against the walls without finding the famed exit to the sky.

> It was the height of activity in the market and the strand of the day was filled with snails and ripe tomatoes. Before the miraculous facade of the cathedral I could understand perfectly how San Ramón Nonnato could cross the sea from the Balearic Islands to Barcelona mounted on his cape, and how the ancient Sun of China becomes infuriated and leaps like a cock over the musical towers made of dragon meat.

Dragon meat! Of course. And musical towers. Snails, ripe tomatoes, the same world, undone by the poet's glance. Where are we? And the text answers by inviting us into a city where it rains little copper bells. I hear them now, thinking of my life.

———

When we returned, everything was changed. The tender trees in the forest, our birches peeled back to their shrimp-pink bark meat, swung outside the windows and sang, but bitterly, of the coming winter. Love shuffled along, raking the leaves, but it was too late. That winter, during a thaw when I got out onto the roof to brush away the wet snow to prevent a collapse, one lung at a time, the task became impossible: Plainfield, Vermont.

In Lorca's story, the traveler arrives at the Inn of Santa Lucía. We find out very little about this Saint. Apparently, she died in a bed of flames. Lorca exploits religious iconography, violently and lightly, and the general sense of alienation travelers feel. What begins as a Homeric journey becomes an inward one of disintegration, mirrored in the landscape. Written half a century ago, his tale of disorientation and transformation is familiar and powerful. The traveler's typical actions are undone at every turn; when he visits a church, night arrives like the head of a mule with leather blinders. When he gets hungry, he sets out toward the inn, which is a long way, by the cathedral and the railroad station. There we have the three locations. We begin at the inn, and shall return to it. On the way, the traveler stops at San Lázaro train station. Lorca's references to light (Lucía) and the dead (Lazarus) are profoundly Spanish. He once said, "Spain is a nation open to death. In all countries death is a finality. It arrives and the blinds are drawn. Not in Spain. In Spain, they are opened." Anthropomorphic activity abounds: sadness loosens the electrical cables and raises the doorway tiles.

———

San Lázaro himself is quite strange; before he died, he had a "predilection for the sound of another orbit, one that dragged along fishes." Never mind. "When he died he was as hard and laminated as a loaf of silver bread." It is at this station that our traveler meets another traveler, for one final shock (of course, it is midnight). Lorca's games abound; the traveler confuses himself for the second traveler, and ends up at home, with an empty suitcase, and only the spectacles and the duster of someone else. In short, what happens? An inn, a station, a church: the nouns are stable in the tale. Movement, confusion, symbolic images, surreal events are represented in the adjectives, the verbs, the modifiers, which all fly in the face of reason. In Lorca's hyperreality, poetry itself is legendary. Unnerving, hallucinogenic moments, a traveler's destabilized reality, occur in bed, on the street, on the way to dinner. The familiar in the arms of the unfamiliar.

When we arrive, late, to the hotel, our room is tricolored minimalist, black, white, and gray, those three destinations. Further, the gray breaks into chrome, aluminum, slate. The whole small room has the large flat feeling of geometry. The mattress is flat to the bed-frame, the pillowcases very tight to their down pillows, and the square white tiles in the bathroom angle down and away like a vanishing point in a twenty-first-century glass airport. The tub looks porcelain, etched with hairline cracks, and therefore the room is touched with a slightly Asian sensibility in this and in the saturation of the gray color, silty and rich. Behind the white window shade, which snaps up roughly to my touch, lies the steel and chrome blue-tone symphony of the city.

The bed, the bath, the city. We turn on the TV and click through a dozen American shots, a pick-up truck navigating the prickly pear and mesquite of the Southwest (the plotless narrative commercial); then Ingrid Bergman, in profile, a symbol of simplicity and elegance, but why? because her hair is pulled tightly back like ancient Helen's, who we associate with suffering? Is suffering elegant? We discuss this issue feverishly, physically, beginning to weaken, to relax; after the film, a talk show with a nearsighted, fake background of New York's theater district; (a commercial for) exercise equipment in which two superbodies dangle from an enlarged arachnid . . . We cruise them silently, Ingrid Bergman's head in the slick London rain, large and sculpted, as if held up on a stick like something beheaded carried around the Greek plaka. Then the dusty American male icon, huge, slamming the cab of his truck while the blond dirt of the foreshortened desert plain stretches out behind him, barrel cacti giants in the glare the same size as the bare mountain.

Click. Two men having sex in a bed without a room, to blaring music, which I silence. Their rhythm is remarkably stable, then imperceptibly quickens, but never stops. It loops endlessly in postmodern irony, until it becomes sexless, mechanized and, close up, the shadow of a line of ants on one of them, or just a shadow darkening the sex of one and the arm of another. Then the grinding in full artificial light. Cut-aways, close-ups, repetition. We make love with the porn movie on, but not to it, only with images from it on our private mental screens, and in our own timing. Her hair smells of perfume and the food of the journey, our Chinese take-out from last night, slightly gingered, like an orchid. And of the city, its garbage, gasoline, sweat, and faintly sweet, stale cooking oil. I glide slowly down from the top of my erotic journey into her arms, as tomorrow morning I shall glide down the long winding staircase from the mezzanine to the grand, muted lobby in an ether of winter clothes. Outside, an explosion of height and proximity; of steel, and of magnesium fires, and of the thousand and two faces swathed in fiber and hair, wax, makeup, and smoke: Paramount Hotel, New York, New York.

"The room had a mirror. I, half a comb in my pocket." Lorca loves to work with oppositions and comparisons, but he's not interested in balance. *Half* a comb, the qualifier is intense. Things being never quite equal, there seems to be no reason to try to pretend they are. But if they aren't equal, they are intimate. And if they are intimate, they are, possibly, devoted, and therefore neither would consider abusing its power. One part of the equation is never better, only at an impressive angle from the other. Here he goes again, "While I slept, the exquisite minuets of goodnights got lost in the streets." *But of course they did!* we want to shout, but do not, because we fear we may not have fully understood. That is the point. That which remains somewhat mysterious to us leads us on. As we approach enlightenment, mystery and magic breathe deeply in our midst, yet we are alone. Lorca places us in a state of readiness; we are alone in a shared space.

It is midnight, no doubt, when we hear the shots. They seem to be very close, but it's hard to tell. Sound expands, without interruption, in the cold desert. Behind the bold light of the helicopter fanning above our house, I see the flashes of a blast. Then a spray of color over the distant mountains. Behind the fading lights, the bodies of the constellations, the archer and the dippers, in frozen animation. The celebration of New Year's breaks into our sleep, hammering. Our bed is in a bowl of mountains. The bowl sends the sound round. The helicopter shines its circle of light on traffic, that of the thoroughfare and that of the dream I was in. What suspect is loose? We have gone to bed early on the last day of the year. The wind crosses our bed with eucalyptus air. We are stiff with fear, our journey interrupted. Was I dreaming of the moon above the open-air station? . . . the last light in the claustrophobic station?: Tucson, Arizona.

"The traveler walked along the platform . . . he went back and forth without observing the long sad parallels awaiting the train." The inn, the church, the station. These are the Andalusian poet's temporary rest stops, in a long Spanish night, "a barbarous night, with exposed breasts surprised by a single telescope." The action is identified, but the participants are barely sketched, or partially sketched. The moment is luminous and mysterious. The telescope itself is a force, never mind who is holding it. The implications are rampant. The world of a thousand objects and places and colors, numbers and fractions, fragments, is shaken free for us as if a wind has loosened the fruit from the trees of an immense garden.

Here is a little more of the ending of "Santa Lucía and San Lázaro": "I have been home only a few minutes. I found my suitcase empty. Only some spectacles and the white duster. Two themes of a journey. Pure and isolated." Who are these last two characters, adjectives given the status of archetypes? The parts of speech stare back at me, from Lorca's legend, in tin, with purple globes, "with voices that will, of necessity, call out." If we rummage around a Lorca legend, we may never get back, we may find our real home. No sooner do we meet someone, we become him. No sooner do we leave the church, the church has vanished. Upon arriving ("At midnight I arrived in the city"), the traveler asks for and receives the best room:

> "I like it." (I saw my "I like it" in the green mirror.) The innkeeper shut the door. Then, with my back turned to the little frozen quicksilver field, I exclaimed again, "I like it."

Above, Lorca has hung one of the famous mirrors of legend, where things seem not as they are but, magically, become what they seem. Wherever I go, Lorca shows me the windfall from the field of quicksilver.

LYDIA MILLET

* * * * * *

The Wife Killer

Blue Beard wanted his new wife to find the corpses of his for-mer wives. He *wanted* the new bride to discover their muti-lated corpses; he *wanted* her disobedience. Otherwise he wouldn't have given her the key to the forbidden closet; he wouldn't have left on his so-called business trip; and he wouldn't have stashed the dead Mrs. Blue Beards in the closet in the first place. Transparently, it was a setup.

In the postmodern world Mrs. Blue Beard doesn't take the bait.

She says, No, honey, you keep the key. Really, I insist. I want to respect your personal space. But by the way, while you're at it would you mind holding the key to the liquor cabinet? I'm on the Ninth Step. And listen, here's the key to the kitchen. Keep me away from the fridge, would you? I'm doing Jenny Craig. It's such a wonderful program. You're kind of getting a beer gut there sweetie, you should try it yourself.

Blue Beard's descendant lies glumly in his recliner, remote control drooping from his right hand, swilling beers, drowning in lassitude, advancing into sure senility. On Super Bowl weekends he munches on pretzels and swears half-heartedly when his office pool-picks lose, all the while dreaming of a secret locked closet where the decapitated beauties of a golden moment of conquest and barbarity lie sleeping as a testament to his virility.

The real closet contains only shelves, lined with dusty old wrestling trophies. These days he doesn't even go in there anymore to look around, the way he used to. It's depressing.

His ancestor was a tyrant, a polygamist by nature, and an executioner. But he had an honor code, thinks Blue Beard. He was the consummate host to his last wife, after all. She could have had anything she wanted—riches unbounded and prime real estate. Just don't use the key to the closet, he said. Those were his terms; they were clear. Was it so much to ask? So symmetrical, so paternalistic, an authority grounded in unilateral rules. So mafia. So Old World.

Still. All those dead wives. The only reason the last one got away with her life was her brothers, who came charging to the rescue at the eleventh hour. That last wife was no saint, after all. She had no real sterling qualities to qualify her for redemption. After her husband was killed by her brothers she gave them some blood money, took the rest of the estate for herself and used it as a dowry to marry someone else. Possibly an earl, down on his fiscal luck. Couldn't she have used at least *some* of it to found a battered women's shelter or something?

Blue Beard's ancestor was foiled in the end, but that didn't help the wives who had already died.

Why did he do it?
He was a romantic.

My wives: when I touch them they begin to disappear. Oh, not their eyes; not their legs, not their armpits, stomachs, or breasts. These things stay. They stay too much. They turn into a room that I live in—all walls and no windows. Or, if windows, smudged and hung with cheap curtains. Dust clings there on the homely square weave like caterpillars, worms of dirt in dry brown chrysalis. But *they* disappear. What they could be is lost, and what they are is the residue. What they could be, at the beginning, is beyond words and flesh. It clothes itself in flesh and words and in the symphony of these two elements, but lies within them and without at once and shows of itself only glimpses.

Take eyes. The first time I see the eyes of a future wife, they're light out of the shadows of flesh. Their glance, the angle of their contact with me moves and settles, flickers away and vanishes. Anything can be behind the lids of those eyes. And chance is infinite. I follow the eyes and I accept, with a great lift of excitement for the new I say: I also go. We go together. We go to union, to its gorgeous illusion. When do I go? Whenever I can, in the turn of an instant. And why? The earth is flat, whatever science says. The world is flat. There are mountains: I see that. But once I stand on them, even they are flat beneath my feet.

Seen from a great distance, the world may look like a sphere, for all I know. Through distance things assume their true form. Close up they are nothing: the nothing of the familiar. The flatness of the everyday.

So take the forms of all my wives.

The first was the best, and too the most horrible. When I say she killed me I'm not exaggerating, since melodrama takes away a man's credibility; but I rose like a phoenix, burned straight to the bone through the soles of my feet and then born again, and a fanatic, like everyone who comes back transmogrified from the dead. The feet turned clawlike after that and I was a bird of prey. Will you ever know the bliss of the dive? I say no, and I'll give you good odds.

Of course I wasn't old then and I knew nothing and believed it all, that is, what I was told. I was gawky with ignorance. Men and women fall in love and they get married and they live: happily, ever after. A great lie, one of the greatest. A great lie is an empire, with cities a thousand miles high that sparkle in the night and draw flies. It was a bedtime story. It was a lullaby and it still is. Be meek the lambs, be meek the sheep. Be meek and be industrious. Stay in your houses, submit your lust and the communions of your spirit to the pews and aisles, the courthouse, the town hall. And never go outside again, for that will keep the order.

We all stay in our homes and over the country roam the hungry wolves while we are sleeping. Wearing our skins to walk among us but drooling quietly out of the dry woolen mouths of our dead.

Was there a mention of the sameness of it all? Of one day, identical to the next? Was there a mention of the wallpaper, whose designs repeat themselves and are not worth repeating? How new words and flesh melt the walls and the paper, the fences and the calendar? How they are only more life, and not less? There was no mention. None at all.

I know it now for what it was, with my first wife—I knew it

then and now I know it still. It was the state of rapture. It was ecstatic. What they call *to be in love*, which is so different from *love* because love is only gratitude and tolerance and does not stimulate. I don't even like to defile my first wife with words: she can't be captured for a moral or a platitude.

I should say, it was ecstasy until it was not.

And that time came. And they all do.

At the beginning wherever we went we were paragons. If we were not we felt we were, and to feel is to be. Or is enough of being, at the least. Every movement of my first wife was a sweep of pride for me: she was perfect under my gaze and her perfection spread to me. I was taller than I ever had been before that, tall, rampant, cloaked in alertness, wanted for wanting. Everyone saw me as I wished to be seen. When we entered a place we owned it. At the start, even alone, we were transformed. We had an invisible audience spellbound by the performance of ourselves, extravagant and splendid.

But then we were at home again. After a while I knew her toenails and her bitten fingernails, her knees, the blemishes that barrooms and theaters covered in subtle darkness. I knew the dust in the cracks, the dust of habit and routine, of gray and brown and aimless passage through time, without mission, without trajectory, and all the surfaces of bare floor and sallow bottles for the retention of smoothness. I knew her preparation and the slow and actual unrolling of the days. One morning I woke up and the rapture had washed away in the drain, coiled sticking down the pipes like the long hairs that fell from her head when she washed.

And after that we were nothing wherever we went. I was shrinking and I forgot my quick grandeur and the manners of my desire. More and more my limbs were awkward again and my functions those of a slave, who works without pay and never knows the pageantry of envy.

Then one night we were drunk and full of spirits. I had drunk enough to drown me, I was so drunk I stole a corkscrew from the bar though of course I did not need it. And it was almost like before. We ran, coming home from the warmth of all our friends around a glowing hearth. We ran laughing stupidly through the fields and there was the white disc of the moon and clouds and light rain.

And then we stopped and turned and saw each other. I looked at her eyes, drunk as mine. And in that instant I saw how something in her had turned, and the drunkenness masked it and brought it out at once, because she had the carelessness of drink but also its naked truth. I saw myself in the tears of her eyes, and saw I was a dwarf and the stupor of the wine was temporary for us both. I'd never known the anguish of my diminution before then. I knew that she had grown into furniture, yes, but not myself, to her, and there it was. I thought I would wrinkle and droop right there. My disappointed bones were crumbling, I was spineless. Before I thought I clutched her back and drove the stolen corkscrew through her skin between the ribs.

So she died in the field. The bliss that was gone and would never come back soared above us like music, finer then than it had ever been.

It was the most I ever felt.

I lay there with her all night, sobbing, I'm not ashamed to say. My nose was running and I had no voice left by the end. My mouth was so dry I had to try to drink the rain, but there wasn't enough. And I had doubts. I don't deny it. But in the morning I found I'd fallen asleep on her body. And I saw the sun and felt my regrets drain into the ground beneath her limp heels. I picked a wet blade of grass from her ankle. She would never grow old. And she died in euphoria.

With my second wife I designed a ritual. But my first wife was impulse: a surge, wind, a flight. I always wanted to ascend again, and never knew the same height. My fourth wife was only a child, and the fifth was blind. Some were undeniably beautiful and some only to me, but I have loved them all. And once I saw that rapture was the dance of the new, I never let the new get old.

At last I grew old myself and I saw that without a known and seen history I was going to be nothing again. And my wives are all my history, the history of having been adored and adoring. It is nothing less than religion: the history of ecstasy. I fought like a lion against this flat earth.

This last was given a key, and a law to break, the way I'd learned to break them. If she had liked my history I would be living still, and so, for a time, would she.

But I am dying like the rest.

And I had a glorious life, while it lasted.

Between an egoist with high expectations and a sociopath stretches only the fine thread of empathy and identification. Yet in social terms the egocentrism of the romantic is no more re-markable than that of the so-called well-adjusted person, as long as the "well-adjusted" is held to be a person comfortably conformed to the rituals and trade-offs of status quo social in-tercourse. The hegemonic state has its own rationalist insanity of human sacrifice, which it prefers served tepid and garnished with statistics.

In contemporary American ideas this imbedded structural pathology is a descendant of such philosophies as social contract theory and utilitarianism, now codified and practiced in the cost-benefit-calculus of neoclassical microeconomics—which styles itself as the ultimate in systemic rationality. And the personal formulation of this political doctrine calls itself "realist," where realism is functionally equivalent to selfishness (a standpoint that Americans, in particular, choose tragically to mistake for "individualism," to which only noble impulses are ascribed). I use "realism" as it is most often used in speech, to refer not to any particular Realist theoretical assertion but to a simpler intuitive evocation: the *realistic* is that form of ontological compromise that mediates, to the conceptual or moral satisfaction of its proponent, between the actual and the ideal.

Of course, the claim that such mitigating realism equates with selfishness is debatable. Historical examples of perfect social forms are reluctant to present themselves; our sleeping culture dreams of utopia through a multitude of artistic and narrative articulations while operating, awake but not self-aware, in a perpetual debasement of ethical and aesthetic conscience it ruefully terms *society* and seems to conceive of as a moderate and necessary evil. Leibniz's infamous determination that *we live in the best of all possible worlds* rings of bitter irony to the reflective, as well as to such directly interested parties as the materially disadvantaged or oppressed, but apparently provokes no gag reflex: the aggregate political spirit of the middle-class American of the nineties is a passive organism, atrophied through disuse.

The realist equation is therefore straightforward, since "I am fine" slides easily and gracefully into an essentially meritocratic conceptual decision that "we are fine"—meritocratic because the free-market paradigm of competition is so deeply ingrained in our collective psyche that we believe socioeconomic losers deserve to lose. In the chaotic mudslinging of confused political labels that substitutes for serious public discourse on values in the mainstream media, the only clear semantic distinction between "liberals" and "conservatives" that remains is this: the latter group believes losers deserve to lose, while the former is morally offended by this assertion, but evinces in the face of it no urgent or active compulsion toward change. Inklings of guilt generated by this abrogation of personal social responsibility are chalked up to a wise cynicism, tempered by sad resignation, which places the ideal and the real in distinct categories such that never the twain shall meet—a dualistic rationalization of the failure of courage.

Nor does the conviction that losers deserve to lose translate into a belief that winners deserve to win, although this is inevitably the other half of the equation, in logical terms. On the contrary: the spirit of the contemporary American bourgeoisie, which represents itself through the myriad unquestioned assumptions of a corporate media culture, openly admits to extreme cynicism where the moral character of the wealthy and the powerful is concerned—an oddly righteous censure, colored green at the gills with envy.

Thus we staunchly defend our system of governance and our modes of cultural discourse, reviling their detractors as traitors to a vision we cannot define, while simultaneously despising the formal (elected) executors of the social order—politicians—and loathing its informal (self-appointed) administrators—the super-rich. "Corruption" and information manipulation on the part of political leaders are widely held to be both inevitable

and incidental: inevitable because human character is acknowledged flawed, incidental because these flaws are seen not as
products and producers of the sociopolitical and cultural order
but as regrettable and individually isolated, if infinitely multi-
plicable, exogenous events. We believe in the heroic dream of
democratic capitalism and deplore its effects. We insist we are
free but act as though we are prisoners: for a prisoner is simply
a person who cannot substantively influence the structural
terms of her existence, who has no capacity to define the
norms and rules under which she lives. A prisoner may decorate the walls of his cell as he pleases, within limits, but may not
venture beyond them. Our ahistoricism, our consumerism, our
passivity in refusing the responsibility to redesign the existen-
tial buildings we inhabit—all these we view as luxuries to
which we are entitled.

Both human character—except when classified as aberrant
and thus pathologized—and social inequality are viewed within
the dominant paradigm as stable factors. The individual self is a
fixed quantity, subject to linear improvement chiefly through
the acquisition of capital and thereby goods and hierarchical
status, and increasingly by means of, among other vehicles,
mass-marketed texts of egocentric conformity that bill themselves as "self-help." The pursuit of happiness, these texts suggest both implicitly and explicitly, persists eternally in the
personal rather than in the social. In this loose and widely
consumed mistranslation of Freudian psychoanalysis to mass-
produced do-it-yourself pedagogy, the self-evaluative self becomes the sole locus of idealization and therefore the only
arena of conception in which improvement is popularly
deemed feasible.

This ideological primacy of the good of the striving, competing self over social or collective good is attested to by a broad range of trends in material production and consumption—including best-selling business how-to books and the massive proliferation of goods and services associated with the achievement of physical fitness—of which the culture-within-a-culture of self-help is merely a single example.

"Realism" is then no more than a mitigating and flexible set of intuitive responses to perceived disjunctions between a desirable social state of general emancipation from want—in Bentham's phrasing, "the greatest good for the greatest number"—and empirical evidence that such a state does not exist. In other words, realism is a euphemism for that form of self-interest that believes the subject is best served by emotional and practical rejection of the good of others as a central motivator of individual behavior.

Our notions of self-interest suffer from a poverty of imagination, formed in response to a culture that asks us only to consume and not to produce—except insofar as income constitutes production. I believe we make our worst mistake when we allow ourselves to be persuaded into a constrained and narrow interpretation of selfhood. Far more tragic than our forced overconsumption of material goods, of which we have some grudging awareness, is our forced consumption of ideas, which we reinforce by replicating in, for example, our authoritarian treatment of individual and cultural difference—a form we recognize for the most part only in passing, on the surface, if at all, with a brief nod in the direction of social determinism.

Romantic constructions of selfhood, indulgence and egotism notwithstanding, have something to offer to the self that considers itself autonomous, rational, and well-adjusted—not least their insistence on the sublime and on the transformative powers of imagination, on the extraordinary and the fluid within human emotional experience. Only a consciousness that is able to imagine sympathetically the new and the fundamentally other can hope to improve its conception of itself in revolutionary and innovative terms; only through reconceiving the landscape of its own construction can the mind reconceive the landscape of power, of deprivation and abundance, of the body politic—in short, the terms and means of a greater happiness. The mind that remains unaware of its birthright as a conceiving organism that is constantly vulnerable to inertia—eternally an unconscious victim of kidnap by minds and mentalities with stronger wills to prevail—will steadfastly mis-recognize the evidence and forms of its own domination.

The problem with romanticism is not chiefly that we seek to view ourselves through its flattering lens, but that the seductive rose-tinted light obscures us from ourselves in the process by blocking out the faces of other figures in the landscape.

In the Charles Perrault version of "Blue Beard," printed in English in the eighteenth century, what begins as Blue Beard's story quickly becomes his wife's. The fairy tale is named for him, yet he disappears as a protagonist as soon as he leaves his house, when the point of view changes. Of which the narrative purpose seems fairly clear: his wife is the fable's moral center. Blue Beard's transgressions are unredeemable, while his wife's betrayal is morally innocuous, if potentially fatal; he cannot, therefore, serve as our friendly narrator.

In this original "Blue Beard," the unnamed wife discovers corpses while her husband is away; finds she cannot wash the blood off the telltale key—the sole magical element in an otherwise straightforward plot—and on her husband's return, after some prevarication, finally hands over the key, which serves as incontrovertible proof of her guilt. Notably, Blue Beard comes home the night after her discovery, and asks her to produce the key only in the morning. In the interim, the text less than subtly suggests, the wife attempts to secure her husband's goodwill with sexual favors. Not surprisingly, given the era in which the story was written, the punitive authority of the modern state is absent: the wife entertains no thought of recourse to police powers to provide her with protection from her murderous spouse, and in the end retributive justice is dispensed with swords by her soldier brothers—a military clan.

The wife may be "Blue Beard's" protagonist by default, but readers aren't primarily interested in her, and neither was the author. He didn't even give her a name. Any interest we have in the story lies with its villain. Countless films have been made about Blue Beard—by Charlie Chaplin, among others—and his story has often been rewritten.

Blue Beard retains his charm by being what most men and women feel they cannot be: an overt articulator of the private fantasy of egomania. At first glance he is simultaneously what we can never be and what we long to be; by implication a sadistic killer, by extension a sexual hedonist, and at the least a particularly earnest misogynist, he is the subject that takes itself for a god. He is omnipotent because he accepts no social compromise; he acts solely in the pursuit of his own satisfaction. We may dismiss him as a fairy tale frivolity, pathologize him as an impossibility, or even think ourselves daring in acknowledging the psychosexual appeal of his transcendent egotism; but we are unlikely to identify with him wholeheartedly.

On the face of it, Blue Beard is presented to the consumers of myth as a fanciful, operatically bloody example of what not to be. We can easily reject the notion that serial murder is a viable option for improving our social lives. Still, the idea of Blue Beard is also the idea of a strange, quasiromantic liberation.

Insofar as romance consists in the telling of a heroic story, the allure of the romantic resides in the desire of individuals to construct heroic narratives of their own lives. The wistfulness with which we often recall or articulate our pasts, our need to identify ourselves with the images of famous people, our collective addiction to the forms of the heroic narrative propagated by Hollywood—all these urges bespeak a powerful compulsion toward self-romanticization. In identifying with sports heroes or participating vicariously in the monogamous passion of pulp romance fiction we indulge in the luxury of glorifying ourselves as we feel we need to be glorified. We are always the main characters in our own stories; other stories may be interesting, but they tend to be most interesting when they cease to be *other* and become our own.

The elements of the romantic are the sensationalistic, the dramatic, the monolithic; and these seem to reside chiefly in the violation of the taboo. In transgressing convention or law, we instate ourselves in history; we recognize that our power to affect the world is greatest when we take action against the constrictions placed on our personal liberty by the preestablished order, by the old rules—by, in fact, any rules, as the context dictates.

Our culture shows us, before all else, that the way to fulfill-ment is most direct through the elevation of our desires and ourselves over the desires and selves of other subjects. Only in holding fast to the goal—possibly private, possibly surrepti-tious—of being ineffably superior, sublimely competitive, for-ever first, do we become romantic subjects in our imaginations. In the process, subjects other than the self become objects, and the romantic collapses into the pornographic.

But who is *we?*

We are not the socioeconomically disenfranchised. The most that can be hoped for, for them, is entry into the stable quotid-ian world beyond material need. *They* may see some of the same movies, we think, or watch the same TV; they may read some of the same books and hear the same music; but at such times, in such moments, we suspect, they live a wholly vicari-ous life. There are millions of them, and they dream of lives they cannot have.

We dream of the lives that we do have. When we have night-mares, we wake ourselves up. And when for a moment we re-flect on the nightmarish quality of the waking lives of these visible-yet-invisible people, we call ourselves realistic to as-suage our consciences and go about our daily tasks.

The descendant of Blue Beard lives a quiet life. In time he does not remember the closet that never really existed; he forgets the mythic dreams of his youth. Occasionally, in the night, he wakes up and looks at his slack-jawed wife, who has fallen asleep with the reading light on and her Silhouette romance open on her chest; he looks at the cover of the book, which bears a portrait of a black-haired man who could be a pirate, and a buxom blonde with flowing locks and a flowing white dress. And then he looks down at himself, in his bed, and is ashamed, reflecting momentarily on all that he might have been; he feels a fleeting urge of savagery—almost of self-expression. But it passes: he leans over his wife, flicks out the lamp, rolls over and goes back to sleep.

JOYCE CAROL OATES

✴ ✴ ✴ ✴ ✴ ✴

In Olden Times,
When Wishing Was Having:
Classic and Contemporary
Fairy Tales

ONE

Whatever is an exit from that country . . .
cannot be an entrance.
—JOHN CROWLEY, "The Green Child"

A gathering of essays on fairy tales by women writers is particularly appropriate because the fairy tale, as a literary/cultural genre, has traditionally been associated with women. Distinguished archivists like the pioneering Charles Perrault (whose *Histoires ou contes du temps passé* appeared in 1697), Jacob and Wilhelm Grimm (whose *Die Kinder und Hausmärchen* appeared in various volumes, 1812–1857), and Hans Christian Andersen (whose collections appeared 1837–1874) have been male, but most of the material they collected was given to them by women. It is of one of these extraordinary sources that Wilhelm Grimm speaks so warmly in the preface to one of the Grimms' editions:

> *[This woman] retains fast in her mind these old sagas—which talent, she says, is not granted to everyone. She recounts her stories thoughtfully, accurately, with uncommon vividness and evident delight—first quite easily, but then, if required, over again, slowly, so that with a bit of practice it is possible to take down her dictation, word for word.*

The very expression "fairy tale" calls to mind a quintessential female sensibility: the tales are "old wives' tales," "Mother Goose tales." The association has long been an ambiguous one, not altogether flattering to women, and frequently disturbing.

For the term "fairy tale" is itself ambiguous. Sometimes it is frankly pejorative, dismissive. Its received connotation has to do with benign, rather brainless fantasy: *And they lived happily ever after.* But many fairy tales are nightmares of senseless cruelty and violence (as in "The Girl Without Hands," where a father chops off his daughter's hands to save himself from the devil—and this, one of the "good" fathers in the Grimms' collection); and the terms of "happiness" in others (Hansel's and Gretel's reconciliation with the father, who had left them to die in the forest, for instance; the torture death of Snow White's wicked stepmother) are problematic to say the least. Girls and women are the uncontested property of men, to be handed over by their fathers to virtually anyone the father favors—a murderous/cannibal robber bridegroom, a "frightful beast," the devil himself. The father's wish seems to include the daughter's reflexive response, as if the two were not two but one: when the craven father of "The Girl Without Hands" tells his daughter what he must do to save himself from the devil, the daughter meekly replies, "Dear Father, do with me what you will, I am your child." Simply to be *female* is to be without volition, identity.

In the great majority of the tales, to be a heroine in even a limited sense requires extreme youth and extreme physical beauty; it would not be sufficient to be merely beautiful, one must be "the greatest beauty in the kingdom"—"the fairest in the land" (as Snow White's famously jealous stepmother demands for herself). Young, maturing girls like Snow White, Cinderella, and the White Bride of "The White Bride and the Black Bride" (Grimms) are the natural targets of the homicidal envy of older women; ubiquitous in the tales are "wicked stepmothers" who conspire to injure or kill their beautiful stepdaughters. (If there is a fairy tale in which a stepmother befriends her stepdaughter, or even treats her decently, I seem to have missed it.) Even Sleeping Beauty, whose mother loves her, attracts the animus of a wicked (female) fairy, for her possession of a "bright resplendent beauty [that] had somewhat in it luminous and divine" (Perrault). The lot of women in a patriarchal society which privileges them as valuable possessions (of men), or brands them as worthless and contemptible, made it inevitable that women should perceive other women as dangerous rivals; that there are so many "step"mothers in the tales suggests how frequently women died in childbirth or as a consequence of constant childbearing; how frequently they were replaced by younger wives. Even for princesses like Sleeping Beauty, the optimum marriage age is fifteen or sixteen.

Fairy tales, like ballads, to which they are closely related, are a communal folk art of the uneducated, nonliterate class, yet they are politically and morally conservative to a degree that seems puzzling. Caste goes unquestioned even in such pica-resque, spirited tales as "Puss-in-Boots"; individual merit is rarely celebrated except in terms of the fixed social order. Contrary to popular assumptions, Cinderella, for instance, is not a commoner but a girl of aristocratic birth whose misfor-tune has been to lose her mother; when her father remarries, as fathers inevitably do, she finds herself displaced in the household by a cruel stepmother and stepsisters, made into a char-girl ("Cinderella": "of the cinders"). To interpret "Cinderella: or, The Little Glass Slipper" as a populist rags-to-riches romance is to totally misinterpret its fundamental story, which has to do with the putative injustice of denying one of aristocratic birth her rightful privilege, and with the drama of disguised worth; though Cinderella sleeps in a chimney corner, is forced to wear rags, and is abused by the females in her house-hold, nonetheless she is "a hundred times handsomer than her sisters" in their costly attire. Her physical self, including her small, dainty, beautiful feet, is the expression of her aristocratic virtue, and so she will be recognized by her prince because such virtue will assert itself; how very different from a tale in which a cinder-girl, or match-girl, or beggar-girl, is plucked for ro-mance by a nobleman. In a crucial sense fairy tales work to sub-vert romantic wishes, for they repeatedly confirm "order" and redress dislocations of privileged birth while leaving wholly un-challenged the hierarchical basis for such privileging. Amid the countless tales exalting the aristocrat over the commoner, "The Princess and the Pea" is a rarity in its suggestion of satire. In the most commonly known version, popularized by Hans Christian Andersen in 1835, aristocratic hyperesthesia is celebrated tongue-in-cheek: a self-declared princess is put to a secret test by her prospective mother-in-law, a queen, sleeping on a bed of twenty mattresses and twenty featherbeds laid upon three peas with such discomfort that, in the morning, she complains that her body is black and blue with bruises—proof to the queen and her son that she is the genuine article, a true princess fit to marry a prince, "for it was quite impossible for any but a true princess to be so tender." Hans Christian Andersen, of working-class origins, concludes the tale with a slyly ironic aside: "Now was not that a lady of exquisite feeling?"

Few fairy tales, however, are so playful as "The Princess and the Pea," nor do they suggest subversive attitudes; the world as it appears is not to be questioned, still less resisted. "Progress" in the social-evolutionary sense would be anathema to the fairy tale atmosphere of fateful resignation and what might be defined as a causeless consequence: your fate is deserved because it happens to you, it doesn't happen to you because it's deserved. All "good" heroines accept their fate passively, unquestioningly. To express even normal distress at being viciously mistreated would be in violation of the narrow strictures of fairy tale "goodness."

For fairy tale heroes and heroines are children, and the fairy tale derives from the childhood of the race when there would seem to have been, for most people, no coherent sense of "history," only an unchanging, static present encompassing an infinite cycle of seasons. The very concept of "history"—the male province of deliberation, analysis, action, acquisition, and control—springs from a grasp of individual self-determination, not mindless passivity and acquiescence. The traditional fairy tale begins *Once upon a time*—bland, blurred, stereotypical language that thwarts the more vigorous intellectual desire to know *when, where, how, why*. And *who:* for while recorded history is a chronicle of specific rulers and their governments, a complex mosaic of individual names, dates, allegiances, careers, the fairy tale world is ahistoric and timeless, politically static, its abbreviated dramatis personae a perennial cast of Kings, Queens, Princes, and Princesses; there are wealthy men and poor men, merchants, huntsmen, woodcutters, millers; there are beautiful daughters, handsome young men, and wicked stepmothers (before the Grimms' discreet alterations, some of these were wicked natural mothers): beyond this, characterization does not exist; of the growth, development, and evolution of human personality there is none. (Except in those instances in which a vain princess repents of her ill treatment of a disguised prince, or wicked stepsisters repent of their ill treatment of a stepsister who has married a prince.) Of course there are fairies—good, wicked, and "godmothers" (though rarely godfathers); there are giants, ogres, talking beasts of every species, including bears who are likely to be bridegrooms and talking cats likely to be helpers. There are always wolves, and wolves are "bad."

Many a fairy tale turns upon a secret word-formula or a secret, highly potent name: to utter "Rumpelstiltskin" is to save the life of one's baby. To have access to a magic knapsack and hat (as in the Grimms' tale "The Knapsack, the Hat, and the Horn") or to a cloak of invisibility (as in the Grimms' tale "The Twelve Dancing Princesses") is to save one's own life and to reap great riches. As in Ovid's great poem *Metamorphoses*, there are abrupt, magical changes: young men become swans, or ravens, or boar-like beasts and frogs yearning for human love to redeem them; sometimes, though rarely, as in Hans Christian Andersen's "The Swineherd," a disguised, begrimed prince will reveal himself in anger to the princess he would have married, and reject her. In Andersen's famous tale "The Little Mermaid," a cruel bargain requires that the heroine relinquish her siren's voice in return for a human shape and human love on earth—a disturbing parable of women's place in the world of men. (To be different in any respect, for a woman, or even to be suspected of "difference" is dangerous by fairy tale logic, for the categories of women are few, and divisive: in the cruel, darkly comic cautionary tale "Clever Elsie," [Grimms'], a mentally defective girl is boasted to be clever, married off by her father under false pretenses, and soon shut out of her house by her disgruntled husband, who has outfitted her with bells.) As in Homer's *Iliad* and *Odyssey*, the fairy tales are filled with fantastical interludes in which benevolent or malevolent beings of supernatural origin intrude in human affairs, with the astonishing omnipotence of parents exerting their power in an infant's life. Above all, human beings are surrounded by invisible forces which cannot be controlled but which, if one knows the secret rite or word-formula, can be placated, like the Judeo-Christian patriarch-god.

(How odd it seems to us, in fact, that the European fairy tale world coexisted with a powerfully institutionalized and politicized state religion; an essentially anti-Christian, pagan world populated with mysterious non-human beings like fairies, trolls, and witches who ceaselessly involve themselves in the affairs of mankind. The Grimm brothers collected a number of Christian fairy tales under the title *Children's Legends* which are about such holy figures as St. Joseph, the twelve apostles, the Virgin Mary, the Christ-child and God Himself; little-known tales lacking the dramatic force and arresting images of the more traditional tales.)

What is troubling about the fairy tale world and its long association with women is precisely its condition as mythical and stereotypical, a rigidly schematized counterworld to the "real"; an enchanted, or accursed, world whose relationship to reality is analogous to that of our dreams to our waking lives. As if the province of women must be unreal, trivial. As if women are fairy tale beings yearning for nothing more than material comforts, a "royal" marriage, a self-absorbed conventional life in which social justice and culture of any kind are unknown. Which helps to account for why fairy tale endings are nearly always absurd. For instance,

> As they spoke a splendid carriage drove up with eight beautiful horses decked with plumes of feathers and golden harness, and behind rode the prince's servant, . . . then all set out full of Joy for the Prince's kingdom; where they arrived safely, and lived happily a great many years.
>
> "The Frog Prince"

> And a magnificent princess alighted from the coach and went into the mill, and this princess was the little tabby-cat whom poor Hans had served for seven years . . . [She] took her faithful Hans and set him in the coach, and drove away with him. They first drove to the little house which he had built with the silver tools, and behold it was a great castle, and everything inside was made of silver and gold; and then she married him, and he was rich, so rich that he had enough for all the rest of his life. After this, let no one ever say that anyone who is silly can never become a person of importance.
>
> "The Poor Miller's Boy and the Cat"

In the yet more transparent wish-fulfillment fantasy "The King of the Golden Mountain" (Grimms), a king takes revenge on his unfaithful queen and a court of kings, princes, and councillors by brandishing a magic sword and uttering the words "All heads off but mine!" with the immediate gratifying result—"All the heads rolled on the ground, and he alone was master, and once more King of the Golden Mountain."

TWO

Beauty is a simple passion, but, oh my friends, in the end you
will dance the fire dance in iron shoes.
—ANNE SEXTON, Transformations

Of course, I've been unfair to the very nature of the fairy tale: it *is* crude, it *is* transparently wishful, it does reflect the unquestioned prejudices of a conservative patriarchal folk culture. Yet fairy tales contain an incalculably rich storehouse of mysterious, luminous, riddlesome and ever-potent images, a vast Sargasso Sea of the imagination. Though characterization is minimal, plots are bold and original; if endings often have a hasty, perfunctory quality, nonetheless fairy tales can encompass in the space of a few fluid passages complete miniature narratives. Like the folk ballads, the tales spring from a diverse and anonymous communal source, mysterious in their origins as language itself.

Jacob and Wilhelm Grimm believed that the myths of ancient times had descended first into heroic legend and romance and finally into folk tales with an appeal to children. Before the Grimm brothers, it was fashionable to revise and "improve" the tales to make them pleasing to an educated reading public, but after the Grimms began to publish their monumental work, respect for the oral folk-source was observed; it would come to be considered a violation of principle to alter the purity of the fairy tale source. Only in recent times has the fairy tale been reclaimed by writers and artists for their own imaginative and frequently subversive purposes. Such experimental, postmodernist work draws upon tradition while boldly "revising" it, often from a feminist perspective as in the work of Anne Sexton (*Transformations*, 1971) and Angela Carter (*The Bloody Chamber*, 1979).

Anne Sexton's brilliantly inventive poetry sequence retells sixteen classic fairy tales, among them "Snow White and the Seven Dwarfs," "Rumpelstiltskin," "Rapunzel," "Cinderella," "Red Riding Hood," "The Frog Prince," "Hansel and Gretel" and "Briar Rose (Sleeping Beauty)"; it is also the confessional document of "a middle-aged witch, me." The poems are notable for their characteristic Sexton flights of romantic lyricism, black comedy and bittersweet irony; each poem is preceded by an autobiographical preface—"Take a woman talking,/purging herself with rhymes,/drumming words on a typewriter,/planting words in you like seed grass." ("Iron Hans") "Snow White" faithfully recapitulates the fairy tale in contemporary/vernacular language: "The dwarfs, those little hot dogs,/walked three times around Snow White,/the sleeping virgin. They were wise/and wattled like small czars." Unlike Donald Barthelme's droll metafiction *Snow White*, Sexton's poem does not explore the sexual possibilities of a virgin residing with (male) dwarfs; Sexton's Snow White is a virgin even after her nominal marriage to a faceless prince, a younger version of the wicked stepmother who dies in the dance of red-hot iron shoes: "Meanwhile Snow White held court,/rolling her china-blue doll eyes open and shut/and sometimes referring to her mirror/as women do." Sexton's feminism is radical enough to expose and condemn the deadly "femininity" of women who refuse to acknowledge their masculine, aggressive selves: "Inside many of us/is a small old man/who wants to get out . . . /one part papa,/one part Doppelganger." ("Rumpelstiltskin") Cinderella's tale is "that story"—made banal by familiarity and repetition, yet never entirely believable:

> *Cinderella and the prince*
> *lived, they say, happily ever after,*
> *like two dolls in a museum case*
> *never bothered by diapers or dust,*
> *never arguing over the timing of an egg,*
> *never telling the same story twice,*
> *never getting a middle-aged spread,*
> *their darling smiles pasted on for eternity.*
> *Regular Bobbsey Twins.*
> *That story.*

"Red Riding Hood" is the most complex of the poems in *Transformations*, freely mixing the poet's anguished personal life ("And I. I too./Quite collected at cocktail parties,/meanwhile in my head/I'm undergoing open-heart surgery") with the familiar tale of Little Red Riding Hood deceived and devoured by the wolf and saved by the fortuitous intervention of the huntsman ("It was a carnal knife that let/Red Riding Hood out like a poppy,/quite alive from the kingdom of the belly"). The poem is an anti-lyric, heavy with irony, able to make little of the overfamiliar tale, which resolves itself all too easily in a "happy" ending:

Those two remembering
nothing naked and brutal
from that little death,
that little birth,
from their going down
and their lifting up.

"The Frog Prince" is an occasion for a hallucinatory stream-of-consciousness linking the poet's confused inner life with the symbolic Other, the Frog: "My guilts are what/we catalogue./ I'll take a knife and chop up frog." Not the Frog as Prince but the Frog simply as Frog captivates her.

Frog has no nerves.
Frog is old as a cockroach.
Frog is my father's genitals.
Frog is a malformed doorknob.
Frog is a soft bag of green.

The moon will not have him . . .

Once Frog becomes Prince, the poem ends abruptly; as in "Hansel and Gretel" the fairy tale swiftly dissolves like a bad dream, with a coda in which the poet speaks ironically: "Their mother, you'll be glad to hear, was dead." Sexton's most personal identification seems to be with "Briar Rose (Sleeping Beauty)" whose experience parallels the poet's own wavering pilgrimage "from Bedlam and partway back" (the title of her first book of poems, 1960): "Consider a girl who keeps slipping off,/arms limp as old carrots,/into the hypnotist's trance,/into a spirit world/speaking with the gift of tongues./She is stuck in the time machine,/suddenly two years old sucking her thumb,/as inward as a snail,/learning to talk again./She's on a voyage." Sexton's Briar Rose, saved by her prince, is released from the prison of catatonic sleep only to fear normal sleep forever, dependent upon "the court chemist/mixing her some knockout drops/and never in the prince's presence." The poem's elliptical revelation is a shocking one: Briar Rose has been sexually molested by her king-father, a "theft" committed upon her as a child.

> *There was a theft.*
> *That much I am told.*
> *I was abandoned.*
> *That much I knew.*
> *I was forced backward.*
> *I was forced forward.*
> *I was passed hand to hand*
> *like a bowl of fruit.*
> *Each night I am nailed into place*
> *and I forget who I am.*
> *Daddy?*
> *That's another kind of prison.*
> *It's not the prince at all,*
> *but my father*
> *drunkenly bent over my bed,*
> *circling the abyss like a shark,*
> *my father thick upon me*
> *like some sleeping jellyfish.*
> *What voyage this, little girl?*
> *This coming out of prison?*
> *God help—*
> *this life after death?*

A nightmare ending of the boldly revisionist *Transformations*, this plea from the child-self, locked in the heart of the adult woman. *Is this life after death?* may well have been the plea of Sexton's life, and Briar Rose/Sleeping Beauty the poet's most poignant expression of her suffering.

In Angela Carter's similarly iconoclastic collection of stories *The Bloody Chamber*, a lush, fevered prose style expresses the exoticism of the fairy tale world in a way that, ironically, the pedestrian, serviceable prose of the fairy tales themselves does not. (Angela Carter, a scholar/translator of Perrault's *Histoires ou contes du temps passé*, defined their essence as "heroic optimism," the principle that makes possible "happy" endings.) A postmodernist fantasist, an experimenter in form and voice, Carter created for her tales a florid, self-conscious, overwrought prose, as in these musings of the seventeen-year-old virgin bride of Bluebeard: "I felt so giddy as if I were on the edge of a precipice; I was afraid, not so much of him, of his monstrous presence, heavy as if he had been gifted at birth with more specific *gravity* than the rest of us, the presence that, even when I thought myself most in love with him, always subtly oppressed me . . . No. I was not afraid of him; but of myself. I seemed reborn in his unreflective eyes, reborn in unfamiliar shapes. I hardly recognized myself from his description of me and yet, and yet—might there not be a grain of beastly truth in them? And, in the red firelight, I blushed again, unnoticed, to think he might have chosen me because, in my innocence, he sensed a rare talent for corruption." The "talent for corruption" in fairy tale virgins is one of Carter's most provocative revisionist-feminist themes, often equated with food, drink, perfumes and flowers, in sensuous prose: "the reeling odor of a glowing, velvet, monstrous [rose] whose petals had regained all their former bloom and elasticity, their corrupt, brilliant, baleful splendor." ("The Lady of the House of Love")

In Carter's revision of the Bluebeard legend, the collection's title story, the virgin-bride of the murderous marquis is saved, in an unexpected ending, by her own mother, a huntswoman who arrives at just the right moment: "You never saw such a wild thing as my mother, with her hat seized by the winds and blown out to sea so that her hair was her white mane, her black lisle legs exposed to the thigh, her skirts tucked around her waist, one hand on the reins of the rearing horse while the other clasped my father's service revolver . . . And my husband stood stock-still, as if she had been Medusa, the sword still raised over his head as in those clockwork tableaux of Bluebeard you see in glass cases at fairs"—to fire a single bullet through his forehead. (A ridiculous ending, perhaps, but no more ridiculous than any other fairy tale ending, the feminist Carter seems to be saying. And why not, for once, feminist wish-fulfillment?) In Carter's similarly lush, sensuous revision of "Beauty and the Beast," titled "The Courtship of Mr. Lyon," the mythical marriage of innocent virgin and good, decent beast evolves into ordinary domestic marital happiness: Mr. and Mrs. Lyon walk in the garden; "the old spaniel drowses on the grass, in a drift of fallen petals." (How welcome, for once, a fairy tale ending that subverts the fantastic altogether.) In an artful variant of this marriage tale, "The Tiger's Bride," a female sexuality emerges passionately from a lifetime of repression, conquering "nursery fears made flesh and sinew; earliest and most archaic of fears, fear of devourment. The beast and his carnivorous bed of bone and I, white, shaking, raw, approaching him as if offering, in myself, the key to a peaceable kingdom in which his appetite need not be my extinction." Beauty craves

Beast as Beast craves Beauty; in erotic union, female and male are perfectly conjoined: "And each stroke of his tongue ripped off skin after successive skin, all the skins of a life in the world, and I left behind a nascent patina of shiny hairs. My earrings turned back to water and trickled down my shoulders; I shrugged the drops off my beautiful fur."

Carter's females are hardly "good" girls but complex, morally ambiguous individuals, not to be defined or predicted by gender, as in "The Company of Wolves": "See! sweet and sound she sleeps in granny's bed, between the paws of the tender wolf." And females can be as cruelly rapacious as males, in "The Snow Child" (in which a decadent nobleman's wife conspires in his brutal rape and murder of a young girl, the "child of his desire"); and "The Werewolf," in which, unexpectedly, the grandmother herself is the wolf against whom the shrewd young virgin must defend herself with her father's knife and a public denunciation of her grandmother to neighbors: "They knew the wart on the hand at once for a witch's nipple; they drove the old woman, in her shift as she was, out into the snow with sticks, beating her old carcass as far as the edge of the forest, and pelted her with stones until she fell down dead." The tale ends abruptly with the girl (never identified as Red Riding Hood) moving into her grandmother's house and "prospering." *The Bloody Chamber* revels in such startling reversals, dramatic surprises that suggest the tales' schematic intentions rather more than they evolve from a graceful conjunction of character and tale itself.

Like Sexton's more slapdash, idiomatic poems, Carter's prose fictions recapitulate familiar fairy tale forms from radical angles of perspective. Sexton's women are trapped in their legends like puppets on strings, while Carter's are more realized

as protagonists, willful and often perverse creations who define themselves against their seemingly prescribed fates. Not
"heroic optimism" after all but "defiant self-dramatization" most
accurately describes the mood of *The Bloody Chamber*.

Though the story is not derived from a specific fairy tale,
Rachel Ingalls's novella *Mrs. Caliban* is clearly of the fairy
tale/wonder tale mode, notable for its matter-of-fact tracing of
a companionable love affair between a housewife and a "frog-
man"—a creature six feet seven inches tall, with a dark green
skin, indigenous to the Gulf of Mexico. Ingalls's fantasy is compelling for its being so realistic as prose, unlike Angela Carter's
fantasies; though weakened by a hurried, rather sketchy de-
nouement, in which the woman's unfaithful husband dies in a
car crash, *Mrs. Caliban* has the melancholy, bittersweet air of a
romance that has come to no significant resolution, but simply
ends with the departure of the frogman-lover.

Like Ingalls's alien being, the mysterious green-skinned children of John Crowley's "The Green World" (collected in
Crowley's slender volume of fabulist tales, *Antiquities*, 1993)
have come from a world, or a counterworld, to which they can
never return: ". . . from a land below the earth [where] there
is always twilight. Whatever is an exit from that country . . . is
not an entrance." This enigmatic tale of children who have lost
their way out of their own world and are exiled in another
opens: "This story is recorded by Ralph of Coggeshall and by
William of Newbridge, both of whom say it took place in their
time, in the middle of the twelfth century, in West Suffolk." The
mode of narration is resolutely undramatic, however astonishing the events narrated. One of the green-skinned children, a
boy, dies of malnourishment; the other, a girl, survives, able to
consume human food and, in time, losing most of her green

color—"though her eyes remained large and strangely golden, like a cat's, and she never grew to proper size." Like most of the tales of *Antiquities*, "The Green Child" invites symbolic interpretation while pressing for no obvious meaning; nor does it move to a dramatic resolution, inviting us to ponder the mystery of "fairy" children as they might have been perceived in an authentic historic setting. The surviving girl marries, but

> . . . if there were children, and children of those children, so that in some way that green land elsewhere and also the distant bright country glimpsed across the wide river entered our plain human race, it must surely be so diluted now, so bound up and drowned in daylight and red blood, as not to be present in us at all.

Some of our most distinguished contemporary writers have drawn imaginatively upon archetypal fairy tales, interpreting them in a distinctly feminist manner. Jane Smiley's *A Thousand Acres*, for instance, is a realistically rendered revisioning of Shakespeare's *King Lear*, itself a bold revision of an ancient Anglo-Saxon legend (in which not daughters but sons "betray" the aging former king); in Smiley's interpretation, the tragic action derives not from the experience of the tyrannical, self-absorbed father, a Midwestern farmer whose ambition has been to own "a thousand acres," but from the largely repressed, debilitating experience of his three daughters, who have been victims of their father's incestuous lust. (Significantly, the old man never acknowledges his brutal exploitation of his daughters, never repents.) Margaret Atwood's *The Robber Bride* is an ebullient, rather farcical modern-day variant of the nightmare tale of female victimization, and her more realistically depicted short story "Bluebeard's Egg" conflates variants of the classic

Bluebeard legend, including a little-known version that pre-dates Perrault. In this variant, not a key but an egg is the object of Bluebeard's temptation of his young wife. At the conclusion of Atwood's story we are left to contemplate with the betrayed and now-frightened house-wife-heroine her mysterious husband, a surgeon, who in his impenetrable maleness would seem to be, himself, Bluebeard's egg: "This is something the story left out, Sally thinks: the egg is alive, and one day it will hatch. But what will come out of it?"

In Shirley Jackson's curious version of the Bluebeard legend, "The Honeymoon of Mrs. Smith" (subtitled "The Mystery of the Murdered Bride"), a story never published during the author's lifetime but probably written in the early 1960s, the murderous husband's seventh wife, "Mrs. Smith," is mysteriously, maddeningly passive in her role as victim, as the Bluebeard-figure is himself passive. The author seems to be suggesting in this enigmatic, rather low-keyed tale that the Bluebeard archetype of the murdering husband/helpless bride repeats, and repeats, and repeats through history; individuals lack all volition, caught in the impersonal cycle of murderer and victim, sexual psychopath and bride. The story ends:

> "*A week of marriage was too much for you,*" [Mr. Smith] *said, and patted her hand.* "*We'll have to see that you get more rest.*"
>
> *Why does it take so long, why does it take so long? Mrs. Smith thought . . . and turned and said to her husband,* "*Well?*"
>
> "*I suppose so,*" *Mr. Smith said, and got up wearily from the couch.*

A. S. Byatt's "The Story of the Eldest Princess" mimics the quest-motif of fairy tales and legends by following the episodic fortunes of a princess who seems to know that she is "caught in a story" not of her own devising; her meeting with an old woman (fairy godmother) instructs her to find a way out by realizing that "many things may and do happen, stories change themselves, and these stories are not histories and have not happened." In "Ursus Triad, Later" by Kathe Koja and Barry N. Malzberg, the tale "Goldilocks and the Three Bears" is transmogrified as a hallucinatory erotic fantasy of Goldilocks's sexual subjugation to the bears, her masochistic accommodation to violation by the nonhuman:

"You wanted to be filled? their postures asked her as they came upon her. Then *be* filled. To bursting." The innocent virgin becomes, through sexual degradation, Queen of the Bears, "the queen of the magic forest and the empty house, daughter of the night born to gambol in stricken and ecstatic pleasure . . . to pour and fill and to become." Beneath the classic fairy tale of a child blundering into a house not her own, a self-annihilating fantasy.

That the artful re-visioning of fairy tales has become a popular genre is attested by the commercial success of a series of anthologies edited by Ellen Datlow and Terri Windling with such titles as *Black Thorn, White Rose; Snow White, Blood Red; Ruby Slippers, Golden Tears.* Among these stories is a variant of "Beauty and the Beast" titled "The Beast," by Tanith Lee, in which the inner, secret bestial nature of a handsome prince-like lover is revealed at his death; a variant of "Hansel and Gretel" by Gahan Wilson updates the fairy tale to the Depression, conjoining it with a parable of wealth, privilege and exploitation in which brother and sister coolly supplant the malevolent witch who would destroy them. Kathe Koja's "Waking the Prince" reverses stereotypical male activity and female passivity in a narrative that moves in parallel time-dimensions, one quaintly fairy tale and the other achingly contemporary. "The Huntsman's Story" by Milbre Burch is an anti-fairy tale about a psychotic serial killer and a child victim (Polly Klaas) abducted by a parolee with a lengthy criminal record and murdered in California several years ago. The deep melancholy of the narrative excludes all magical transformations, the sleight-of-hand of elevated language:

> *She followed him mutely, not out of literary convention, but because he bound her mouth with duct tape. . . . No seven small men to befriend her. When it's time, there will be six pallbearers. The huntsman came unbidden.*

It is instructive to note that the contemporary fairy tale in its revised, reimagined form has evolved into an art form that subverts original models; from the woman's (victim's) perspective, the romance of fairy tales is an illusion, to be countered by wit, audacity, skepticism, cynicism, an eloquently rendered rage.

THREE

Blue-Bearded Lover

I

When we walked together he held my hand unnaturally high, at the level of his chest, as no man had done before. In this way he made his claim.

When we stood at night beneath the great winking sky he instructed me gently in its deceit. The stars you see above you, he said, have vanished thousands of millions of years ago; it is precisely the stars you cannot see that exist, and exert their influence upon you.

When we lay together in the tall cold grasses the grasses curled lightly over us as if to hide us.

II

A man's passion is his triumph, I have learned. And to be the receptacle of a man's passion is a woman's triumph.

III

He made me his bride and brought me to his great house which smelled of time and death. Passageways and doors and high-ceilinged rooms and tall windows opening out onto nothing. Have you ever loved another man as you now love me? my blue-bearded lover asked. Do you give your life to me?

What is a woman's life that cannot be thrown away!

He told me of the doors I may unlock and the rooms I may enter freely. He told me of the seventh door, the forbidden door, which I may not unlock: for behind it lies a forbidden room which I may not enter. Why may I not enter it? I asked, for I saw that he expected it of me, and he said, kissing my brow, Because I have forbidden it.

And he entrusted me with the key to the door, for he was going away on a long journey.

IV

Here it is: a small golden key, weighing no more than a feather in the palm of my hand.

It is faintly stained as if with blood. It glistens when I hold it to the light.

Did I not know that my lover's previous brides had been brought to this house to die?—that they had failed him, one by one, and had deserved their fate?

I have slipped the golden key into my bosom, to wear against my heart, as a token of my lover's trust in me.

V

When my blue-bearded lover returned from his long journey he was gratified to see that the door to the forbidden room remained locked; and when he examined the key, still warm from my bosom, he saw that the stain was an old, old stain, and not of my doing.

And he declared with great passion that I was now truly his wife, and that he loved me above all women.

NOTES

Works consulted in the preparation of this essay are:

Arwood, Margaret. *Bluebeard's Egg.* Boston: Houghton Mifflin, 1986.

Carter, Angela. *Burning Your Boats: The Collected Short Stories.* New York: Holt, 1995.

The Classic Fairy Tales. Ed. Iona and Peter Opie. New York: Oxford University Press, 1992.

Caught in a Story: Contemporary Fairy Tales and Fables. Ed. Christine Park and Caroline Heaton (England: Vintage, 1992). Contains "The Story of the Eldest Princess" by A. S. Byatt.

Crowley John. *Antiquities.* Seattle: Incunabula, 1993.

Grimm, Jakob and Wilhelm. *The Complete Grimms' Fairy Tales.* New York: Pantheon, 1976.

Ingalls, Rachel. *Mrs. Caliban.* Cambridge, Mass.: The Harvard Common Press, 1983.

Jackson, Shirley. *Just an Ordinary Day.* New York: Bantam, 1996.

Off Limits: Tales of Alien Sex. Ed. Ellen Datlow. New York: St. Martin's Press, 1996. Contains "Ursus Triad, Later" by Kathe Koja and Barry N. Malzberg.

Ruby Slippers, Golden Tears. Ed. Ellen Datlow and Terri Windling. New York: William Morrow, 1995.

Sexton, Anne. *The Complete Poems of Anne Sexton*. Boston: Houghton Mifflin, 1981.

Smiley, Jane. *A Thousand Acres*. New York: HarperCollins, 1991.

Warner, Marina. *From the Beast to the Blonde: On Fairy Tales and Their Tellers*. New York: Farrar, Straus & Giroux, 1994.

✳ ✳ ✳ ✳ ✳ ✳

Rapunzel
Across Time and Space

Baldheaded. This word flew through a restaurant in a country club I was in recently. Spoken by one of a group of young black girls I was dining with, it sailed stealthily. An invisible boomerang. Purposeful. Well-aimed. It quietly whizzed above our water glasses, bowing the heads of the candle flames, pulling laughter up the slender throats of the girls.

Baldheaded is one of those encoded words. It is one of *our* words. A black word. You can look it up in a dictionary, but you will not find the meaning that we have wrapped it in. For those girls and me, that word did not mean someone with no hair, or some man who is balding on top. This is what it meant:

> **baldheaded** *a. referring to a black female with very short, especially kinky, hair.*

The girl who had flung the word that night in the restaurant explained to me that she only wanted me to answer a question—why the character Sarah in a children's book I'd written was baldheaded. She and her friends thought the question was funny. The whole notion that a girl whose hair was no longer than the snap of a finger, whose hair was so nappy, so kinky, so picky, so beady, so woofy, so wooly, so rough, would be given such a prominent role in a book probably would have seemed laughable to me when I was their age. And what would have seemed even more outlandish was that Sarah *was not* the comic relief. She was not the butt of all the children's jokes because of her hair, but rather was intelligent and compassionate and skipped some mean double dutch to boot.

If I had come across a character like Sarah when I was a girl, I would have been stunned. I don't recall seeing black girls in the books when I was little in the late sixties. I read about Pippi and her long stockings, the Strawberry Girl and Ramona—that pest. If I had found Sarah in a book, I would have loved her. Secretly. Gone to the bookmobile and checked out over and over every book she appeared in. Read them at night in bed with one of my sisters. Stared at her face so much like mine, finding her secretly beautiful. But I would have wondered the same thing the girl in the restaurant wondered.

My hair was long, in two thick braids that fell past my shoulder blades. Why couldn't Sarah's hair be like mine? Pretty. I knew my hair was pretty because it was long, not because of what my mother said, or what my father said. Because I never heard them say that. It was comments from girls in the projects where we lived, girls at school, who made it clear to me that my sisters and I and other girls with long, thick hair had pretty hair. Nice hair. We did not have "good" hair. Because good hair was something you were born with. It was hair that was naturally straight or curly. My sisters and I all got our hair pressed with a hot comb. So all our hair could aspire to was being pretty, and for me, that was enough. Pretty hair.

Sarah could have had that, I would have thought. Long braids shiny with grease. The author could have given her braids tied with ribbons or affixed with shiny barrettes the way my mother did my hair. I would have thought that, not knowing the straightening comb had not been invented until this century, well after the time the books Sarah is in are set. I would have thought that the author made a mistake by making her bald-headed, but never said that to the author if I ever met her.

My parents are Southerners, and like many Southerners, they raised my siblings and me to be unfailingly respectful and polite to both children and adults. They did not approve of us throwing encoded words around, certainly never at a dinner table, and not even in the wilds of the school playground where it seems a child would like to throw them. I would have kept my feelings about Sarah hidden in my heart with my other se-cret—my love for Robert, a boy with skin like copper, who sat in the front row of my fourth-grade class. I would not have been open about the way I felt about Sarah because at ten, even at eight, I knew the connotations of baldheaded. Not only was Sarah's hair ugly, she was ugly, unlovable, deserving of ridicule. I knew these as facts of life. They were truths, like the rising sun in the east and the inconstant face of the moon shining in my window at night. I don't know when I learned them, on what day I sat down and was told about girls like Sarah, the direction of the rising sun, the fickleness of the shining moon. But I knew. On the playground and in the alleys around my house, I heard girls who looked like Sarah told to "Get out of here with your ugly, baldheaded self." I saw them dismissed, heard them dismissed, not for something they ever did, or said, but just for *being*. I never called those girls names, but I was capable of laughter like the girls in the restaurant. I could giggle along with those girls who knew how to throw well. Girls who could have been raised in the outback two hundred years ago, in a world created in the Dreamtime.

The restaurant I was sitting in, a virtually all-white country club one of the girls' family belonged to, was a world hundreds of light-years removed from the world I grew up in. In all my nights of dreaming as a girl, I never dreamt this world, never dreamt these girls. Despite what Einstein says about the impossibility of time travel, the barrier of the speed of light, I've traveled through time. Maybe that is why I don't expect questions about baldheaded girls. It would seem that black girls would be beyond that now, especially these girls, wealthy and privileged and beautiful. It would seem they would not be part of the cult of Rapunzel, paying homage to some girl in a fairy tale whose story they might not even remember well.

I know I don't always remember fairy tales well. I remember bits of stories, trolls, straw spun into gold, poison apples, witches, wicked stepmothers, handsome princes. Rapunzel, I'm sure of, is about hair. The girl has long hair and meets a handsome prince who sees her hair shining golden in the forest, climbs it, falls in love with her and later marries her. They go on to live happily ever after. End of story. But when I went and reread the story recently, I discovered I knew less than I even thought.

The fairy tale does not even begin with Rapunzel. It begins with her parents, a barren couple who have all but given up hope of having a child. The mother sees some rapunzel, a bitter lettuce growing in a witch's garden. The father, seeking to please his wife, goes and gets some for her. At night he scales the wall surrounding the witch's garden and gets his wife the rapunzel. He even returns a second night for more. This is when he is caught by the witch and she makes him promise to give her the child the wife will bear. He swears he will and keeps the promise once the child is born. The witch names the child Rapunzel.

Rapunzel is very beautiful with golden hair. The witch takes her off to the middle of the forest when Rapunzel is twelve. She locks her in a tall tower that has a window only at the very top. The only way the witch can reenter the tower is by Rapunzel's hair. Rapunzel ties it onto the window latch and the witch climbs up. One day, a young prince is out in the forest and hears Rapunzel singing. He is moved by her voice, finds the tower, but can't figure out a way to enter it. He returns the next day and hears the witch call to Rapunzel to let down her hair. Once the witch leaves, he does the same and meets Rapunzel. He wants to marry her and take her away, but Rapunzel reminds him there is no way for her to leave the tower. She tells him to bring skeins of silk and she will make a ladder. One day, Rapunzel tells the witch that when the prince comes to see her, he does not pull her hair as hard as the witch does when she climbs. In a fit of anger, the witch cuts Rapunzel's hair and sends her away. The witch then attaches the hair to the window latch and when the prince comes, she tells him he will never see Rapunzel again. Distraught, the prince jumps from the tower window. His fall is broken by a patch of brambles that scratch his eyes out. The prince wanders for years until he comes to a desert, the place Rapunzel has been banished to. She is now the mother of twins, a boy and girl. The prince hears her voice and he follows it. Rapunzel recognizes him. She cries and her tears cure his blindness. The prince takes her back to his kingdom and they live happily ever after. End of the story.

This is the end of the real tale, not the one I remembered. It has left me angry with the father, a thief of a man who steals from the garden of a known witch, not once, but twice. Sure it is to please his wife, but they would have all been better off if he had given her some arugula he bought at a farmers' market. This foolish man then has the nerve to give away a child he and his wife have longed for. It is best that the story jumps then to Rapunzel, sparing us the grief of her parents, both their mouths made bitter by their longing for Rapunzel, the daughter they will never know.

I'm amazed by two things about Rapunzel's life in the forest. One is the length of her hair. I knew that it was long, but I had forgotten its length—twenty ells. That's seventy-five feet! I can't imagine how many pounds that is, or where she actually kept all that hair before she let it down. The other thing that amazes me is that the prince is *not* attracted to Rapunzel's hair. He is not even attracted to her face, a crescent of it shining in the corner of the window, the fullness of it hovering above a canopy of leaves. It is Rapunzel's voice that brings him to her. It is the beauty of her soul that makes him want to ascend the tower.

The prince is attracted to what he cannot see, what he cannot touch. He is not attracted to the beauty of Rapunzel's hair. It is not an end; it is merely a means, a way of climbing into her life. That is why even after throwing himself out of a seventy-five-foot tower and having his eyes scratched out, the prince is able to recognize Rapunzel again.

Rapunzel's tears are very powerful, restoring sight to a man who has no eyes. Perhaps their power comes from Rapunzel's lifetime of sorrow—being given away by her father to a witch, locked in a tower, having her head shorn, being banished to a desert, living in misery with a set of twins fathered by whom? The girl has truly suffered and deserves some happily ever after, especially since she has found a man willing to accept two children whom he may not have fathered. He deserves his sight back and Rapunzel deserves all seventy-five feet of her hair back, coiled around her head like the rings of Saturn, trailing behind her like the tail of a comet. I hope as the story ends, Rapunzel has her hair, a reminder of the time she has traveled, the space she crossed to come to a life that may seem like a dream come true to someone looking at it from the outside but from the inside looks nothing like a world she dreamt, but one that should have been all along.

I hope the children I spoke to in the restaurant study Rapunzel's life, remember the details of it better than I did. They are still young and most likely will grow out of their fascination with long hair. I grew out of mine in college when I realized not only had I never gotten Robert all those years ago, that I had never gotten Henry or John or Dennis or Craig while I was in college. I went to the hairdresser and had her cut my hair off. I was sick of relaxing it, of combing it, of using it to pull men up into my life. Having my brains pulled out, bit by bit, little by little. There was no way I wanted to end up some vapid, shallow woman with an ell of a lot of hair but nothing underneath it. I had the hairdresser make me baldheaded and when she spun me around to look in the mirror to see what I saw of her creation, I did not have to hold the secret inside. I thought I looked quite fine. That my hair looked pretty. That it looked good. It was good.

My hair is now more of an accessory than anything else. Since college I've let it grow back and cut it again, let it grow back and cut it again. Now it is growing back, getting long again. I straighten it with a hot comb, or jump in the shower and let it get good and nappy, good and woofy and wooly and rough. I braid it, twist it, or wear it in a big nappy ball on the top of my head. When I feel like being baldheaded again, I will go to a hair-dresser and make it so, knowing that not only do some little black girls dismiss baldheaded women, sometimes grown black men do also. But that is all right with me because there is a day in every woman's life when she hears a voice inside herself that tells her what she needs to do, that tells her what needs to come out and be heard, even if it is only from a tower, only in a forest. And if any man is wandering by and hears it, he had better have a ladder and the strength to endure the power of her tears.

This is not the kind of thing you can say to a child who asks a simple question. *Why is Sarah baldheaded?* The girl who asked it is still shedding baby teeth. You have to answer a question like that simply. Speak like a child. You have to say, I wanted Sarah to have short hair because I thought she looked beautiful that way. I saw a picture of a girl taken just before slavery ended. She was dark, thin and had very short hair. She had big dark eyes that looked sad and I thought she was a very beautiful little girl. That is what you say. What goes unsaid is what a child of that age cannot understand.

When I saw that girl with those eyes, I thought her face as beautiful as the dark side of the moon. The side we never see because we are told the moon rotates and revolves at the same time. Because it has this captured rotation, we are told, the moon always keeps the same side toward Earth. Being one who has traveled through time, I don't think the scientists' story is true. I think they have bad memories and maybe have forgotten parts of their own tale.

Maybe, once upon a time, the moon did show her other face, proudly, boldly, for just one night. It shone down on Earth below just as the other side does, bathed in silver light, brilliant in its fullness. But this face was dismissed for *being* what it was not—just like the other side. Since that night the moon turned that face forever-more into the darkness of space refusing to let anyone on Earth see it and was called fickle. She was hurt by being made fun of, for being called fickle, and sang out her sorrow from the dark side of her face. People hear her voice on windless nights. Part of a chorus people used to call the music of the spheres. Its beauty haunts us, draws us to look up into the sky at night.

We want to hear her voice more clearly, but the moon will never turn its other face to us again. We will have to cross time and space to pull ourselves into her life, make a ladder of our own hair. Nappy. Curly. Straight. Braided. Dreaded. We will have to shave our own heads, all of us become baldheaded and beautiful, weaving a ladder that stretches to her to hear the full beauty of her voice, to see the beauty of the face cloaked in darkness. We will feel the power of her tears as they fall into our eyes. Though not blind, we will see that she was never the one who was fickle. We were. Then we will all live happily ever after. End of story.

FRANCINE PROSE

❋ ❋ ❋ ❋ ❋ ❋

Sleeping Beauty

It seems, we might think, the very simplest of tales, this romantic and hopeful story about the power of love to reverse all the weaker enchantments and in the process rouse young girls from their insensate virginal comas. Its elements (the pricked finger, the drop of blood, the long swoon, the Prince who slashes through the bramble hedge to deliver the saving kiss) are so naively transparent, their sexual content so naked that we may be reminded of those textbook-Freudian dreams in which the dreamer's teeth fall out, or trains disappear into tunnels. How embarrassing to observe one's mysterious and fascinating subconscious surfacing in narratives so predictable, so banal.

It seems, we might think, a paradigm of the feminist critique of how our culture programs girls, of that psychic footbinding designed to send them—blinded, hobbling—from the cradle to the altar: Just close your eyes, dearies, and lie perfectly still until the handsome Prince happens along and his desire initiates you, introduces you to your real life. No other story, no other fairy tale sets it all out so diagrammatically, or so strictly prescribes the division of active and passive along, as they say, the most gender-traditional lines. Cinderella, Rapunzel, Little Red Riding Hood—all those endangered and rescued maidens were at least apparently awake, and, strictly speaking, conscious.

Conversely, we might think "Sleeping Beauty" emblematic of something hardwired into the species, DNA-encoded, cellular, deeper than culture and representative of all the untidy, inconvenient and ineradicable instincts that make the feminist's tiny daughter pine for the nail gloss and lipstick. As girls, we loved this story best of all for its heartening promise that the long nap we knew we were taking would eventually end; perhaps when we least expected it, the mystical—predestined—kiss would provide the piece of the puzzle that, even fast asleep, we knew was missing.

Or we might think, as I do now, that the story is yet another of those madeleines manquées, those memory-jogs that don't quite work, that fail to restore our youth, one of those markers, those startling reminders of how far we've come, and of all we've gone through and learned. How much smaller our childhood homes seem when we revisit them as adults, how different that buttery tea cookie tastes when we must weigh the health risks they pose. And oh, how the beloved fairy tale can suddenly reveal that dark subterranean detail, that knotty little plot twist squirming under the surface that we never registered, never suspected, all those years ago.

So let's begin again, this way: imagine the Prince's surprise when the Princess (Is she comatose? Is she . . . dead?) turns out to be alive! No one could for one moment pretend that what inspired his lustful or curious kiss was her vibrant animation. Those eyelids blinking open, that look of wonder or distress, the inevitable consternation when the awakened dreamer figures out that she's somehow slept through the last hundred years—none of that was exactly what the Prince had in mind as he braved the wild beasts and sliced through bramble thicket.

Gradually, with age and time, and often through the medium of art (which so often traffics in the hidden, the taboo, the unspeakable), we begin to collect a few hints, a few vague shadowy clues to that most baffling and intriguing enigma: the opposite gender's sexuality—not its garden-variety lusts and marketplace fixations but the cobwebbed corners of rarely visited attics. Sometimes these are facts that are commonly known by (let's say) one-half of the population but prudently concealed from the other half. These are home truths that our soul mates, our most dearly beloveds, would just as soon choose to keep quiet—that is, if they knew them themselves and could put these intuitions into words. For sometimes these are secrets judged not merely too dangerous to admit, but too anarchic and subversive to permit oneself to think.

And really, why should men trust us with secret information that (given our momentary or lifelong feelings about males in general or in particular) we may use against them, as evidence of insufficiency, or villainy, or hopeless and incurable testosterone-linked disease? Alternately, if our experience has caused us to feel fondly toward men (as individuals, needless to say, not as governments or armies), we may find ourselves struck by the astonishment that overcomes us when we're obliged to admit that someone is genuinely—someone dares to be—different from ourselves.

Back to Sleeping Beauty, then. By now it's probably clear that what I'm talking about is a sort of modified necrophilia: not exactly sex with a corpse—literal graveyard amour—but rather sex with a woman who only *appears* to have left the world of the living.

Once you look it's everywhere, though mostly—again—in art, since not even one's most voluble, open, forthcoming, least paranoid male friends (and certainly not, for obvious reasons, one's husband or lovers) are about to confide that their deepest secret fantasy is sex with an unconscious woman (now commonly thought of as rape) or with an inflatable sex doll or ingenious female robot.

And yet it can be imagined, and *has been* imagined, again and again, by the likes of Basile and Charles Perrault (the original authors, transcribers—or whatever—of "Sleeping Beauty"), by Edgar Allan Poe, by E. T. A. Hoffmann, by Heinrich von Kleist, by Tommaso Landolfi, by Thomas Hardy, by the great and eccentric Uruguayan fabulist Felisberto Hernandez, by Yasunari Kawabata, and, more recently, by Alfred Hitchcock. (What one wants to point out is that none of these writers are man-hating feminists raving that what men want, what men really want, is not a living, breathing woman but rather a barely sensate automaton or a receptive pillowy sex toy. . . .) It's men who have imagined this—that is, imagined *other* men capable of falling in love with an artificial "woman" or a living woman convincingly impersonating a dead one.

In another fairy tale, "Snow White," the Prince falls in love with Snow White while she is insensate in her coffin. In the Volsung Saga, Sigurd loses his heart to the fast-asleep Brunhilde as soon as he removes the armor from her unconscious body. For Poe, of course, the perfect lover is the dead Annabel Lee, whom no living (or full-grown) woman can ever hope to equal. In Hoffmann's "The Sandman," it's Olympia, the piano-playing but nearly mute, icily pretty automaton whom the young Nathaniel much prefers to his flesh-and-blood fiancée, Clara. In Hernandez's "The Daisy Dolls," it's the larger-than-life-sized mannequins engineered to look progressively more animated and "natural" as a rich man and his wife play an increasingly treacherous game involving elaborate practical jokes, passion, betrayal and murder.

In von Kleist's "The Marquise of O," the heroine faints dead away in the aftermath of an assault during the siege of her family's castle—and, in that unconscious state, inspires her gallant rescuer, Count F—, to rape her and father a child. In Hardy's *Tess of the D'Urbervilles*, somnolence holds a similar attraction for the amoral Alec D'Urberville, who takes advantage of the sleeping Tess to rob her of her virtue. Landolfi's "Gogol's Wife" is an inflatable doll with mucous membranes whom Gogol murders in a fit of uncontrollable jealous rage; the old men in Kawabata's *The House of the Sleeping Beauties* pay large sums of money to patronize a bordello where they warm their old, chilly bodies by lying beside the warmer flesh of slumbering young women.

By far the most disturbing example of this peculiar subgenre is Alfred Hitchcock's masterpiece *Vertigo*, with its loopy, lush excesses and its gaping plot holes through which we can glimpse the master wrestling with his private demons, a struggle so all-consuming that he inevitably loses his grip. In this film (so dreamy, so hallucinogenic, so nearly out-of-control compared to the logical, bloody-minded meticulousness of his other work), Hitchcock appears to be operating in a fever-haze of rampant sexual obsession. His compulsion is almost indistinguishable from the passion that drives his hero, Scottie, to turn the warm-hearted, down-to-earth Judy into an exact replica (a mannequin) of the icy, ethereal—and, by that point, dead— Madeleine (who was herself supposedly possessed by the spirit of another dead woman, Carlotta Valdes).

In the film's most fascinating, horrifying and titillating sequence, we watch the play of torment, longing and desire on Scottie's face as he cajoles and bullies Judy into changing her wardrobe, her style, dying her hair, transforming herself, inch by inch, into the woman Scottie fell in love with when he rescued her—unconscious, half-drowned—from San Francisco Bay. (Like Sigurd in the Volsung Saga, Scottie undresses his beloved while she is still passed out—before she has awoken, or recovered.) And we know that Scottie will never be satisfied until Judy *becomes* the lover whom he was finally unable to keep alive, helpless to save (or so he thinks) from suicide and violent death.

The first time I saw the film, I was a freshman in college, and afterward I stayed awake, terrified, all night, seized by a sort of anxious vertigo not unlike poor Scottie's. Since then I've seen the film perhaps a dozen times and gradually come to understand what it was that so unnerved me during and after that first viewing.

That was in the late sixties, when one heard a lot of talk about the ways in which men reduced women to fetish objects. But none of the men *I* knew did that; they all seemed perfectly capable of telling (and in fact quite grateful for) the larger and smaller differences between a female college student and a Barbie doll. Moreover, the male's inability to see women as fully human and his powerful impulse to fetishize them has always seemed a somewhat overelaborate reading of the fact that construction workers whistle at female passersby.

Vertigo convinced me that such impulses were very real, and what I felt was a fear akin to (if not as severe as) what we experience the first time we're forced honestly to confront the fact of death, or the existence of evil. I realized that it could happen, I glimpsed what that sort of fetishization would—and did—look like, and I understood that all of us (not only men) might be capable of acting on that impulse but in fact might be (consciously or unconsciously) powerless to resist it.

I realized that these constructs we nurture so lovingly—that is to say, our individual *selves*, those intricate collages of memories, experiences, opinions, feelings, quirks, etc.—finally mattered far less than some sort of template that we either matched or didn't, some abstract erotic response to images and desires programmed into the system long before birth, or in the earliest weeks or moments of life; we might as well be ducklings, imprinting on a real or artificial surrogate mother duck.

It all seemed so reductive, so terribly unfair, like some sort of sexual Calvinism, erotic predestination—the unchangeable fate, incapable of being altered in the slightest by all our illusions of self-knowledge, by our fancy pretenses of rational (or irrational) choice. What does it matter what we *are* if we are all simply obeying some biological imperative triggered by a suit, a glance, a gesture, the color of someone's hair? And what could be a more perfect repository for these inchoate longings, a more suitable scrim on which to project these mysterious desires, a cleaner slate on which to draw the ideal creature who embodies all these most hidden and urgent needs than an artificial woman, a woman asleep or dead, a woman who will not spoil the moment of blissful consummation by insisting so distractingly that she's Judy—and not Madeleine.

So perhaps the story of Sleeping Beauty is not so much as promise of future romantic awakenings as a warning, an etiquette lesson, a prescription for behavior. It's not so much that we *are* asleep, on ice till the Prince comes to rouse us. It's that—if we want the Prince to come . . . well, forget the makeup, the curlers, the short skirts, the feminine wiles, forget the flirtation, the conversation. The surest route to a man's (or to some men's) heart is to pretend to be unconscious: I'm asleep, dear . . . and actually, to tell the truth, I may not even be . . . real. I'm what you've always dreamed about. Do with me what you will.

If fairy tales are the alchemical distillation of our collective desires and dreams, then perhaps what Freud said about dreams may apply to these stories too: their details, their entirety, the sum of what actually happened are finally less significant than what we remember and misremember, fragment and distort.

This, then, is how we remember the story of Sleeping Beauty: the Princess, the castle, the brambles, the Prince . . . and, of course, the kiss. Some of us (the more logically or causally minded, those interested in first principles) may even recall that the source of the enchantment was the malevolent curse of some typically malcontent witch. Wasn't there a pricked finger involved? A telltale drop of blood? Something about a spinning wheel? Or was that . . . Rumpelstiltskin?

So what have we forgotten? What is the "real" story? What elements of the narrative have been selectively edited out by the bowdlerization of the nursery and by the omission of the more disturbing details with each retelling, each generation?

Let's look at Charles Perrault's "La belle au bois dormant," the very first story in his 1697 *Histoires ou contes du temps passé*. Here, the romantic awakening (no kiss, it seems, was required; the Prince had merely to kneel before the Princess for the spell to be broken) is a bright little nugget sandwiched between two dark chapters on the theme of female vengefulness, envy and rage. The love story provides a brief interlude of grace (in one lovely detail, the ladies-in-waiting take care not to tell the newly awoken Princess that she is dressed in the fashions of somebody's great-grandmother—though she looks very beautiful anyway) between two much longer and profoundly harrowing sections.

The first movement begins with the King and Queen's passionate longing to have a child, a wish which after many barren years is ultimately granted. Overjoyed, they stage a lavish Christening, to which they invite all the kingdom's resident fairies, with the understanding that each elfin godmother will give the newborn a magical gift.

Alas, the royal couple forgets to include an elderly, reclusive and obscure fairy, who shows up uninvited, her offering a curse. She promises that the Princess will have her hand pierced by a spindle and die of the wound—a malediction which a younger fairy mediates by changing the death sentence to a mere hundred-year sleep. (Hosts, hostesses, makers of guest lists and indeed of *any* lists—the most fashionably dressed celebrities, the notable books and films of the year, the richest CEOs, the best writers or artists under the age of forty—

would do well to consider the daunting number of fairy tales that begin with catastrophes whipped up by somebody in a rage at having been excluded.)

As a prophylactic measure, spindles are outlawed throughout the kingdom. One wonders what its residents did for clothing during the intervening years until the teenage Princess, wandering through a palace, finds an old woman in a tower room so remote that she has apparently never heard about the prohibition against spinning. Of course, the Princess sticks herself and nods off for a hundred years until the Prince arrives, and so on. (The kiss—so central to our modern understanding of the story—is thought to have been added during the centuries when "The Sleeping Beauty" was a standard repertoire plot for traveling marionette shows; this fact may tempt us to reimagine the kiss as a sort of abrupt thunking peck between two wooden puppets.)

No sooner has the Princess woken than it begins to seem as if the long sleep has been a blessed idyll, a prudent restorative nap before the struggle-to-the-death about to ensue when the Prince (now the King) goes off to war, leaving the Princess (who by now has borne him two children) with his mother. The worst-case nightmare mother-in-law is, as it happens, an Ogress whose craving to eat her two grandchildren and her daughter-in-law (with Sauce Robert!) is thwarted at the very last minute by the King's return. Is this, then, one moral of the tale: that the long sleep of girlhood is a brief, welcome interval of peace between the battles (with other women!) that deform childhood and adult life?

And now let's search a bit further back still, to see what Perrault himself forgot—or what he chose to leave out—in his borrowing from an earlier version of the story in Basile's 1636

Pentamerone. Here there are no uninvited vengeful fairies; rather, a wise man predicts that harm will come to the Princess through a splinter in a skein of flax. But here again female malevolence is the truly lethal splinter; after the King awakens the Sleeping Beauty (whom Basile calls Talia), it turns out that her gallant savior is already married; like the Ogress in Perrault, his understandably furious wife tries (with horrifying near-success) to cook and eat her husband's mistress and her two children, Sun and Moon. And where did these children come from?

That is the major—and most startling—difference between Perrault and Basile. For the King in the Neapolitan tale acts on the impulse which later generations of literary heroes some-how managed to resist. That is, he rapes Sleeping Beauty, and in the process fathers two children, who are miraculously able to nurse although their mother remains unconscious. Finally, one of the infants, in a sort of feeding frenzy, mistakes her fingertip for a nipple, sucks out the poisoned splinter and brings the Princess back to life.

So now, it seems, we've come full circle, and then some. The insensate, slumbering woman is not only the ideal lover and mate, but also—as it turns out—the perfect mother. The kiss that returns the Sleeping Beauty to her waking state requires two generations. Or perhaps it's not love—but motherhood—that finally makes a girl's eyes blink open in this seemingly sim-ple (but actually complex) story, this seemingly romantic (but in fact deeply disturbing) narrative, this eternally haunting fairy tale with its peculiar take on death and life, on women and men, on the continuance of the species.

LINDA GRAY SEXTON

✳ ✳ ✳ ✳ ✳ ✳

Bones and Black Puddings: Revisiting "The Juniper Tree"

I open the blue, hardbound volume of the Grimms and Andersen fairy tales my mother gave me when I was young, and flip through the pages. Though we never read these stories aloud, they captivated my imagination for many years. This book is one of the very few I have on my shelf today that accompanied me into adulthood, surviving years of winnowing and small apartments with their lack of shelf space. Its binding is unwinding in my hands, its tissue-thin pages are smudged with the greasy fingerprints of the girl I was, yet still it influences the writer I have become.

The flyleaf bears several inscriptions, the first, at the top, in the block-like printing of fourth grade: "Linda Sexton, September 15, 1961." In the middle runs a sentence of loopy cursive letters, all the *i*'s dotted with circles and a fancy curlicued flourish for emphasis: "*I Still Have It: May 29, 1967.*" And at the bottom, in a hand practicing the streamlined adult look: "Now I understand it, Jan. 10, 1970."

I read the book cover to cover many times, though I tended to dip into the Grimms' section most often, savoring its more primitive folksy style, so unlike the other things I read during those years: the standard children's classics like *The Yearling* and *Old Yeller*, *The Red Pony*, *The Little Princess*, the entire Black Stallion series and, inevitably, each Nancy Drew adventure. In sixth grade I grew up to Kafka's *Metamorphosis* and Dickens, but somehow I never quite left the Brothers Grimm behind until I went away to college.

As a teenager, I returned home from school each day and made myself a bowl of canned soup. Religiously I always chose one of two varieties: vegetable by Campbell or clam chowder by Snow. Then, in order to be hands-free, I propped a book open in front of me at the kitchen table, weighted it down with a salt shaker or a knife, and let myself sink into a swoon of reading, dribbling soup down my front as I became absorbed. From Mother's adjacent writing room came the sporadic clatter of her typewriter as she worked. I was silent, and therefore safe, for she allowed no noise around her—not even the hush of quiet voices—when she was working. My sister retreated to her bedroom upstairs, or else went to a friend's house, but I learned early to tailor myself to a writer at work.

In between devouring *Gone With the Wind* and *Madame Bovary*, I continued to read and reread the fairy tales, which I stowed just around the corner from the kitchen in my mother's study, on a shelf convenient for quick access, always the same shelf for safety. It was easy to lose a book in our house; sometimes you were right in the middle of reading something when it was simply swallowed up by the tide of other titles, never to be located again. Books multiplied like toadstools after rain, tilting precariously on bedside tables and coffee tables, overwhelming our many shelves, overflowing from my mother's writing room, and burying the small wooden desk on which I elbowed them aside to do my homework.

There was something comforting about reading the same stories over and over: I knew them as well as a child knows the lyrical repetition of a Dr. Seuss book, and in our chaotic household, whose atmosphere climbed and dipped in sync with the barometer of my mother's manic depression, repeated suicide attempts and hospitalizations, the ability to predict how the story would end provided me with a stability I craved, the ritual of reading myself into a world other than my own accompanied by the warmth of a bowl of soup. Soup and story went on to protect me at dinnertime, when my parents argued angrily after their private cocktail hour, my sister and I choked food down our tense throats, Mother sometimes became dissociative or hunched over the toilet to vomit up the meal my father had cooked. Sometimes I helped her leave the dinner table and took her upstairs to put her into bed.

Fairy tales were the only short stories I read repeatedly. Already I preferred the larger, rich form of long fiction, and this preference would shape my life: unlike my mother, I did not become a poet, but a novelist. Yet, why were *these* the stories I chose to reread again and again? In his introduction to my edition, W. H. Auden suggests that the fairy tale is "a dramatic projection in symbolic images of the life of the psyche." The tales themselves tapped into something particular both in me and my life that O. Henry or Somerset Maugham could not. The only other author who came close was Edgar Allan Poe, and his macabre stories I also read over and over.

When I got a bit older, at twelve perhaps, my mother used to emerge from her writing room after I had finished my soup and my read, just before I retreated upstairs to start my home-work, to show me what she was working on. She began asking for my opinion, and in this way she drew me into her world of writing, where words were the building blocks. And when I was sixteen, my mother got curious about my fascination with the fairy tales and asked which were my favorites. I wrote down a list with black felt pen on a paper napkin: "The White Snake," "Godfather Death," "Briar Rose," "Iron Hans," etc. . . . The napkin still exists, in her archive at the University of Texas at Austin (at least, I believe it does, though possibly only in my imagination). Borrowing my Grimms', Mother wrote a poem called "The Gold Key," in which she envisioned herself as a storyteller whose task it was to retell these old, half-forgotten, well-remembered tales. She began to spin the poems the way Rapunzel once spun straw into gold, reinterpreting the stories with an emphatically modern twist.

Transformations was published in 1971, the event that surely led to my self-consciously clever inscription regarding under-standing the stories at last, which I had written in the front of the blue volume that had once been solely mine. I see now that I had "understood" the tales—with both heart and psyche—long before Mother began to work on them, and that under-standing is what gave shape to my fascination. I realize, too, that once I left my childhood home for college, I stopped reading the Brothers Grimm. I do not believe I even took it with me. I left both it, and my mother, behind. For a while, free of her strong influence in my life, I thought I did not need it anymore.

It's late lunchtime for me today, midweek, the kids not home from school yet. Midwinter has come to northern California, rainy and raw, and I make myself a bowl of vegetable soup: I al-ways stock plenty of cans in my pantry as my sons, Alexander, thirteen, and Nicholas, twelve, eat it by the cartload, and I confess, I still enjoy it myself. At my own kitchen table, I now sip and leaf through the blue volume, dipping, browsing, looking for a subject, unraveling the years in my own head and remembering the pleasure these stories brought me. Yet "Cinderella" and "Snow White" have become too much a Disney product. I cannot think of "Sleeping Beauty" without seeing the fairy godmothers wave their wands as they argue about the color of the princess's dress while she waltzes with the prince: pink to blue, blue to pink, and back again. Like so many other little girls raised in the early fifties, I did have fantasies about being swept up by a prince, about being married in a beautiful dress that cinched my waist reed-thin and elevated my breasts over neckline's edge, fantasies about living happily ever after—but those fantasies are not the ones that, in the long run, interested me or drew me to the book. And stubborn now at forty-three, I refuse to choose to write about a tale my mother once selected from my own list.

How horrible so many of them are: not because they are violent or gory—though surely this is true—but because in nearly all of them the women are such losers. In so few does the woman manage to outfox the man set in opposition to her. If she does, either she is brought to heel and punished, or she is cast in an evil light. To critique the subject from my own feminist viewpoint would certainly be politically correct, but somehow it lacks appeal. I keep looking.

The book's pages fall open naturally to a particular story, the binding perhaps pressed flat from the weight of the salt shaker I had used to keep it open some thirty years earlier. Unlike so many of the others, this story has remained incredibly sharp in my mind. Not one of those my mother chose to retell in her

Transformations, nor one of the many with which most people are familiar, it is the saga of a murderous mother and her persecuted children.

As the story of a child's triumph over the adults around him, "The Juniper Tree" involves the most intense of childhood fantasies. As I reread it, it makes me shiver. But it also makes me grin. I know instantly that I am going to write about it because I see my life reflected in it, and that, as Auden pointed out, is the key to the fairy tale—that symbolic projection of our own psyche, no matter how bloody or savage or strange.

Instantly I recognize that once again I am in the midst of choosing family relationships as my subject: fathers and daughters, mothers and daughters, mothers and sons—and I despair that I will ever write about anything else. Is this how early fixations become midlife obsessions? Don't I have one good mystery in me, one adventure set in the Soviet Union with spies, one Brazilian romance complete with snakes and voodoo and large turquoise stones? Did the difficulties of my early life— mirrored so precisely in these stories of family triangulations, manipulations, and greedy little deeds—shape so entirely the kind of writer I would become?

I get up and put my soup bowl in the dishwasher. My son Nicholas, twelve years old, is rollerblading up the driveway. I check my watch: three P.M. Alexander appears, only a bit behind his brother, on his bicycle, struggling to balance himself under the weight of his incredibly enormous eighth-grade backpack. I start thinking about what snacks they are going to want.

The back door slams, they appear in the kitchen, looking for me. Alexander avoids questions about his day, grabs a bag of chips and a soda, and disappears into his bedroom. His stereo booms bass—Primus, an alternative rock band. Nicholas hangs around, telling me about drama auditions as I make him a grilled cheese sandwich and then he, too, is gone, but with a kiss, to sneak a little TV before starting his homework. I go back to the table and pick up the book again, making notes this time.

As I had remembered, "The Juniper Tree" is a great story, and longer than the others in the section told by the Brothers Grimm, where lengths of only a single page are common. This one takes a full seven of tiny print—more novel than short story as fairy tales go, and therefore part of its attraction, I suppose, to one who would eventually become a novelist.

It begins two thousand years ago, when a rich man and his beautiful, pious wife discover they are infertile despite their years of prayer. In the front yard stands a juniper tree; one day in winter the woman pares an apple while standing beneath it and cuts her finger, which bleeds onto the snow. She wishes for a child as white as snow and as red as blood; soon she conceives a child. The months of her pregnancy pass in largely symbolic prose: she flowers as discreetly but abundantly as does the tree. Nine months later, a little boy is born to her, as white as snow and as red as blood, but "when she beheld it she was so delighted that she died."

Pausing at the conundrum of the way death and delight merge here, several parallels strike me and I get up from the table to make myself a cup of tea. Alexander's stereo still blasts. I wonder if I'll have to tell him to turn it off and start his homework.

Like the mother in "The Juniper Tree," I struggled with infertility; when, after three miscarriages, I became pregnant with Alexander, my pleasure had been so acute I well imagined

I might die from it—if not from the pain of the thirty-six-hour labor itself. When Nicholas followed, eighteen months later, the sensation of pain and pleasure again mingled at frighteningly intense levels. Mothers, it seems to me, live balanced on the fine edge of this emotional pendulum.

I lean against the counter to drink the tea, steeped black and strong. My own mother could move in an instant from love to rage, from reading to us to beating us. And there have been more times than I want to acknowledge when I understood her urges all too well—that terrifying rocket I used to make from one emotion to the next when my children were small and I wanted to hit them, to tower over them the way I was once towered over. I feared that my children would be the death of me, or eat me alive: they would either kill me with joy and laughter and pride, or with frustration, anger, and fury. Love has many facets—and all of them are edged with razor-sharp intensity.

Alexander's stereo cuts out mid-song and the house resounds with silence. I breathe a sigh of relief: one more altercation avoided. He's at the age where he still does what I tell him, but never without an argument. The taste of the tea lies on my tongue, heavy as an herb.

The wicked stepmother is a staple of the childhood fairy tale, and so it comes as no great surprise that, after the bereaved husband buries his beloved wife beneath the juniper tree in their front yard, he marries again. Stepmothers, in our imagination, and even in reality perhaps, represent all those aspects of our own mothers that we loathe or by which we are frightened. Reading about the evil stepmother enables us to conquer our fear of Mother, especially when we see her defeated or vanquished, or better yet, killed.

The stepmother in "The Juniper Tree" dislikes her new son so intensely that she reviles him with cruel words and beats him. Then "the devil enters her" and she begins to plot against him. I look at the clock on the stove and think about dinner— it's getting close to five. But the truth is that suddenly I am exhausted by the idea of taking this story apart and discovering myself inside of it. Suddenly it seems beyond me, both intellectually and emotionally.

I don't, however, allow myself to give in to the comfort of a domestic routine just yet. Instead I push myself to imagine such a woman, the devil entering her, the sexuality of the scene. And then, my conscious brain both focused on and distracted by that image, I flash onto something else: my own mother, her private devil snapping into her, up through the spine outward to the skin, rage overcoming reason as she tantrums on the floor of her study, beating her fists and feet against the gold wool carpet, screaming at me. Insanity was the devil. When it entered her, it transformed her into a woman out of control, someone who hated me. And I hated her back.

Remembering my mother this way always upsets me, and today is no exception. I allow myself to go to the refrigerator now, to soothe myself by gathering together salad ingredients. Salad is always the easiest way to start, with its no-nonsense chopping of obvious ingredients. I stretch to take down the oval wooden bowl John and I received as a wedding present seventeen years ago, and find comfort in its smooth grain between my hands: it is the distance between this life and that. I use it to push back the monsters of my psyche, the wolf under the bed, the creak on the floorboard.

But "The Juniper Tree" is not a simple salad, and abuse is not enough to appease the stepmother's greedy appetite. She plots to kill the little boy so that she and her daughter will inherit all her husband's land and money. One afternoon she arranges for the little boy to reach into an open trunk in her bedroom in search of an apple and as he bends over it she slams the lid down, severing his head. This boy, as white as snow, as red as blood: his purity embodied by how innocently he reached into that trunk; his destiny—the red spill of his blood—predicted several years earlier by his unsuspecting mother.

The stepmother arranges the boy's body in a chair outside the room, ties a handkerchief around his neck to hide the gaping wound, and balances his head back atop the corpse. The ill-fated apple is set in his hand. Then she manipulates her daughter, Marlinchen, into asking him for the apple. When he refuses his sister with his silence, the stepmother counsels her daughter to "box him on the ear." Marlinchen asks her brother once again, then boxes his ear as directed and gets the shock of her life when his head rolls onto the floor.

She runs downstairs, screaming with fear, to tell her mother that she has killed her brother. The stepmother encourages Marlinchen's automatic assumption of the blame and gives her no comfort. "What have you done?" she says. "Be quiet and let no one know it."

I begin to slice the lettuce, throwing it by the handful into the big wooden bowl. Nicholas comes in and offers to help; he likes to cook, but this time I refuse. I want to be alone. I am working the story out in my mind as I use my hands. I picture myself as that little boy and know that in seeing something of my life in his I have forged a link between us: I am remembering what it was like to be small and afraid; I am remembering what it was like to be twenty-one and afraid, reading my mother's letters for the first time in my role as her literary executor, discovering passages wherein she refers to the times she tried to choke me in my crib.

I begin to seed a green pepper, realizing suddenly that at the point in the story where Marlinchen assumes the blame for the crime, I have suddenly moved beyond empathizing with the dead woman buried under the juniper tree or the murdered boy. Now I also want to cry for the little girl who suffers the hell of her unearned guilt. Childhood, with its attendant and inevitable magical thinking, has guilt enough to spare. How many years did I feel that if I could just be a better child, a more likable daughter, my mother would not try to kill herself. I was convinced that I was the one responsible for her self-destruction. Now I know the truth, but when I was small I thought I could be Joan of Arc. I sweep the peppers into the wooden bowl, and then consider olives, tomatoes, onions. I sharpen my knife again.

The body must be disposed of, of course, so the stepmother chops her stepson into pieces as easily as carving a turkey and then makes him into "black puddings." Marlinchen weeps without ceasing and so there is no need of any salt for the seasoning. Over dinner that evening, the father swallows his wife's lie that the son has gone to visit an uncle, and eats heartily—blindly—of his son's body. He is so taken with the black puddings that he gorges on them, tossing the bones under the table, bones that Marlinchen retrieves and takes to bury beneath the juniper tree, weeping tears of blood.

The juniper tree comes to life as she approaches with the bones, "as if someone were rejoicing." Surely this animation is the renewed spirit of the boy's buried mother. A mist rises from its branches, a fire ignites, and from the midst of the fire a beautiful bird flies out, singing a song of intense beauty. The bones in Marlinchen's hand disappear, and I remember how I longed to have a mother who could resurrect my childhood for me, to restore to me the safety I so craved, to relieve me of my responsibility for the one adult I most adored.

The bird flies over the town, singing merrily, drawing attention to himself with his beautiful song, but the various townspeople who listen to him seem unable to recognize or to hear the words of the song—yet they are enchanted by his music. The lyric tells the truth of what happened to him: "My mother she killed me, my father he ate me, my sister, little Marlinchen, gathered all my bones, tied them in a silken handkerchief, laid them beneath the juniper tree." It is as if he is singing a poem in a language they cannot interpret: the language of death, about which so many of us—including me, still standing at my chopping board—do not want to hear. Yet, the townspeople are so entranced by the song's beauty that they ask him to sing it repeatedly. The bird cockily refuses to do so without being paid and thus he receives a gold chain from the goldsmith, a pair of red shoes from the shoemaker, and a millstone from the miller's men. Bearing his gifts he flies back to the juniper tree and begins the song once again.

Inside the house, the family still sits eating their supper of black puddings, but the stepmother feels uneasy and anxious. "My teeth chatter," she says, "and I seem to have fire in my veins." The father is entranced by the bird's song and goes out to listen to it. He does not hear the words either, only the beauty of the music, and as he stands there, listening happily, the bird drops the golden chain down around his neck. Inside the stepmother lies writhing on the floor as if poisoned, plugging her ears; she, it appears, understands the lyric only too well.

From the house comes Marlinchen, who, significantly, is the only character in the story to receive the honor of a name. She listens to the bird's splendid music, and receives a gift of the red shoes. Skipping back to the dining room, she tells her mother how good she feels. The stepmother rises, her hair standing on end "like flames of fire," and goes out the door. The bird lets the millstone drop on her head and she is crushed; smoke and flames rise from the spot; her body vanishes and out of the ashes steps the little boy. He and Marlinchen take each other's hands and go back to have supper with their father, as if they are starting life all over.

Marlinchen was the only one who cared enough to sweep up her brother's bones and bury them. After my mother's suicide, there was a three-year interval during which general family procrastination allowed her crematorium box to wait in my father's closet; no one was willing to settle her remains in a permanent location. One day I picked up the box that held the chips of her bones and used the seatbelt to strap it into the passenger seat of the car. I drove it to the cemetery to make arrangements. I too was the caretaker, free storage for lost souls.

The salad is finished and I turn on the oven. I mix oil, balsamic vinegar, and herbs for dressing. I snap green beans and put a big kettle full of water over the flame. The children pass in and out, moving like fish through the underwater action of my kitchen, the heart of my home. I watch them and think about all the different ways in which the children in "The Juniper Tree" are ultimately extremely powerful. The vengeance they enact is a very simple solution to a truly complicated situation—that in and of itself was the stuff of my most powerful childhood fantasy: in the end the underdogs conquer the world. Those who were victims become victors. When I was small I dreamed of the day I would be powerful and strong enough never to be at the mercy of adults who were out of control again.

In our home, language itself was of prime importance: my mother labored long and hard over each syllable she wrote; my father gloried in crossword puzzles; when my sister or I asked the meaning of a word, we were told to go and look it up in the big dictionary that lay conveniently open on the counter in my mother's writing room. Yet in "The Juniper Tree," the townspeople do not hear the words the bird is singing; they do not want, or are not psychologically equipped, or perhaps just do not care, to comprehend the truth of the slaughter—like the townspeople of Oscwiecim in World War II who watched the cattle cars stuffed full of Jews clatter down the steel rails, who lived next to Auschwitz's ovens and pretended not to notice the black stench that filled the sky. Despite the fact that people turn aside from *what* the bird sings in favor of *how* he sings, the bird tells the truth and so ultimately his beautiful, finely crafted song becomes the tool with which he vindicates himself. He requires payment to sing the song more than once and then uses that payment to vanquish the woman who killed him.

While I set the table with knives, forks, and spoons, I reflect that "The Juniper Tree" is also a lesson in spiritual afterlife, and this aspect, too, took root and flowered in the imagination of the child I was. Marlinchen was the keeper of the bones and she brought her brother back to life by guarding them well. When

I was young, I believed that I could save my mother from her own death wish. Long before she committed suicide, however, I had to come to terms with the fact that this was only a fantasy, that I could never succeed in saving her if she were truly determined to die. This was a realization that nearly killed me, for there was a time when I would have traded my life for hers— or, put more accurately, there was a time when I did not want to live if I had to be separated from her. Her numerous hospitalizations often did separate us, continually restimulating my greatest fear of the most lasting separation: her death. In "The Juniper Tree," however, the good mother lives on in the tree, giving strength to her son, being present throughout all the seasons—her spirit transformed but forever watchful over her son's welfare. Her spirit resides inside that tree—fueled by the intense love so many mothers bear their children.

The little boy is actually reborn twice—first as a bird, then as himself—both times through the healing fire of his mother's love. The fairy tale gave voice to my childhood fantasy that I would be reborn into a loving family, where the parents took charge with authority and love, and that my mother would be reborn into a woman both steady and sane.

The story's first climax comes when the bird flies out of the tree and the bones disappear from Marlinchen's hand, the second when he drops the millstone on the head of the stepmother. For all the fantasies I had of saving my own mother, or of gathering her bones and helping her to be reborn, I had an equal number, I am certain, of retaliating for what I felt were her inadequacies. And so, when the little boy returns from the dead in the form of the beautiful bird to kill the stepmother who murdered him, I see just how the stepmother operates in my mind—perhaps in every reader's mind—as a surrogate for my own mother's undesirable aspects. On some level, it did not matter to me that my mother had struggled against her own lack of control in her loathing of me, had struggled not to use me badly or beat me. In fact, sometimes the very idea that she had struggled to be a better mother enraged me further: I didn't want to know she had tried because it was easier just to think that she had been monstrous, literally, a wicked step-mother. In those moments, I wished I could have been as clever as the bird with his millstone, or as strong as Gretel with her magnificent, soul-affirming push. I wanted to shove my very own witch into the oven in the small brick colonial we called home.

At the end of *Searching for Mercy Street*, my memoir about my relationship with my mother, I retold a dream I had while I was finishing the final chapters of the book. At the unconscious root of the dream lies the metaphor of Hansel and Gretel, that old story of maternal cannibalism. In this dream I am part girl, part woman, lost in the forest of my own grief over her death, following a path that leads to a reunion with my mother, who by then had been gone twenty years but who had described herself in one of her early poems as "a possessed witch/haunting the black air, braver at night; dreaming evil . . . twelve-fingered, out of mind."

Finally I reach a clearing and the witch emerges from her gingerbread house, both delighted and despairing over the ways in which we have both changed during the last twenty years. As she stands there, poised on the cusp of the last moon of her life, I can see from her expression that she envies my youth. She takes my hands and we dance in a circle, then sit down to feast on coconuts filled with milk. I watch her eyes "twitch over the fat of my breast, the long sinew of my thigh. I am her chicken biddy. I am her drumstick."

Though I still fear her intentions, she is old now, and she does not challenge me: once again, apparently, I am the person in charge, but this time appropriately so. She offers me food and then, in the dream, I offer her a poem I have written. Poetry was the language in which she was accustomed to speak and thus left no room for misunderstanding. Today the poem seems to me something of a gauntlet thrown down, a younger woman's challenge to the older, an insistence that ancient powers be passed on, a sharp retort to that original theft of my book of fairy tales. I had dreamed a poem while she could only write them.

The dream's and poem's meanings both whirl around the central image of cannibalism—as does "The Juniper Tree," where the stepmother and father eat the child. When I awakened from the dream in the middle of the night, I went immediately into my office to write it down. With it I buried my mother's bones at last, releasing us both from the winding sheet of my grief.

Mother,
we know what we are about.
The oven door
is a hungry black mouth. It
waits.

I have what you need.
I have what you want.
Love binds

desire. Is it a dream
that I slide you into the black
water of the oven?

Is it a dream
that I launch your long
motionless body, well-kept
with my devotion, sleek
with my love?
Is it a dream
that you go
without a ripple
just
my face
salt-slicked
at your smooth glide
out?

The whole of *Transformations* was filled with an abundance of gluttonous culinary metaphors, new babies like artichokes and toddlers like lamb chops, the young girl in Rumpelstiltskin pictured as luscious, sleek, and round as a grape. In "Godfather Death," the princess is as ripe as a tangerine, and in "The Maiden Without Hands," the wizard wants to lap her up like strawberry jam. How often did my mother tell both my sister and me, "I love you so much I could eat you up!" as she nuzzled our ears, our cheeks, our hair. She nicknamed me "Linda Pie" and "chicken biddy"; in her version of Hansel and Gretel, as the witch lights her oven at 350 degrees, she refers to the child as "my fritter, my bubbler, my chicken biddy!"

The imagery she employed in *Transformations* undoubtedly

took some root in the fairy tales themselves: in the Grimms' version of "Rapunzel" the name Rapunzel means rampion—a species of precious salad leaf the pregnant woman craved and for which she sent her husband over the wall into the witch's private garden. In exchange for some lettuce, the flesh of a child: thus was Rapunzel named for the food for which her mother had abandoned her.

As I shred carrots in the food processor I think about the most vivid detail of "The Juniper Tree": not the glossy bird or his beautiful song, not the abrupt beheading, not the tears of blood that Marlinchen weeps, but instead those indescribable black puddings the stepmother makes from the boy's body. I imagine a black pudding to be something like a blood sausage. Ground finely and seasoned highly, rich in oozy organ meats, black with blood and baked in a shallow pan like a lasagna. Nasty but very rich. I can see her now, her apron stained, her spatula reddened, as she strips the bones and cranks her meat grinder. Reading this scene gave me a ghastly sort of thrill—as if I had crept into a house of horror to witness, undetected, the unimaginable. And yet was it really so hard to imagine? I had grown up in a home dominated entirely by the devil who plagued my mother with hospitalizations, the uncontrollable siren's song of art, and last but not least, her admitted desire to kill both her children and herself.

There is a now-and-then aspect to reading fairy tales: I remember the child I was as I read today, but I drag in the woman I am as well. The full cycle of my life is captured in this one seven-page story: the abused child, the child with fantasies of revenge, the child with fantasies of rescue, the child who both adored and hated the omnipotent parent who controlled everything in her life; and then the mother I am today as well, who identifies with the woman dying from joy at her child's birth, who empathizes with the stepmother raging with envy at her child, who rejoices when that stepmother is vanquished by that child. I am the mother who refrains from tagging her own children with edible terms of endearment and yet finds it difficult not to nibble and nip along the irresistible length of their growing bones and ripening cheeks.

As I put the finished salad into the refrigerator to chill, I wonder why I never read any of these fairy tales aloud to my own children. They knew Mother Goose but never Mother Gothel. Why didn't I ever give them the book, or provide them with a copy of their own? Why didn't I ever suggest they check it out of the library? My kids, raised on politically incorrect pistols and Terminator movies, haven't been sheltered from the gore of nineties entertainment; after all, Alexander's favorite author is Stephen King. Still, maybe Grimms' fairy tales is my version of an X-rated movie. Nothing I want my children to see. Or hear. Or experience.

From time to time, I still pull this book down from the shelf, especially when I am writing; recently I discovered details from "The Maiden Without Hands" and "Godfather Death" popping up in the novel on which I am currently at work. I found myself rereading the stories, mesmerized once again; I was startled to realize that the fairy tales were still deeply twined into my unconscious life, and because the act of writing taps the vein of the unconscious so silently, the tales flood back into my current stories with their metaphors and morals at the times when I am most unaware, most deeply immersed in creation. I had thought I could leave the Grimm brothers behind, but—as with any strong and complicated relationship—it has not proved to be nearly as simple as that.

I turn the oven on, string my stained apron around my neck, and take out three kinds of ground meat: one pound beef, one veal, one pork. I pull my largest stainless steel mixing bowl from beneath the counter and open the packages wrapped in white butcher paper. I chop celery, garlic, and onions and set them frying in the skillet. I line up bay leaf and thyme on the countertop, work eggs and bread crumbs into the bloody meat with my hands. The mixture squishes through my fingers and I remember my mother teaching me how to blend a meat loaf, lightly but firmly, enough to mix it but not hard enough to make it heavy. I still use her recipe, altered somewhat for flavor. What, I wonder now, is the recipe for black puddings? Surely the wicked stepmother used the one her own mother had given her, the one passed from generation hand to hand, its basic formula altered only by time and the touch of each woman's individual craving.

MIDORI SNYDER

* * * * * *

The Monkey Girl

When I was a girl reading fairy tales, I appreciated those courageous maidens tromping off in iron shoes or flying on the back of the west wind to find their future husbands where they, imprisoned by trolls or cannibal mothers, waited to be rescued. I admired those young women and their single-minded purpose. They were bold, resourceful, and spirited. And they were certainly a far cry from the "waiting-to-be-awakened" girls or the girls expecting to be fitted with a shoe, a Prince, and a future all at the same time.

Yet even in their plucky natures and heroic tales, there was still something about them that troubled me. Perhaps it was the assumption of happily-ever-after, or at least the seeming surrender of all that reckless adventure. Their rites of passage completed, the journey to find a husband over, there was an expectation that life for these young women would settle once again into neatly defined roles and an untroubled routine. This assumption didn't sit well with me at all. I knew from my own family that such happily-ever-afters were not true. I had parents who had met and married in a passion, and then just as passionately argued, accused, betrayed, and divorced each other. The photographs of their early years depict the blissful expressions worn by most newly married couples, but the later years proved ugly, full of dark misadventures and contentious battles over money. Though I left home at seventeen, inspired I think by the example of those stalwart maidens, I roamed the world in iron shoes forged by my parents' issues and no other goal in my mind except to escape their battles. Eventually, my money dissolved, the shoes became as thin as paper, and I returned home.

What a surprise then to discover a scant year later that home had all but disappeared. A Central Asian scholar, my mother had boarded a bus in Istanbul and traveled for two weeks across Afghanistan, following the Silk Road up to India, where she was now living, indefinitely it seemed. My father and his new wife returned from Africa and moved to another state. My older brother and I temporarily inherited the house along with its mortgage and one of my mother's dysfunctional, melancholic friends as a roommate. I received phone calls from my mother at odd hours of the night, from Delhi, Calcutta, and Bombay, mostly asking me to wire money. During the days I worked at a movie theatre, selling popcorn and watching *Dirty Harry* play to a nearly empty house. It didn't seem right. She was out there reinventing herself and I was here, stuck. I wanted to be angry with her, but the truth was I admired her. She was difficult, unpredictable, but also interesting and indomitable. I concluded that she had needed that difficult spirit to survive the dismal destruction of her happily-ever-after.

At the end of my eighteenth year I enrolled in college and

met my husband. It happened with the unreal grace of a fairy tale—a single sentence really. There was an introduction, a smile, a night and almost immediately we were attached at the hip. As pleased with each other as we were, it was disconcerting to find our joy not shared by our friends. According to his family and certainly his suburban friends from high school, I was an unlikely choice, a disaster, and an aberration. It was the seventies; I was too political for them, too opinionated; I wore flannel shirts and glasses and said "fuck" earnestly and often. His friends whispered that he had been snared by a girl who wasn't playing by the usual rules. I was neither compliant, nor pretty in the way one expects of an accessory, and I was known to have claws, verbal comebacks that stung. His parents were convinced that I was the reason he strayed from the church. I was a fornicator, from the wrong class, a pathetic child of a broken home who could only spell disaster for their errant son.

Yet on the other side of the field my women friends from the university shook their heads in equal disapproval. Self-proclaimed radical feminists, these "Red Sisters" argued that marriage was bourgeois, that women in such bonds were no more than property, and they determined that the only way to avoid the trap was to sleep with one anothers' husbands and boyfriends, swapping them like shoes or sweaters. I refused such invitations—I had already seen where that road led and I wasn't anxious to retrace my parents' footsteps. Monogamy and true love may have been reactionary, but I found them challenging, full of creative possibilities, and, among my girlfriends, mostly untried.

Still, it was difficult and lonely to be on the margins of two worlds, so I remember the thrill I felt recognizing a kindred spirit the first time I encountered "The Monkey Girl," a tale

from the Kordofan people of the Sudan. The youngest son of an
Emir is asked to choose a bride from the eligible maidens of his
village. The Prince rides his horse up and down, spear in hand,
ready to cast it at the door of the chosen girl. But he seems unable to decide and, in a moment of frustration, casts the spear
far out into the desert. For two days he journeys after it only to
discover the spear embedded in the trunk of a lone tree, and in
whose leafless branches sits a monkey. As the Prince approaches, the monkey inclines her head and in a gentle voice
accepts the proposal of marriage. And the Prince? Well, he is
the hero, a man of integrity, true to his word, so he pulls the
monkey up behind him on the horse and together they return
to the village to be married.

As one might imagine, it's difficult for the Prince. The Emir
is appalled; the Prince's brothers, married to wealthy brides,
pity him. Hearing the Prince's heavy sighs, the monkey makes
him an offer. "Return me to the desert and I promise there will
be another woman, more beautiful than you can imagine, waiting for you on your return." "And you?" the Prince inquires.
"What will happen to you?" "I will die," she answers simply. The
Prince is a decent and compassionate sort, and though it would
improve his situation immensely, he refuses to sacrifice the
monkey's life. Yet when the Emir decides to dine in each one of
his sons' homes, the young Prince is overwhelmed with dismay
for their house is a dark hovel, their meals poor fare. The monkey repeats her offer, but once again the Prince refuses. The
monkey tells the Prince to invite his father for the evening meal
and that all will be ready for his arrival. When father and son
enter the house, the Prince is astonished to discover a miraculous transformation. Beneath the golden gleam of a hundred oil
lamps the once-barren rooms are now sumptuously decorated.

There are plush carpets patterned with flowers, embroidered silk pillows on which to recline, and low tables spread with silver and copper platters of rich, steaming food. The men are amazed, and for the first time, the Prince begins to wonder about his bride.

What follows is a delicious, slow striptease as the monkey unveils her secrets to the Prince one pale limb at a time over a number of nights. Three times the curious Prince spies on the monkey and manages to catch sight of her sitting before a mirror and deftly peeling back a portion of her furry hide. By moonlight he can see a slender wrist, the curve of her ivory breast, a naked shoulder. Each time he moves toward her, she twirls her finger and a sandstorm fills the little room, blinding him. Only when she is at last ready to emerge as a lovely young woman is the Prince able to steal the skin and burn it. As she stands before him in all her splendor, the Prince is appropriately humbled and awed by his fantastic bride. United at last as a couple, their marriage is now on a sure and heroic footing.

That should have been enough of a happy ending. But it isn't and with good reason. How can a woman of power, of fantastic substance from that world beyond the boundaries of the human world, be tamed, slotted into the narrow role of a wife? What indeed would be the point of reducing her to the ordinary? The Prince and the Monkey Girl are happily married, but the happily-ever-after is threatened when the Emir begins to lust after the young woman. He imposes impossible tasks on his son, proclaiming death if the Prince fails to complete them. Of course, it is his fantastic bride who rescues him. Effortlessly drawing on her power, she makes the gardens bear fruit overnight and just as easily consumes a storehouse of food during the second night. In the final task she tricks the Emir into agreeing to his own death should the Prince succeed in making a newborn infant learn to walk and talk in a single day. The following morning the child walks into the hall announcing the Emir's death sentence and the ascension of the young Prince to the throne. Not just a pretty face, this monkey girl, but wise and adept at managing agriculture, politics, law, and dangerous men.

What fascinated me the most in this story was not the obvious ugly monkey to beautiful woman transformation. It was the idea that the Monkey Girl controlled not only the destiny of her own rite of passage, but also that of the Prince. Through the agency of the spear—a wonderful manipulation of the phallic sign—she brings the Prince out into the fantastic realm to her to begin his journey. Similarly, cloaked in the animal skin, she embarks on her own rite of passage, journeying back to the human world while the storyteller in her recounts in figurative language the scenario of her death as an adolescent girl and her resurrection as an adult woman ready for marriage. She uses her disguise not only to complete her rite of passage, but also to test her husband's worthiness, his integrity, his compassion, and the strength of their bond. Little by little, she reveals herself to him, gradually making him aware of the considerable hidden power she possesses. Can he handle it? Will he be frightened? Or worse, will he try to control and possess her like the Emir?

It is the task of the hero to wrestle with the ambiguous power of the fantastic world and return with its fully creative potential in hand. The young Prince proves his loyalty and compassion, and from the monkey's bestial skin there emerges a beautiful bride. This bride is unlike her mortal counterparts, no matter how brave and courageous they may appear in the other tales, for she represents a union, a partnership between the human hero and the creative forces of the fantastic world. In their marriage, hero and fantastic bride work together as equals to enrich each other's lives and strengthen their community.

But this is one bride who must never must be underestimated or taken for granted in the happily-ever-after. The beastly bride, while she may shed her skin or commit herself as a sensual partner, never surrenders her power and therefore always remains a little dangerous, a little unpredictable. There are beastly brides who hide their scales, their fur, and don the bodies of women in order to marry men for their own reasons and have children. Perhaps these brides should come with warning labels—disrespect us at your own peril! Husbands transgressing by peering into keyholes to learn the hidden truth about their wives run the risk of losing all the privileges such fantastic women provide them. And while the tales of beastly brides may be regarded as the cautionary warnings of a patriarchal society convinced that the difficult woman hides a furry tail, scaled thighs, or a demon's appetite, I, for one, rejoice in them. They force the essential questions of marriage: Can you respect the power I hold, the secrets that are mine, the space that is reserved for me alone and still be loving? Can marriage be a union of two forces each with their own gifts to be offered freely, mutually acknowledged, respected, and supported? And if the answer is no and the marriage hits a bump, a snag in the happily-ever-after, these women pack their bags and leave for the forests, the deserts, the deep oceans, or India, angry, but undaunted. Years after their divorce, my father confessed to me that he had often told my mother in their bitter fights that it seemed she couldn't decide whether to be a mother or an academic. It was with regret that he had recognized too late that

had he supported her, she could have been both. A beastly
bride, my mother was too difficult and too rich in resources for
my father to appreciate and love until she was gone.

The tale of the Monkey Girl gave me what I needed most at
a critical time in my life: the image of the creative and complex
woman, unique to herself but willing to share those considerable gifts with a man capable of intuiting the wealth of her
worth hidden beneath the skin. But more than that, the
Monkey Girl also suggested that I need not be afraid of the fragile happily-ever-after, that I had resources of my own, and that
I would not have to contort myself into a restrictive social role
for fear of losing that fairytale ending. There was always travel.
I gained courage resisting the tyranny of those opposing sides:
the one that argued I was too radical and sharp, and the other
that insisted I was a deluded, romantic traditionalist caught in
the jaws of a bourgeois trap. Thirty years later, still happily married to the same man, I feel a debt of gratitude to the powerful
example of the fantastic bride.

When I began to write novels I experienced again the presence of the Monkey Girl at my shoulder, pushing me, encouraging me. What better teacher could I have had? For out of the
mysteries, the imagination, the realm of all things fantastic, she
creates and transforms life: gardens out of the desert sands,
wealth out of a hovel, feasts out of dry bread, precocious children out of newborns, and a husband out of a promising but
confused young hero. She has a flare for drama, disguise, and illusion. From the moment the Prince releases his spear in her
direction, she controls the story, manipulating the narrative,
repetition fueling a smoldering sexual anticipation that cli-
maxes when she at last reveals herself quite nude and available.

But behind the Monkey Girl there is another woman, the

one who tells this tale, the one who repeats it over and over again so that we may always remain respectfully awed by the provocative and resplendent power of the fantastic bride. Who could resist admiring the skill of such a potent storyteller? Certainly not me, and so it is in my own work that I follow this well-worn path and take pleasure in writing the tales of difficult women, ambiguous and fantastic women, women whose fairytale-like stories I never grow tired of imagining.

FAY WELDON

* * * * * *

The Journey to Mr. Fox

Reader, I married him. The ring slips upon the finger. What is *Jane Eyre*, what is many a well-known novel which penetrates the archetype, that tells of transformation and destiny, but a fairy tale bereft of the trappings of enchantment? What we long to know, what we yearn to hear, happy endings for the well-intended, (so long as you keep to the rules, but first decipher the letters of fire) misfortune for the bad, true enough in a Jungian sense, just not in the real world. Swinegirl (little Jane Eyre) catches Prince (Mr. Rochester). Froggish Mr. Knightly, in Jane Austen's *Emma*, turns marriageable when kissed. Madame Bovary takes arsenic and meets her destiny. A likely and rewarding tale, this happy-ever-after in the head, and justice done: the unquiet fairy tale settled into novel form. You never know: perhaps the tellers of the tale, bards and novelists alike, in their obsessions, in their imaginings, in their picking up of trifles of misremembered sayings, the collective unconscious forging ahead, dream adding to dream, hark forward into a future, not backward into a misty past. How would we ever know?

Reader, I married him. In 1992 I fell in love with and married a Mr. Fox, in spite of the warnings in a fairy tale I knew well, having written an admonitory novel around the tale back in 1976, calling it, quite directly, *Words of Advice*. In the U.K. the title, as it happens, was changed to *Little Sisters—Words of Advice*, sounding too like a book of moral strictures, which it was, for the comfort of British publishers. The tale was that of Lady Mary and Mr. Fox: its instruction and warning—be bold, be bold, but not *too* bold. Evil presents itself as good: penetrate that evil to discover it: keep your wits about you, and righteous rage will save you.

Let me tell you the story of Mr. Fox and Lady Mary, as told by Gemma, rich and beautiful, to Elsa, poor and pretty, in this novel of mine, *Words of Advice*.

Lady Mary the High Lord's daughter was betrothed by her father to the noble Mr. Fox. The day before her wedding, too inquisitive for her own good, she'd stolen into Mr. Fox's house to see what she could see. BE BOLD was written in letters of fire above the first door, and all within was grand and quiet: BE BOLD was written above the second door, and there too all was orderly and peaceful. But above the third door flamed the words BUT NOT TOO BOLD. Just a door, thought Lady Mary, like any other door, and in she went on tippy-toe. The other side of the third door she found a charnel house and her beloved Mr. Fox feasting with his friends. A robber baron, that he was, her Mr. Fox, the meal he ate was human flesh. As Lady Mary crouched hidden in her dark corner, watching, a severed fin-

*ger flew across the room, and fell into her lap and on that finger
she saw a ring. So she slipped the ring from the finger, and crept
away with it and that night showed it to her brothers; and when
the next morning came and with it her marriage day, and handsome Mr. Fox came up the aisle to marry her, her brothers fell upon
him and killed him; and so justice was done.*

In the end it is the evil Mr. Fox who is too bold, allowing himself
to be discovered, and so destroying himself: not Lady Mary,
whose boldness saves her: and the ring, of course, symbol of
safety, though it clearly failed to help its original owner. In the
novel Gemma is married to a millionaire and is confined by a
hysterical paralysis to a wheelchair. She has taken her nineteen-
year-old houseguest, Elsa, under her wing, and persists in giving
her unwanted advice by means of fairy tale. The author herself
does much the same for the reader, using the novel as vehicle.

In familiar telltale singsong rhythms, if not content, the novel
begins thus:

*We all have friends who are richer than ourselves and they, you
may be sure, have richer friends of their own. We are most of us
within spitting distance of millionaires.*

Spit away——if that's what you feel like.

*But after the manner of these things, Elsa, who has not a
penny to her name——except the remnants of last week's pay
packet——knows Victor, who is an antique dealer, who knows
Hamish and Gemma, who are millionaires.*

*And Victor and Elsa, one Friday evening, cursed or lucky
things, sit in Victor's big new light-blue Volvo at the gates of*

Ditton House, where Hamish and Gemma live, and wait for the
great teak veneered doors to open and let them through.

 Victor is forty-four. Elsa is nineteen, and his mistress. A year
ago, when Victor was still a tax accountant, he fished Elsa out of
his typist's pool. She flapped and wriggled a little, and then lay
still, legs gently parted.

(Elsa—as I describe her, and I come to this novel almost as a
stranger, since I haven't referred to it, let alone read it, for
twenty years, and I daresay I barely read it then—writing a
novel is so entirely a different matter from reading it—is
"abundantly lovely," she is the robust woodcutter's daughter
rather than the princess who can feel the pea under the pile of
mattresses. That's Gemma's style: in *Words of Advice* the two archetypes meet and battle it out.)

She (Elsa) weighs twelve stone four pounds and is five feet eight
inches tall. Her swelling bosom and rounded hips give ample
promise of pneumatic bliss. Her skin is white; her cheeks red; her
hair browny-gold, and thick, and long. Her face is perhaps rather
heavy and her expression sleepy; but whether that is good or bad
depends on what you want her for. Her blue eyes, when she can be
induced to raise them, are innocent enough. This evening Elsa is
wearing her best: old jeans whose every tattered seam she knows
and loves and a faded mauve shirt with a button missing.

 Ah, she's beautiful; lush and not louche. Another button pops
now, as she bends.

(Victor is six foot two, weighs fourteen stone and is an established antique dealer. He is not a prince; rather he is Emperor.
And swinegirls and kitchenmaids are meant to consort with

potential princes, not established men of middle years. Trouble
of some kind is bound to ensue.)

*And behold, gliding down the long paneled hall to meet them, her
powered wheelchair moving with the silence of the most expensive
machinery, comes Gemma.*

*Seen from a distance she is a child: her smile radiant and full
of expectation. As her chair approaches, years pass. She is twenty,
twenty-five, thirty, thirty-five—older, older still. Or is that just
a trick of the light? Because she lives in pain, or longs for death?
And that is all her expectation.*

*Gemma stretches out her pretty hand to greet first Victor, then
Elsa. She is young, after all. Barely thirty.*

(After their initial meeting, in which Gemma insists on mistak-
ing Elsa for Wendy, Victor's daughter, Elsa is sent without ceremony to her room.)

*Elsa is embarrassed to the point of tears—(how she overflows, al-
ways bubbling and erupting into the outside world: she blushes,
she cries, she stumbles, she is sick; she gets diarrhea or cystitis at
the drop of a hat; she coughs up phlegm; her nose runs; as if there
was far more of her than could ever easily be contained).
Sniveling, Elsa is obliged to follow the servants along ever-
narrowing corridors to a small room overlooking the central
nexus of the house—the work area where the kitchens are, and
the dustbins, and the compost heap, and the coal cellars. Then up
and up they go to a room as chaste and ordinary as Gemma's was
luxurious. It has cream walls, green painted woodwork, a narrow
bed with white sheets and gray blankets, a locker, a basin, a plain*

white towel on a peg and a small yellowy piece of soap in the washbasin. There is no mirror, but under the window stands an old brown office desk. And on the desk is a new typewriter; manual, not even electric. On the floor are stacked reams of typing paper: top, carbons, and flimsy in assorted colors. There is a tin filing cabinet—full of empty folders; waiting, but for what?—and a small wastepaper basket.

Elsa throws open the window, and leans out. She is four stories up. Her long hair falls over the sill and down over empty space. She is frightened.

Elsa lies upon the bed and shivers. She does not like being alone. She is one of seven children. She is not a good typist. She tries, but even if she gets the words correct, sheets emerge from the machine crumpled, untidy and smudged. The typewriter sits on the desk like some unfair challenge; the filing cabinet like some test she knows she will fail: the drop from the window an unspoken threat.

Defenestrated!

A fairy story comes to Elsa's mind: that of the incompetent peasant girl who boasted of her prowess at weaving, and was shut up in the castle by the king and set to work weaving banks of straw into gold. Has Elsa likewise claimed to be what she is not—a secretary, when in fact she can barely type a line without smudges and mistakes? Is her presumption now to be punished? And who is her Rumpelstiltskin to be; the dwarf who visits by night and performs the impossible task, claiming her firstborn child unless she can guess his name?

(Is she to bear a child to Hamish? Surely this too is not required of Elsa?)

Oh, grief so harshly punished! And poor Rumpelstiltskin, fit only to be used and abused! This and many other bitter tales Elsa would later tell her brothers and sisters at bedtime.

But perhaps she is being too gloomy: perhaps the typewriter is coincidental: perhaps her nightly visitor will be the Prince whose face must never be looked at, in case he's seen to be a toad after all. Well, easy enough not to look. Just to lie back and accept.

Or perhaps, since she is so clearly now imprisoned in a tower, snatched out of Victor's double bed by the witch Gemma, her prince will come to rescue her, climbing the tower, using her yellow hair as a rope? But how did that story end? Alas, the Prince was toppled from the tower by the witch, and blinded by the brambles below, never to look on beauty again.

(Go too far and fate will get you! If the Prince had been content with serenading Rapunzel, had only looked but never touched, he might have survived with his sight intact: had the peasant girl at last learned how to weave flax into gold—at night class—she might have defied the witch—her mother, the sexual rival—and come down of her own account.)

Elsa shivers. Although there seems little forbidden to her about her own beauty, perhaps God has other ideas?

The door is pushed open. The Prince? The dwarf? The toad? But no, it is only Victor. He has to bend to enter the room. His high-domed, much-scarred head catches, nevertheless, on the lintel: he cries out in pain. Blood flows. Elsa laughs. Victor carries folders in his hands. Recomposed, he is brisk and businesslike.

"Gemma wants these in triplicate, Elsa," he says. "It's an inventory of all the things she wants sold."

(More flax into gold, if you please!)

*"You mean this is to be a working weekend?" Elsa is plaintive,
dabbing his bald landing strip with tissue. "I thought I was a
proper guest."*

"Well—"

"They wouldn't ask Janice to type—"

(Janice is Victor's wife. Of course Victor has a wife.)

*"Janice can't type. Women should be useful. You are. It's a compli-
ment."*

Elsa is mollified, but still complains and protests.

*"I'll make a dreadful mess of it now. I'm much too tired. I'll
do it tomorrow."*

"But Gemma wants it by morning."

"I'll do it after dinner."

*Even as she speaks, Elsa has the sensation that some fixed pat-
tern of events has moved into place, and is now firmly locked, and
that whatever she says or does now in this household will be according to destiny, and not in the least according to her own desire.*

*Or is it just that, throughout her childhood, whenever Elsa
said "I'll do it later" her mother slapped her? But no—our feelings of doom, our intimation of immutable fate, must surely be
deeper than this.*

*Elsa's suspicions are correct. She is locked into Rumpelstiltskin
mode. She must turn chaff into gold, or be lost.*

(The next day, the typing delivered on time—Hamish crept
into the tower room and did it for her, to the highest standards—Gemma gives Elsa more unwanted advice.)

"You don't intend to stay a typist forever, I daresay," murmurs Gemma.

"No," says Elsa. "Of course not."

"Be careful," says Gemma, suddenly and sharply. "I know what you are thinking and I know where it can end. To be wanton, and yes, you are wanton—with your life, your sexuality, your future—is a dangerous matter. You are greedy and careless at the same time, and have made yourself a hundred times more stupid than you need be. Women do; they have to, if they are determined men shall be their masters; if they refuse to look both into the faces of men and into their own hearts."

Elsa opens her mouth to speak.

"Be quiet," says Gemma. "Say nothing. I know it isn't comfortable. I know that self-knowledge is painful. I know that to think you are a princess and find you are a beggar-girl is very disagreeable. I know that to look at a prince and find he is a toad is quite shocking. I also know, and you will probably never have the opportunity to find out, that to believe you're one of nature's beggar-girls and then end up a princess is perfectly dreadful. Don't do it. Transformation can destroy you."

Elsa blinks, startled.

"If I can read your heart, Elsa, it's because I can read my own. I have a story to tell. It's a fairy tale. I love fairy tales, don't you?"

"A bit."

"I thought you would. Princes, toads, princesses, beggar-girls—we all have to place ourselves as best we can."

Elsa has the scent of triumph in her nostrils, the taste of sexual power between her soft red lips. Something instinctive and nasty surfaces, hardens, takes possession. Other women are her enemy, she perceives. Men are there to be made her allies, her stepping-stones to fulfillment and worldly success. Elsa looks sideways at Gemma and thinks "Why, if I wanted I could have your husband too." (Thin, dry, husk-like Hamish.) "Then where would you be, Gemma," thinks Elsa, "with your unworkable legs and your crippled hand."

(Gemma, like Lady Mary, has lost a finger; her ring finger. How she comes to lose it is the tale within the tale, and it is at this point that Gemma tells Elsa the story of Mr. Fox.)

"Why is this story interesting?" asks Elsa. "I don't see it at all!"

"What is so interesting about it," says Gemma, "is that I heard it one night on someone else's transistor radio, read by Dame Edith Evans. I was on a train: I had a sleepless night behind me and another one in front of me. And the very next morning I met a Mr. Fox and fell in love with him; and rings and fingers, or the lack of them, featured prominently in my life thereafter. Had you never noticed the way the secret world sends out signs and symbols into the ordinary world? It delivers our messages in the form of coincidences: letters crossing in the post, unfamiliar tunes heard three times in one day, the way that blows of fate descend upon the same bowed shoulders, and beams of good fortune glow perpetually upon the blessed. Fairy tales, as I said, are lived out daily. There is far more going on in the world than we ever imagine."

"Just a coincidence," muttered Elsa, disbelieving.

"Just a coincidence! I love Mr. Fox and you say just?" Gemma is outraged. "It was many years ago, as they used to say at the beginning of fairy tales, when the world was fresh and young—and so was I—but it was not imagination. It was in 1966."

The tale outside the tale outside the tale, of course, validating
Gemma's claim that fairy tales are lived out daily, is the author's
falling in love ten years later with a perfectly decent Mr. Fox
and not a single brother stepping out of line to finish him off.
Coincidence, as Elsa would maintain. The world is full of Foxes,
and very few are robber barons.

With the relating of the tale, Gemma is freed from the bonds
of trauma and rises from her wheelchair to walk again: Elsa
runs home to her mother and sisters and drinks cocoa before
bed. The men drift off into other women's fantasies, circling
within their own, as princes will.

I was brought up on fairy tales—the traditional kind which
never made much sense, found in my youth in Andrew Lang's
many-colored fairy books—eleven in all, the *Blue, Green, Red*
collections, and so on—before the days of their literary-
academic deconstruction, before Bettelheim, before M. L. Von
Franz. Lang was professor of philosophy at Oxford at the turn
of the century: his view, later demoded, was that fairy tales
were mere relics of savage customs and thoughts common to
early man—such as the belief that animals can understand and
speak with a human tongue.

The effect of these tales, so far as I could see, was to fill the
heads of little girls with mystery, and provide them with those
archetypes which make for unease—why am I not slim as the
Fairy Princess? why are the Fairy Godmotherly gifts I proffer

not magic? why do I stay the beggar-girl and the Prince just looks the other way? why if I'm Cinderella is there no ball to go to? why are my good deeds not rewarded by fate? why does my goose not lay golden eggs? and so forth. But these magically written yet awkward tales at least acquainted me and many others with a turn of phrase which seemed part and parcel of the language of the King James Bible. And of course provided us all with the resonances of a common folk history and culture, without which the contemporary young—whose fairy tales have to come in Disney form—are so much the poorer.

There were as well, for childhood reading, those other fairy tales which posed as traditional, but weren't—coming as they did from the clearly tormented minds of the Brothers Grimm or the enchanted mind of Hans Christian Andersen, and were, to my mind, the better for their single, or dual, authorship, as a Beethoven variation improves on a folk-song theme. To my mind, stories which have been handed down, verbally, over centuries, are on the Chinese whispery side of validity. You can waste a whole lot of life trying to analyze them, force them into genres, picking them over for nonexistent wisdom. You need the genius of Jung to do it. For myself, as a child, Grimms' "Beauty and the Beast" at least made a kind of sense, as did "Snow White and Rose Red;" and Andersen's splinter of ice in Kay's heart and Gerda's search for her cold lover seemed all too true as parable rather than exercise in archetype; and as for "The Little Mermaid," forget Disney, the story was all too masochistically, romantically accurate. Little girls should not be allowed to read "The Little Mermaid" or they'll be inclined to walk on knives all their lives (or succumb to the cosmetic surgeon, much the same thing) in their hope that the Prince will eventually love them. The transformation from ugly duckling to swan fills the prepubertal child with unreasonable hope. After the wintry ice of rejection, the warmth of sun and acceptance will surely come. Well, perhaps, and hi there, Mr. Fox.

It was only when I stood in the Hans Christian Andersen Museum in a little town in Denmark in the early eighties, and listened to a tape of Laurence Olivier reading aloud the story "The Little Red Hen" (who thought the sky would fall upon her any minute) that I realized how much of that particular style I'd brought to my early novels. The grabbing of the reader by the throat—the urgency of tale-telling, bubbling-over narrative— "Listen, reader!" "Spit away, if that's what you feel like!" which I thought was all my own. No such luck: Hans Christian Andersen, that's all, as read by the child that was me, on the hot dry Canterbury plains of New Zealand in 1936, rewritten by me in somber Somerset in 1976, set in London's Carnaby Street, 1966. But what ever changed? Human nature stays the same: in old fairy tales or new. Even your writer turns willingly into Mrs. Fox, protected by a ring.

Transformation wins, okay.

JOY WILLIAMS

* * * * * *

Baba Yaga

Baba Yaga.

When I was a little girl I was mad for Baba Yaga and I think of her still—the Russian witch who lived in a house on chicken feet far far away at the edge of a deep forest. The chicken feet would turn the house around constantly so that no one could find the door.

For some reason I thought that to live in a house on chicken feet which revolved constantly so that no one would find the front door was fabulous, but I also very much liked Baba Yaga's other accoutrements. For example she had three pairs of disembodied hands that did the housework for her and kept the oven stoked and so forth. She also had a fence around the house made of human bones and topped with human skulls whose eyesockets would glow in the dark but that didn't alarm me overmuch. It seemed a shade excessive, perhaps. No one knew what Baba Yaga did when she left her house on her errands and flew through the air in her unlikely vehicle of choice, a mortar and pestle, sweeping clean away with a broom the trail she had made. Baba Yaga was secretive and didn't like to answer personal questions although she did explain those horsemen who galloped through her woods, overtaking those who wandered there. Dressed in black on a black horse was night and dressed in white on a white horse was day and dressed in red on a red horse was the dawn and setting sun. Baba Yaga had it down. She was no bum living in a cave. She was no common hag, no ordinary ogress with chin hair, although naturally she was bony and frightfully hideous. She had an unusual house which was just as alive as she was and although she had, perhaps, one (clay) leg in the grave, she wasn't Death itself. She was one self-contained granny. Those horsemen were *hers*—they belonged to *her* day. She lived the way she wanted to live, rather domestically. She even had a dog and cat.

Even for a particularly shy and thoughtful only child growing up in a parsonage in Maine, vaguely aware of those other horsemen, the four from Revelation—the fourth one, the pale one being You Know Who—this was probably odd, this equanimicable attitude toward Baba Yaga, this happy fascination. I was never herself, of course, although, as I say, I terribly admired her revolving house. I was instead little Vassilissa, the little girl who bravely trudged there on some stupid errand—I believe I was supposed to get light or something—and escaped being eaten by being good, by being blessed actually, and by listening to the excellent advice of my doll who was always with me and with whom I shared everything. Vassilissa had a pigtail, as did I, and would give her doll bread and tell her her troubles as did I. "Have a bite, dolly, and listen to my unhappy story," Vassilissa was forever saying. (Oddly, Rilke, when speaking of *Dinge*, of dolls and death, wrote *Was it not with a thing that you first shared your little heart, like a piece of bread that had to suffice for two . . .)*

Vassilissa escapes Baba Yaga at one point by throwing a crust to the cat who would have otherwise scratched her, and feeding the dog who would have otherwise bitten her. The birch trees which would otherwise have lashed her eyes out were calmed when the child (myself) tied them back with ribbon. The terrible gates constructed of bones and teeth were mollified with water and swung open. Water! Everything has needs and responds to kindness—the animals, the trees, even the scattered dead.

I was curiously contented then, a little girl in wintry Maine, escaping the house of Baba Yaga over and over again, conversing and confiding with my inanimates. But that was then. Death and solitude weren't boring and inevitable then.

TERRI WINDLING

✳ ✳ ✳ ✳ ✳ ✳

Transformations

Every child needs a fairy godmother, someone to turn to in times of peril. I found my own in the sumptuous pages of *The Golden Book of Fairy Tales* (Golden Books, 1958), translated from the French by Marie Ponsot and illustrated by Adrienne Ségur. Without this volume, fairy tales would have been what they were for so many of my generation: stories of passive princesses dreaming of rescue by rich Prince Charmings as portrayed in Walt Disney cartoons and the picture books they inspired. Instead, through Ponsot's evocative words and Ségur's exquisite, rococo paintings, I was introduced to fairy tales in their thrilling pre-Disney (and pre-Victorian) forms—their darker themes toned down slightly for children, but only slighty. Here Sleeping Beauty woke not to wedded bliss, but to an ogress mother-in-law determined to eat her and her children; and Red Riding Hood was devoured by the wolf, awaiting rescue in his belly. One princess lost her finger; another caused the death of the beast who loved her—for happy endings were not guaranteed, and they always came at a price. The stories in this book were both deeply sad and gloriously triumphant. They were trail maps through the deep, dark woods, pointing the way to the brighter lands beyond. Like poetry, they spoke to the soul in richly symbolic language.

There were two things about this particular book that made it vital to the child I was. First, it contained a remarkable number of stories about courageous, active girls; and second, it portrayed the various evils they faced in unflinching terms. Just below their diamond surface, these were stories of great brutality and anguish, many of which had never been originally intended for children at all. (Although Ponsot included tales from the Brothers Grimm and Andersen, the majority of her selections were drawn from the French *contes de fées* tradition—stories created as part of the vogue for fairy tales in seventeenth-century Paris, recounted in literary salons and published for adult readers.) I hungered for a narrative with which to make some sense of my life, but in schoolbooks and on television all I could find was the sugar water of Dick and Jane, *Leave It to Beaver* and the happy, wholesome *Brady Bunch*. Mine was not a Brady Bunch family; it was troubled, fractured, persistently violent, and I needed the stronger meat of wolves and witches, poisons and peril. In fairy tales, I had found a mirror held up to the world I knew—where adults were dangerous creatures, and Good and Evil were not abstract concepts.

When I look now at the stories I loved the best, I see that they have one thing in common: each has a "wounded hero," a young person physically scarred, disguised, or maimed, forced from home and required to make her own way in the world. As

Midori Snyder has pointed out in her fine essay "The Hero's Journey,"* young men in hero narratives leave home intent on making their fortune, soon finding challenges on the road to initiate them into manhood. "When the trials are done," she writes, "[the young male hero] returns home again in triumph, bringing to his society newfound knowledge, maturity—and often a magic bride." Only rarely, by contrast, do young women stride off simply to seek their fate. Instead, fate comes knocking on their door in the form of crisis, betrayal, or magic, propelling them forcibly onto the path to transformation. Nor are young women often allowed to return again when the tale is done; instead, they must make new lives and new alliances, usually far from home. The mythic structure of such stories was something I came to appreciate later, when my own hero's journey led me on to college and the study of folklore. As a child, I only cared that these girls were desperate, scarred, and scared, like me. Their tales assured me that with perseverance I could find my way to my own happy ending—provided I did not sit weeping in the cinders awaiting rescue. I'd have to *earn* a happy ending, and this was the "magic" that I would need: courage, compassion, determination, quick wits, clear sight, and luck.

"Once upon a time," begins "Donkeyskin" in *The Golden Book of Fairy Tales*, "there was a lucky king. He was strong, noble and wise. His subjects loved him. His neighbors respected him. His wife was fair and good." But the king's luck runs out. His queen

---

* "The Hero's Journey" by Midori Snyder, from *The Armless Maiden*, Tor Books, 1995.

lies dying and summons her husband to her side, saying, "Promise me you will not marry till you find a woman better than I." The promise is made, and the king soon discovers the difficulty of this condition. No woman compares in loveliness to his late queen—except their own daughter. And so the king announces his determination to wed and bed his child. Horrified, the girl runs to her fairy godmother, begging for help. "Tell your father that he must make you a dress the color of the sun," says she. "This he'll never be able to do, and then you will be safe."

But the king procures a dress that shines as gold and bright as the sun itself. Likewise, he fulfills each subsequent demand: a dress the color of the moon, a dress the color of the weather, and the skin of the magical donkey who shits coins of gold, the source of his wealth. When he gives his daughter the don-keyskin, she understands he will stop at nothing—and so she wraps herself in the skin and flees to a distant kingdom. In that new place, she takes a lowly, filthy job as a pig keeper, hiding her royal beauty beneath the dirt and the donkeyskin. Eventually, a gentle prince falls sick with love for Donkeyskin, informing his distraught parents that he means to marry the pig keeper. As he pines away with love for her, his parents give their consent at last. Only then does the princess drop the don-keyskin to reveal her true face. When her tale is told, "the prince rejoiced at her bravery, and fell twice as much in love." The story ends with their marriage and reconciliation with her chastened father.

Variants of this incest tale can be found in cultures all around the world under a variety of names: "Allerleirauh," "Thousand Furs," "Mossycoat," among others. Each version begins with the father, whose word is law, despite his mad intentions. His councillors seem curiously unable or unwilling to stop him. My stepfather was not a king, but a factory worker and truck driver, often unemployed, and usually drunk, sitting slumped in the neighborhood bars. Powerless in the wider world, low in the social pecking order, at home he relished his sovereignty and ruled with an iron fist. In the fairy tale, the queen dies young. In life, my mother was gone as well—not dead, but absent physically, working hard hours at ill-paying jobs, and absent mentally, unable or unwilling to protect her children. This was the early sixties, before strict child abuse reporting laws, when jaded, overworked doctors (all too common in working-class neighborhoods) routinely stitched my brothers and me back together and sent us home. Silence surrounded those cuts and bruises, those scalded hands and broken bones. We didn't use the word "abuse"; this was just something that fathers did. Fathers, I'd learned from fairy tales, were sometimes good and sometimes wicked. Mine, it appeared, was wicked, and so I needed a godmother's advice.

I chose a favorite teacher. She was gentle, kind, and pretty as a Ségur illustration. She had once called me a smart little girl— four words that I treasured like pearls. I lingered by her desk one day and haltingly told my dark little tale, throwing the words like pebbles into the deep well of her silence. I couldn't lift my eyes—I still remember the dusty floor tiles, the black and white of my saddle shoes, my frayed laces tied up in knots, my voice the barest whisper. "Where are you hurt?" my teacher said. "Show me." I mutely shook my head, too embarrassed to lift my skirt to show what lay beneath. "Tell your mother to call me," she said, and then the subject closed. I never relayed the message to my mother. Nothing changed. I grew increasingly silent. One classmate teased me sharply: "You never smile. Do you even know *how?*"

Silence is another element we find in classic fairy tales—girls muted by magic or sworn to silence in order to break enchantment. In "The Wild Swans," another story in *The Golden Book of Fairy Tales*, a princess is imprisoned by her stepmother, rolled in filth, then banished from home (as her older brothers had been before her). She goes in search of her missing brothers and discovers that they've been turned into swans, whereupon the young girl vows to find a way to break the spell. A mysterious woman comes to her in a dream and tells her what to do: "Pick the nettles that grow in graveyards, crush and spin them into thread, then weave them into coats and throw them over your brothers' backs." The nettles burn and blister, yet she never falters: picking, spinning, weaving, working with wounded, crippled hands, determined to save her brothers. All this time she's silent. "You must not speak," the dream woman has warned, "for a single word will be like a knife plunged into your brothers' hearts."

You must not speak. That's what my stepfather said: don't speak, don't cry, don't tell. That's what my mother said as well, as we sat in hospital waiting rooms—and I obeyed, as did my brothers. We sat as still and silent as stone while my mother spun false tales to explain each break and bruise and burn. Our family moved just often enough that her stories were fresh and plausible; each new doctor believed her, and chided us children to be more careful. I never contradicted those tales. I wouldn't have dared, or wanted to. They'd send me into foster care. They'd send my young brothers away. And so we sat, and the unspoken truth was as sharp as the point of a knife.

In "Donkeyskin" and "The Wild Swans," crisis is the catalyst that sends each princess into the world, where she will face more trials, then win her way to a better life. I began to search for other tales of innocent and honorable girls imperiled by parents and other adults, finding their way through disaster. Each ended in marriage, symbolizing the passage from adolescence to maturity, but between family crisis and happy ending there was always a journey to make. Take "The Girl With No Hands," the brutal story of a miller's daughter whose own father cuts off her hands in order to save himself from the devil. The girl's purity defeats the devil; the family is left with a fine sack of gold. "Now all is well," the miller assures her. "Now we can live together in splendor." "No," his daughter tells him, "for you would have given me to the devil himself. Here I can stay no longer. I must make my own way in the world." Handless, friendless, she goes to the woods and begins her metamorphosis. By the end of the tale, she is healed, married, a mother, and wearing a crown. In the universe of fairy tales, the Just often find a way to prevail, the Wicked generally receive their comeuppance—but there's more to such tales than a formula of abuse and retribution. The trials these wounded young women encounter illustrate the *process* of transformation: from youth to adulthood, from victim to hero, from a maimed state to wholeness, from passivity to action.

Fairy tales taught me the lessons of transformation; they schooled me in courage, honor, and endurance. Someday I, too, would enter the woods, and I'd have to be prepared. I bided my time in my parents' house, and my grandparents' house, till I was fifteen. And then the fairy tale crisis came to propel me out into the world. I won't describe that dark day here; suffice it to say that, like Donkeyskin, I knew all hope of aid was past, so I wrapped myself in the tattered skin and fled to a distant land. Now *I* was the princess of the tale: alone and maimed in the heart of the woods. But I knew this story. I knew what to do. I knew that if I was brave and true, I'd find a brighter world beyond the cold of the streets, the dark of the trees, and this knowledge pulled me past each wolf and witch who lay in wait.

And yes, I did eventually find my way to the realm that lies happily ever after—not marriage and wealth, but the thing I wanted more than anything else in the world: a college education, to open the door to a different life. I shed my child-self in the woods, emerged from the trees as a new creature, and on that quiet campus I knew that I'd found safe harbor at last. In the pages of myth and folklore texts, I discovered what it was I had been through: a rite of passage, a shamanic initiation as practiced in cultures the world over, a journey to the underworld and a ritual rebirth. I had a new name, a new role to play, a new family of friends, a new community. My hands grew back, and no one ever asked if I knew how to smile again.

Yet it took some years before I could speak of past. The habit of silence was strong. It was only when my stepfather died that this last spell was finally broken. Until then, I lived inside the old donkeyskin, comfortable, disguised, and safe. There were in those days no shelves full of "self-help" books for people with pasts like mine. In retrospect, I'm glad it was myth and folklore I turned to instead. Too many books portray child abuse as though it's an illness from which one must heal, like cancer . . . or malaria . . . or perhaps a broken leg. Eventually, this kind of book promises, the leg will be strong enough to use, despite a limp betraying deeper wounds that might never mend.

Through fairy tales, however, I understood my past in different terms: not as an illness or weakness, but as a hero narrative. It was a story, *my* story, beginning with birth and ending only with death. Difficult challenges and trials, even those that come at a tender young age, can make us wiser, stronger, and braver; they can serve to transform us, rather than sending us limping into the future. I always hesitate to speak of the good that can come from a traumatic past, for there is no good that is good *enough* to justify a child's terror. My stepfather's actions were clearly immoral. Could I go back and prevent them, I would. Yet in that troubled household I learned something that I treasure today: the secret of spinning straw into gold, fear into courage, misery into joy. I don't thank my stepfather for this gift, but the gift is valuable nonetheless. It's the treasure whisked from an enchanter's tower, from the well that lies at the end of the world: the hero's reward, which comes only after dragons and monsters are faced.

My past is like a patch of nettles, the memories burn as I pluck them up . . . and crush them . . . and spin them . . . and weave them into coats made of words and paint. My own brothers are grown now, but there are others out there still caught beneath their donkeyskins and swan feathers. And so I continue to spin, and weave, and toss those coats made of words to the air—hoping that someday, somewhere, they will set somebody free.

ABOUT THE CONTRIBUTORS

✳ ✳ ✳ ✳ ✳ ✳

ALICE ADAMS's latest book, *After the War*, was published by Knopf in 2000. Her most recent title before that was *The Last Lovely City*. She was born in Virginia, grew up in Chapel Hill, North Carolina, and graduated from Radcliffe. Since then she's lived mostly in San Francisco, currently with two cats, Sam and Lucie.

JULIA ALVAREZ is the author of *How the García Girls Lost Their Accent, In the Time of the Butterflies* (a finalist for the National Book Critics' Circle Award), and *¡YO!* She has also published three books of poetry and a collection of essays. She lives in Vermont and in the Dominican Republic, where she and her husband run a coffee farm.

MARGARET ATWOOD is the author of more than twenty-five books of poetry, fiction, and nonfiction. Her most recent novel,

The Blind Assassin, was awarded the Booker Prize in 2000. Atwood lives in Toronto.

ANN BEATTIE has written essays on photography as well as six story collections and six novels. Her most recent book is *Perfect Recall*. She lives in Maine and in Key West with her husband, Lincoln Perry.

ROSELLEN BROWN is the author of nine books, of which the most recent are the novel *Half a Heart* and a collection of poems, *Cora Fry's Pillow Book*. She teaches in the M.F.A. in Writing Program at the School of the Art Institute of Chicago.

A. S. BYATT's novel *Possession* won the Booker Prize in 1990. Her other fiction includes *Babel Tower, Angels & Insects*, and *The Djinn in the Nightingale's Eye: Five Fairy Stories*. She taught at the Central School of Art and Design in London and at University College, London, before becoming a full-time writer. Her critical works include *On Histories and Stories, Degrees of Freedom: The Early Novels of Iris Murdoch, Passions of the Mind*, and, with psychoanalyst Ignês Sodré, *Imagining Characters: Six Conversations About Women Writers*.

KATHRYN DAVIS's most recent novel is *The Walking Tour*. She lives in Vermont with her husband and daughter.

CHITRA BANERJEE DIVAKARUNI is the best-selling author of the novels *Mistress of Spices, Sister of My Heart*, and *The Vine of Desire*; the story collection *Arranged Marriage*, which received the American Book Award; and four collections of prize-winning poetry. Born in India, she lives in the San Francisco area.

DEBORAH EISENBERG is the recipient of a Whiting Writer's Award and a Guggenheim Fellowship. She lives in New York City and teaches at the University of Virginia.

MARIA FLOOK is the author of two novels, *Open Water* and *Family Night* (which received a PEN/American Ernest Hemingway Foundation Special Citation); a collection of stories, *You Have the Wrong Man*; and a memoir, *My Sister Life*. She is the recipient of a National Endowment for the Arts Fellowship and a Pushcart Prize for fiction. She teaches in the Graduate Writing Seminars at Bennington College.

PATRICIA FOSTER She is associate professor of English at the University of Iowa. She has received writing fellowships from Yaddo and the Florida Arts Council, and was awarded the 1993 PEN/Jerard Fund Prize for women's nonfiction as well as the 1993 Mary Roberts Rinehart Award for nonfiction. She is the editor of *Minding the Body* and *Sister to Sister*, and the author of *All the Lost Girls: Confessions of a Southern Daughter*.

Author of *The Situation and the Story*, *Approaching Eye Level*, and *Fierce Attachments*, as well as several other books, **VIVIAN GORNICK** has written for many publications, including *The New York Times*, *The Village Voice*, and *The Nation*. She lives in New York City.

LUCY GREALY is an award-winning poet and author of the highly acclaimed memoir *Autobiography of a Face*. She lives in New York City and is working on a novel.

Cultural critic, essayist, poet, and feminist theorist, **BELL HOOKS** is the author of fourteen books, most recently *Here We Stand: Class Matters*.

FANNY HOWE has published several novels and books of poetry, including *Indivisible, The Lives of a Spirit, The Deep North, Saving History, Nod, Robeson Street, The End*, and *One Crossed Out*. She has also published four books for young adults. She lives and teaches in California.

FERN KUPFER is the author of a memoir, *Before and After Zachariah*, and three novels—the latest, *Love Lies*, a comedic mystery. She has written for *Family Circle, Redbook, Woman's Day, Cosmopolitan, The Women's Review of Books*, and *Parents* magazine. Since 1993 she has been a columnist for *Newsday*. Currently she teaches creative writing at Iowa State University in Ames, Iowa, where she lives happily ever after with her husband, Joseph Geha.

URSULA K. LE GUIN was born in 1929 in Berkeley, California. Among her honors are a National Book Award, five Hugo and five Nebula awards, the Kafka Award, a Pushcart Prize, and the Harold D. Vursell Memorial Award from the American Academy of Arts and Letters. She lives in Portland, Oregon.

CAROLE MASO is the author of nine books, including the novels *The Art Lover, AVA*, and *Defiance; Break Every Rule*, a book of essays; *The Room Lit by Roses: A Journal of Pregnancy and Birth*; and *Beauty Is Convulsive: The Passion of Frida Kahlo*, poems in prose. She is professor of English at Brown University.

JANE MILLER is the author of six collections of poetry, including *Memory at These Speeds: New and Selected Poems*. Among earlier collections are *The Greater Leisures*, a National Poetry Series Selection, and *August Zero*, winner of the Western States Book Award. She has also written *Working Time: Essays on Poetry, Culture, and Travel* in the University of Michigan's Poets on Poetry Series.

LYDIA MILLET is the author of *Omnivores*; *George Bush, Dark Prince of Love*; and *My Happy Life*. Millet was born in Boston in 1968 and grew up in Toronto, Canada; she now lives in New York, where she works during the day as a writer for the National Resources Defense Council.

JOYCE CAROL OATES is the author of a number of works of fiction, poetry, and criticism, including most recently *Middle Age: A Romance* and *Beasts*. She has been a past winner of the National Book Award and is the 1996 recipient of the PEN/Malamud Award for Achievement in the Short Story. Since 1978 she has lived in Princeton, New Jersey, where she is professor of humanities at Princeton University.

Novelist **CONNIE PORTER** is the author of *All-Bright Court*, *Imani All Mine*, and the Addy books in the American Girl series. She lives in Virginia.

FRANCINE PROSE's latest novel is *Blue Angel*. Among her other books are *Guided Tours of Hell*, the novels *Hunters and*

Gatherers, *Primitive People*, and *Bigfoot Dreams*. Her short fiction has appeared in *The New Yorker*, *Atlantic*, *The Paris Review*, *Antaeus*, and *The North American Review*.

LINDA GRAY SEXTON the author of the recent memoir *Searching for Mercy Street: My Journey Back to My Mother, Anne Sexton* as well as four novels. She lives on the West Coast with her husband and two young sons.

MIDORI SNYDER holds a master's degree in literary studies from the University of Wisconsin and has published numerous fantasy novels for adults in the United States and Europe, as well as young adult fiction and short stories. Her most recent novel, *The Innamorati*, inspired by living in northern Italy, draws upon Italian and early Roman mythology and the theater of the Commedia dell'Arte. It won the Mythopoeic Award for best adult fantasy novel of 2000 and has been recently translated and published in France. Ms. Snyder currently lives with her husband and two children in Milwaukee, Wisconsin, where she is teaching English.

FAY WELDON has published more than twenty novels including *Down Among the Women*, *Female Friends*, *Prexis*, *Puffball*, *The Life and Loves of a She-Devil*, *The Hearts and Loves of Men* and *The Cloning of Joanna May*. Dozens of her short stories have appeared in periodicals and have been collected in four volumes, *Watching Me, Watching You*; *Polaris*; *Moon over Minneapolis*; and *Wicked Women*. She was born in England, raised in a family of women (her mother is a novelist) in New Zealand, and took degrees in economics and psychology at the University of St. Andrews. She is married for the second time and has four sons.

JOY WILLIAMS is the author of four novels, two short story collections, and a history of the Florida keys. She has received the Rea Award for the short story and the Strauss Living Award from the American Academy of Arts and Letters. Her latest novel, *The Quick and the Dead*, was a finalist for the Pulitzer Prize in 2000.

TERRI WINDLING is the author of *The Wood Wife, The Winter Child*, and other mythic fiction for both adults and children. She edited (with Ellen Datlow) the six-volume *Snow White, Blood Red* series of contemporary adult fairy tale short stories, as well as numerous other anthologies, book series, and the Endicott Studio for Mythic Arts Web site. She has won six World Fantasy Awards and the Mythopoeic Award for Novel of the Year, and she divides her time between homes in Devon, England, and Tucson, Arizona.

ABOUT THE EDITOR

* * * * * *

KATE BERNHEIMER attended Wesleyan University and received her MFA from the University of Arizona. She is the author of a novel, *The Complete Tales of Ketzia Gold*, and is writing a second novel, *The Complete Tales of Merry Gold*.

Printed in the United States
by Baker & Taylor Publisher Services